My Mother's Wars

Clockwise from upper left: Mary and Goldie (seated), c. 1917; Mary (on right) and Ray, c. 1926; Hirschel and his mother, c. 1935; Moishe, c. 1938

My Mother's Wars

Lillian Faderman

BEACON PRESS, BOSTON

Beacon Press
25 Beacon Street
Boston, Massachusetts 02108-2892
www.beacon.org

Beacon Press books
are published under the auspices of
the Unitarian Universalist Association of Congregations.

Printed in the United States of America

16 15 14 13   8 7 6 5 4 3 2 1

This book is printed on acid-free paper that meets the uncoated paper ANSI/NISO
specifications for permanence as revised in 1992.

Text design by Ruth Maassen

A few names and identifying characteristics of people mentioned in this work have
been supplied by the author's imagination.

Library of Congress Cataloging-in-Publication Data

Faderman, Lillian.
  My mother's wars / Lillian Faderman.
    p. cm.
  Includes bibliographical references.
  ISBN 978-0-8070-5052-1 (hardcover : alk. paper) 1. Jews—Persecutions—Europe,
Eastern—History—20th century. 2. Antisemitism—Europe, Eastern—History—20th
century. I. Title.
  DS146.E852F337 2012
  305.892'407471092—dc23
  [B]
                          2012029270

To my son Avrom:
Here is your grandmother.

Preface

My mother kept no secrets from me about her strange and difficult life before I was born. For most of my growing-up years, she and I lived together in a single furnished room, "by a missus," as such living arrangements used to be called. I think our symbiosis was probably much more powerful than the usual between mother and child because most of the time there was no one but the two of us, no other presence to distract or divert. The intensity of my focus on her was compounded, I imagine, because our daily life was played out in the space of no more than ninety square feet. In that tight proximity, she told me things because she had no one else to tell them to. I saw things because she had nowhere else to go and hide. I struggled to understand things because she was my constant care and study and love.

But the older I got, the less I understood. In the glorious hope and brashness of my young womanhood I knew only that the choices she'd made, which had brought her, and me along with her, to that lonely, airless furnished room of my childhood, had been incomprehensibly foolish, and that her mistakes would never be mine.

Thirty years after my mother's death, my young-womanhood long gone, a sadness suddenly came upon me with the thought that though I'd known all her secrets, I hadn't known her. I think that sadness was triggered because I'd been trying to relearn Yiddish, the language I usually spoke with her before I started going to school; and in a book I'd bought in order to practice reading in Yiddish, I came upon a lullaby by the writer Sholem Aleichem; it was one I remembered her singing when I was a child.

> *Bay dayn vigl zitst dayn mameh,*
> *Zingt a lid un veynt.*

Vest amol farshteyn mistame
Vos zi hot gemeynt.

I translate it this way:

Near your cradle sits your mother,
Singing a song and weeping.
Perhaps someday you'll understand
What her tears meant.

My Mother's Wars is my attempt to understand.

———————

My mother—who was not yet my mother—was kicked out of the home of her half sister Sarah and her brother-in-law Sam several months after she came to America. She was seventeen, and she didn't mind very much being kicked out because by then there was somewhere else she'd much rather be living. Of course she couldn't know in 1914 that she would pay dearly, even to the day she died, for Sarah and Sam's anger with her. And though I wouldn't be born for many years yet, I would pay, too: I think it's fair to say that I grew up in the shadow of my mother's tragedy, which, as things happened, had been made inevitable by what she'd failed to do before she was thrown out.

In her shtetl in Latvia, she'd seen them only once. That was when Sarah, already a grown woman, came to say goodbye to their father before she and Sam left for America. Mereleh, as my mother was called, was five years old then, and she hid behind *der tateh*'s legs because she felt bashful when the stranger, who looked like a rich gentile lady in a big feathered hat and long white gloves, called her *shvesterl*, little sister. She was scared too of the man they said was her brother-in-law, though he ignored her as though she were a piece of the scant furniture. He was stiff and thin like a clothespin, with a scraggly pointed beard that wriggled like the one on the goat that had followed her down the street, pulled her little babushka right off her head, and started to eat it. In the next years, whenever der tateh got a letter from his eldest daughter and her husband in America, Mereleh remembered about them only that Sam had frightened her and that Sarah had dragged her from behind der tateh's legs and hugged her to her big bosom so hard that even after their carriage drove away Mereleh's cheek bore the indentation of a knob-like coat button.

Yet there she was, twelve years later, living with them in America, sleeping on a Murphy bed in their front room. It had happened because in Latvia, even before Mereleh got her first period, she'd been sent out to be an apprentice, first to a milliner and then to a dressmaker, and with loathing she'd believed the needle would be her whole life. Then one of the girls with whom she worked at the dressmaker's told her about a sister who'd gone to New York and was already an actress on the Yiddish stage and getting paid good money for it. That was when Mereleh began to dream. Why not? She'd danced at the Purim festivals in Rezhitse for several years, and every single time, the other dancers stopped to watch her and applaud. Though no one had ever taught her dancing, she knew exactly how to make her movements copy the clarinet's moan, the accordion's chortle, what to do with her hands, shoulders, legs, hips. After she danced at one Purim festival, a bunch of boys came up to her to tell her she was as graceful as a swan. It was ecstasy for her when she was dancing, like she was in a magical trance. When the dressmaker for whom she worked sent her on an errand and she had to walk through the forest, she even danced there, all alone, humming her own tunes and bowing extravagantly to the tree throngs as though they'd applauded. Why shouldn't she go to America and become a dancer on the stage?

How she convinced der tateh to go along with her plan she could never remember, or at least that's what she told me: she only knew that he begged his oldest daughter and her husband to help her; and that Sam kindly sent money for her passage and gave an affidavit saying that if the authorities would allow her into the country, as her male relative he would take responsibility for her.

Young as she was, my mother realized it was no small thing for Sarah and Sam to bring her to America and give her a place to live and food to eat, and she tried to show she was grateful. Every evening after she ate supper with them at the little table in the kitchen, she carried all the dishes to the sink and washed and dried them and put everything away in the cupboard. On Sunday mornings she gathered up all the dirty sheets, towels, Sam's shirts and pants, everyone's nightclothes, and she brought them down to the basement where she scrubbed them in the big tub and then carried them up to the rooftop and hung them on clotheslines, and when they were dry she ironed everything that needed ironing. She swept and dusted and washed the kitchen floor, too. "No, sister, I really like to," she insisted when Sarah tried to take the mop from her hands and said she didn't have to do so much around the house.

But in truth, she felt awkward with Sarah and Sam—not shy as she'd been when she was small and they came to say goodbye, but never at ease. It jolted her in the beginning when Sarah introduced her to the neighbors as "my sister," because Sarah seemed so old, more like an aunt than a sister, and there'd been no chance for sisterly feelings to develop between them. With Sam she was the most uncomfortable. He barely glanced at her and hardly ever said more than good morning to her. She worried that he resented having had to give the affidavit swearing he would be responsible for her. She felt she must get a job right away and start paying him back for all the expense she'd been to him.

She didn't know yet how you went about becoming a dancer on the stage—she planned to find out as soon as she learned a little more English. But she did know how to sew very well because she'd been doing it since she was a child, and Sam told her that on the Lower East Side, where there were sewing factories, everyone spoke Yiddish so she didn't have to wait to learn English to work there. She soon found a job in a shop on Delancey that made pinafores; and every Saturday evening she counted out five dollar bills from the nine dollars and twenty-five cents in her pay envelope and handed them to her brother-in-law. "Listen, Mereleh, we're not starving, and we're your family, so you don't need to worry yourself so much about paying us back right away," Sarah always said.

"You're a good girl, very serious and responsible," Sam pronounced tersely each time, folding the bills neatly into his wallet. His wagging goatee reminded her still of the goat back in Preil, though it didn't frighten her as much as it once had.

She was seeing almost nothing of America but a Brooklyn apartment and the pinafore factory where she worked six days a week. Nobody ever came to visit but Sam's rotund cousin Esther and her husband Marvin, who was partners with Sam in the harness-making business. Every Sunday afternoon the four of them played pinochle until nightfall, cubes of sugar held between their teeth, sipping hot tea which Sarah would keep serving from a kettle on the stove that always emitted a low, monotonous whistle. Esther offered to teach Mereleh how to play, and because Mereleh didn't want to seem standoffish, she tried it a couple of times; but she couldn't see the sense or pleasure in it. While they played at the kitchen table, she sat at the front-room window and looked out at the movement of people and the horse and buggies and the automobiles turning off Ocean Parkway onto Ditmas Avenue. She would have loved to be part of the action in the streets, but when she announced one Sunday before Esther and Marvin arrived that she was going out for a walk, Sam said, "All by yourself?" and she knew by the expression on his face that he thought it wasn't proper for a young girl to go out walking all by herself.

It felt like her old life in Latvia had happened a hundred years ago, yet she was tied to this new country only by the thin thread of her half sister and brother-in-law. At night in the dark, her cheeks and pillow were often wet with tears, and she scoffed at her foolish dream that all she would have to do was set foot in America and she would become a famous dancer. She asked herself, If this is all there is in America—hard work and a Murphy bed I have to pull down from the living room wall every night and put back up again every morning—why did I leave my home, my tateh and mameh, my little brother Hirschel, everyone I loved, just to come here? For what?

She missed them so much, her real family. She kept thinking of the last time she saw them all . . . her tateh, his face white as salt, holding both hands over her bent head and blessing her . . . her mameh wiping her eyes with a corner of her apron . . . her sisters and little brother lined up like stair steps . . . Buna Rivka, who was the next-oldest after her, had called out in her fog-horn voice, "Don't forget what you promised!" because Buna Rivka too had already been sent off to slave as a tailor's apprentice for room and board and two rubles a month, though her chest was still as flat as a door. Hirschel—her little darling, like her own baby ever since he was born when she was seven years old—would not look up at her. Tears bled down his cheeks and made dark bird's-egg splotches on his thin shirt. The cart driver, who'd come all the way from Dvinsk and had been waiting for his sole passenger for some time already, was impatient to leave. He stood beside his old horse, stroking its mane gruffly as the animal whinnied and flicked its tail back and forth at the buzzing flies. He had to take her to Vilna, where she would get a train that would bring her to Hamburg, where she would get a boat that would bring her to Southampton, where she would get a ship that would bring her to New York . . . She'd been impatient to leave, too, one minute—and the next minute she wished she could send the cart away without her, and she'd live here in her shtetl forever and not have to make the long, scary trip all by herself.

"I swear on my life, as soon as I have the money. All of you!" she'd answered passionately. "I won't forget, Hirscheleh. You'll be the first," she whispered into the boy's dark curls. Then she climbed up on the bench of the waiting cart and placed the bundle she'd made from a tattered blanket on her knees. The driver hoisted himself to his seat beside her and smacked his whip on the horse's rump. She turned her head to fill her eyes with der tateh, di mameh, Hirschel, her sisters—just one more time. She was able to grab no more than a glimpse of them, standing in a row in front of the house, teary and waving, as the animal trotted off, turned at the street corner, and took her out of their lives. . . .

But, as my mother would tell me, before long she made a friend at the pinafore factory. "What kind of American name is Mereleh? Call yourself Mary! And no 'Luft,' for godsakes. *Luft* means 'air,' like you're nothing. Call your last name Lifton." Thus Goldie, who sat across from her at a long work-table, baptized my mother. The first time she saw Goldie, Mary thought she looked like the *nafkas* who used to walk up and down the main street in Dvinsk, where she'd gone when she was thirteen years old to be a milliner's apprentice. But Goldie was just a hardworking seamstress who loved to look pretty and loved to have a good time when she wasn't working. She liked dresses that showed off her figure, though she was a little plump around the arms and belly and was more than ten years older than Mary. She cracked her gum, and when she talked she smelled of peppermint or cloves. She wore bright red lipstick and heavy rouge and blue eye shadow, and her hair swept up in back with tiny golden curls plastered on her forehead. She knew the name of everyone in the big pinafore factory and everyone up and down the block, too; and everyone knew her name. She could go up to a fella as easy as crossing the street and say to him in Yiddish, or even English, "Say, where'd you get those eyes?" and she'd banter with the guy for a long time and sometimes give him her address. She was as different from Sarah and Sam as peacocks are from cows.

"Come on up to my room next Sunday," Goldie said one day and gave Mary her address on Orchard Street. Mary was happy she'd have something to do on a Sunday afternoon other than sit by the window and listen to cards being shuffled.

"Where you going?" Sam asked when Mary put on her jacket that day.

"Oh, just to see a girlfriend from the shop," she answered and slipped out the door before he might say something else. Even taking the streetcar back to the Lower East Side, its streets now empty of the rushing workers and lively with the crowds enjoying Sunday respite, felt to her like an exhilarating escape from Sarah and Sam's Brooklyn apartment.

Goldie had her own private room by a missus and could come and go, no questions asked, which Mary envied very much. She was soon admiring Goldie more than anyone she'd ever met, because Goldie was so full of life and knew everything about what you do and how you act in America and was willing to teach Mary all of it. She was like the true big sister that Mary never had. Goldie took her to the Grand Street stores where you could find real bargains, and she taught her how to pick out a stylish dress, a pretty hat with a peacock feather, patent leather shoes with fancy bows that didn't cost much money at all. She and Goldie would dress up in their finery, and they'd stroll Houston or Delancey arm-in-arm. The night streets were lit bright with lamps, and buzzed and roared with throngs of people and music blaring out onto the pavement from dance halls and saloons. Mary felt as she walked those streets, with all their movement and color and noise, like she was galloping atop a handsome runaway stallion—so scary, so breathtakingly beautiful.

But she knew by the looks Sam gave her and by Sarah's saying, "It's not good for your health to get so little sleep," that they weren't happy with her glamorous appearance and her staying out so late every night. Yet she was having such a good time that she didn't want to stop; and anyway every week she still counted out into Sam's open hand five dollars from her pay envelope. And oh, what fun it all was. Now, finally, she felt like she was living in America. At least a couple of evenings a week she and Goldie went into one of the nickelodeons or the new movie houses, which you could find on almost every main street of the Lower East Side. She learned from Goldie to sigh over the handsome actors, the beautiful actresses, the romantic stories. She couldn't read the words that appeared in English on the screen, but you didn't have to in order to see how magnificent the movie stars were and understand the love scenes they acted out.

Sometimes she and Goldie went to funny movies, which often made Mary laugh till her stomach hurt. Her little brother Hirschel would be so delighted at Charlie Chaplin and Fatty Arbuckle, she told herself, and she swore that as soon as she saved up enough, he'd be the first she'd bring to America. Sometimes as she sat in the movie theater and Hirschel popped into her head, the actors on the screen disappeared in front of her eyes and she watched instead the memories that played themselves out like a movie in her head. She saw that last day like it was yesterday . . . even the bundle she'd made from a tattered blanket. Inside it were an old coat; a woolen dress she'd made for herself; two jars of preserves from an ancient apple tree that grew beside the door of the family's house, which she was bringing as a present to her half sister and brother-in-law; and her only treasure, a photograph of Hirschel taken on his tenth birthday, which she'd wrapped in the shawl her mother had knit for her. All through the trip she'd kept taking the photograph out and clasping it to her chest like it was all she had to hold on to.

One night after she and Goldie had gone to see the Keystone Kops, she dreamt she was sitting in a movie house with Hirschel by her side. They were laughing hysterically at the Kops chasing a robber whose pants were falling down as he ran. But when she turned to kiss the top of Hirschel's head, he wasn't there. She woke up with terrible fears and a pounding heart. She'd been in America for almost half a year already, and she still had no idea how she could get the money to send for him. She remembered bitterly her silly dreams, how she thought she would come to America and right away become a dancer. Oh, the foolishness of her illusions. She had absolutely no inkling how you'd go about becoming anything but a seamstress. And though she'd been working sixty-six hours a week for months now, she still made only nine dollars and twenty-five cents a week. How many years would it take to save up enough money to bring over just her baby brother?

I won't buy any more clothes or run around spending money foolishly, she promised herself. But after a long day's work she couldn't just go home to Sarah and Sam's and have a boring supper and go to bed. She needed so much to have a little fun, to see things and do things that would get her mind off how hard it was to make pinafores eleven hours a day, six days a week. When Goldie introduced her to dance halls, they were like a wonderful drug to her tired spirit because when she was dancing it didn't matter that she'd been wearied to the bone at the pinafore factory; she was never too tired to dance the night away. When she was dancing she felt like she was a movie star. Goldie took her to Liberty Hall, Progress Assembly, the New Irving, the Golden Rule—dance halls with glittering chandeliers and shiny wooden floors, and hundreds of young people fresh from the shtetlach of Eastern Europe, mastering the two-step, the Charlie Chaplin wiggle, the grizzly bear, the turkey trot, the bunny hug. She caught on so quickly to all of them. She and Goldie had to pay ten cents apiece to get into a dance hall, but always some big spender who admired the way she danced would want to treat her, and her girlfriend too, to something to eat and drink, and so she and Goldie wouldn't have to shell out anything for their supper. "You're a regular man magnet," Goldie told her with a wink. It was true, she was, though she didn't like it at all when men thought that for a hot dog and a soda they had the right to get as fresh as they pleased. A lot of them seemed to think that. Octopuses, Goldie called such fellas.

When Mary was running around with Goldie and having a good time, she was happy with herself for having been bold enough to leave her dreary home and come to America. It seemed like everything was all right or would be all right in some vague future about which she didn't need to think right now. But sometimes, alone at night in her Murphy bed, even when she sank into it exhausted by fun, she was lonely and missed her family so much. When she couldn't sleep because of missing them, she got up and turned on the light so she could look at the picture of her little brother Hirschel that she'd carried with her in the cart and train and ship and had had framed in gilt when she'd received her first pay. Do they really still exist back there? she asked herself. Sometimes she was overcome with anxiety that she'd never see any of them again.

She got more letters from Hirschel than from anyone back home. *Der tateh says I can come whenever you send for me, dearest sister. It's so lonely since you left for good,* he repeated in each letter. She wanted so much to send for him, to take him to Coney Island and the nickelodeons and to spoil him with candy and to hold him and kiss him like she used to when he was a baby, as though she were his mameh. But all those many months of working so hard in America, and she'd been able to save less than six dollars. I'll ask Sarah and Sam to help bring him over, she decided. After all, he was Sarah's brother, too—and at the rate Mary was managing to save, he'd be an old man before she had the money to send for him. She'd promise them that Hirschel would get a job quickly. He's such a good boy, she'd tell them, and every day she saw boys even younger than he pushing racks of dresses from the factories into wagons that would deliver them to stores, or carrying piles of cloth on their backs to the homes of pieceworkers who would sew them into suits and coats. He'll pay back everything you spend to bring him to America, she would promise Sarah and Sam.

But before she got around to it, serious trouble started between her and them. Even though she still did the laundry every Sunday before she went out, and cleared the dishes from the table and washed them whenever she was home, and made sure to fold the Murphy bed back into the wall the minute she got out of it, and she still gave them five dollars from her pay envelope every week, Sam had become very grumpy with her. He gave her disapproving looks, as though she'd done something bad. It hurt her because most of the time she really tried to please him and because all the things Goldie taught her to love—movies, American love songs, strolling in the lively streets, dancing with a fella even though you don't know him—Sam called *Americana mishegas*, American craziness. Sam and Sarah's only idea of a good time was to play pinochle at the kitchen table. They didn't like Goldie at all. "She's a very bad influence on you. She makes you run around every night and stay out so late I don't know how you can get up in the morning to go to work," Sarah complained.

Goldie couldn't stand them any more than they could stand her. "Old fogeys," she called them. "What kind of life is that for a young girl, to live with people like that?"

Mary sided with Goldie, of course, forgetting that she'd planned to ask Sarah and Sam to bring Hirschel to America. She knew she owed them a lot because without them she couldn't have come to this country herself, but they led old-people's lives, and that's the kind of life they wanted for her. She resented that they wanted her to be just like them. Why did she bother to come to America if not to do things and see things and be free like she couldn't be in Latvia?

But at the beginning of her first winter in America, she got such a bad cold she couldn't even go to the pinafore factory. (Did my mother tell me this story as a cautionary tale, when I too became a wild young thing who would risk life, limb, and good repute for a little pleasure?) Sarah made her chicken soup, and every couple of hours she brought hot tea to her bed in the front room. "See," Sarah scolded, "that's from running around so much when you need to be sleeping." My mother bit her tongue, but it made her angry to be rebuked like that.

About ten o'clock that night, she was dozing, a bit feverish—Sarah and Sam had already gone to bed and closed their bedroom door—and the doorbell rang. It was Goldie, all decked out in her dancing finery, breathless. "I took the streetcar all the way over here because that fella you liked with the wavy blond hair said he'd be at that new hall, the Regent, and he wanted to know if you was coming." Oh, the boy was a wonderful dancer and a real gentleman, not like all the octopuses Mary met, with their groping hands which she constantly had to wrestle. She threw on her silver-spangled dress and dancing shoes, and went to the Regent. Sweat poured down her face and chest, but she and the handsome blond boy danced and danced until 1:00 a.m. He took her home by streetcar, her dress and stockings and underwear drenched in icy sweat.

About four o'clock in the morning, though she didn't want to, she had to bang on Sarah and Sam's bedroom door because her breaths were coming out in sharp whistles and a knife kept stabbing at her lungs and she was scared. Sam ran out to the street to find a taxi. "What's the matter with you that you act like a *vildeh chayeh*, a wild animal?" Sarah scolded when, wearing only a big coat over her tent of a nightgown, her hair straggling loose from her bun, she rode with Mary in the taxi to Brooklyn Hospital. Mary said nothing because she could barely breathe. It was double pneumonia, and she almost died. When she was finally released from the hospital, Sam told her, "We can't take responsibility no more. You come in at two o'clock in the morning. You make Sarah worry herself sick." His scraggly goatee wagged furiously.

"You can stay with us until you get on your feet again, and then it's better if you find your own place," Sarah said sternly, though she dabbed at her eyes with a handkerchief.

Mary felt ashamed and, even worse, she worried they'd write her dear tateh terrible things about her and he'd be so disappointed in her. But she felt outrage, too, she would tell me. To turn her out into the street like she was a goddam dog! Just because she wouldn't let them imprison her as if she were a kid, or as if she were still back in Latvia and wasn't supposed to do anything but work her head off, come home, eat with the family, and go straight to bed. —Anyway, she calmed herself by thinking, Goldie had already asked her to share a hall room on Suffolk Street that had two cots in it. That's what Mary had really been wanting to do for a long time now. And dance. I'd rather dance than eat and sleep, she told herself. Her favorite dance was spieling, which was all the rage at Liberty Hall that year. Goldie called her the spieler champ of the world. People would just stop dancing and stand there, watching her and the boy spiel around the floor. You put your chin on his shoulder and he put his chin on your shoulder, and you joined hands, pushed your butts out, and made your arms go up and down like a pump handle while you twisted and twirled in circles. Squeaks of ecstasy escaped her lips when a good partner twirled her, and she closed her eyes in bliss. It was like her feet never had to touch the ground. The people who watched clapped and yelled, "More! More!" She heard a boy say, "Wow, that girl is a peach of a dancer," and another boy said, "You bet she is!"

Oh, it was such fun, such fun. It made her forget for a little while her long hours at the pinafore factory, and that di mameh, der tateh, Hirschel, everyone she loved, were almost as far away as the dead.

Part I

1

First week of April, 1932

TIME ON THE MARCH

New race in Reich starts with a rush . . . Hitler appeals to women. The campaign for the runoff balloting next Sunday for the presidency of the Reich got under way with a rush in all parts of Germany today. Hundreds of women cheered Adolf Hitler at an open-air meeting in the Lustgarten, when the fascist leader promised that his Third Reich would make it easier for all German maidens to find homes and husbands to support them.

New York Governor Franklin Delano Roosevelt: "These unhappy times call for the building of plans that put their faith once more in the forgotten man at the bottom of the economic pyramid."

My mother, who is still not yet my mother, gets off the train at the Midtown garment district and walks three blocks to a tall gray building that houses several factories where dresses and coats are made. She squeezes into the elevator with a small crowd of other workers and rides up to the twelfth floor. Before she enters the long, narrow workroom of Seidman and Sons, she must pause near the door, take her card from a rack, and get it punched by the time clock. She's been punching time clocks for eighteen years, since 1914 when she worked at the pinafore factory. She's very careful not to be late, because one morning she missed her train and got to work when the time clock showed 8:19 a.m. instead of 8:00 a.m., and the forelady was standing right there, smirking and bowing. "Good afternoon, Miss Lifton. I hope it didn't disturb your sleep to have to come in to work," she said with exaggerated politeness.

My mother doesn't want to lose this job, because it would be hard to find another one these days. She and the other workers at Seidman and Sons have already taken a pay cut. Just last week, the elder Mr. Seidman walked in and stood in the middle of the factory floor, puffing on his big cigar. All the machines stopped. Everyone knew something serious was going to happen. "Listen, people. I hate to ask this of you, but times are very bad. . . . You know, you're all like family to me." Mr. Seidman's eyes shone sentimental tears, but Mary saw his beautiful cashmere jacket, his glittering diamond pinkie ring, his leather shoes that looked smooth and soft as butter, and she thought, Yeah, like the poor relatives. Yet what could any of them answer when Mr. Seidman said, "Who doesn't choose a cut in pay instead of layoffs?"

After Mary punches her time card, she goes behind a long canvas curtain in a corner, gets out of her coat, hat, and dress, and hangs them one above the other on the hooks assigned to her. Then she puts on the cotton shop-dress that she always brings with her in a paper bag, and she goes to her station. Since coming to America she's worked in a dozen shops, as a baster, a finisher, a buttonhole maker, a sewing-machine operator—she's done it all. For years now, she's been a draper, which usually pays a little better than the other jobs. A draper has to fit the various parts of a garment on a stuffed dummy before pinning sleeves to bodice and bodice to skirt; the fitting has to be done just right and it takes a bit of an artistic eye. All the drapers have a stool beside their dummy, because recently the International Ladies Garment Workers Union negotiated it for them, but the forelady doesn't like it when they sit. She says their pinning isn't as good as it is when they stand on their feet and get a better view of the whole garment. And so whenever they're in her sight, which is often, they must stand, arms outstretched, and pin. To Mary the job has seemed harder lately because, as Goldie used to say of women over thirty, she's no spring chicken anymore.

One good thing about working at Seidman and Sons, though, is that her station is right next to a big window, so she can sneak a peek at the sky every once in a while. But it's also near the pressing machines, and in the late spring, when it starts to get hot outside, that's especially miserable. Though the windows are open so that cooler air may come in, nothing seems to come in but flies—even on the twelfth floor. The heat of the pressing machines mixes with the New York humidity, and Mary's work dress sticks to her like shriveled skin. Her sweaty hands leave patches of damp on the material on which she works, but it can't be helped. When the humidity is really bad, all the workers suffer. Sweat pours down everyone's face and neck and back. The hair that covers the chests of the shirtless pressers is shiny wet, like they've just stepped from a bath.

Yet sometimes, when my mother told me about the shops she worked in, she made it sound almost like fun. The talk can be lively and interesting, though you need to shout to be heard above the tat-tat-tat of the buttonhole machines and the whirr of the sewing machines. The only time the chatter stops is when cigar smoke fills the air. Then you know that the boss has come into the factory for one reason or another. But he usually doesn't stay long, and the din picks up again the moment the air clears. In this shop, an Italian presser who has a beautiful tenor voice sometimes sings opera arias, punctuating dramatic or funny lines with the loud hiss of his pressing machine. Last year one of the cutters read *Anna Karenina* aloud in Yiddish during lunchtime. (He hadn't yet gotten to the end of the book when slack season came and everyone was laid off—and when busy season started again Mary took a job in another shop—so she never got to find out if Anna and Vronsky lived happily ever after.) This year another cutter who knows how to read English well has been bringing the *New York Times* to work and reading to the workers who gather over at the cutters' station at lunchtime.

But today at lunchtime Selma, a sewing-machine operator, Mary's closest friend in this shop, tells her, "Mereleh, it's too nice outside to spend our little time for lunch sitting in here. Everyone's going up to the roof. Come on," and Mary goes with her. Selma is about twelve years younger than Mary, a vivacious girl who missed being attractive because scoliosis has made her back look oddly twisted. For the last year or two, Mary hasn't had a real boyfriend; so she and Selma have had a standing movie date for both Saturday and Sunday afternoons, and sometimes they'd go out to eat on Saturday evenings too. But now Selma is keeping steady company with Howie, so she's busy on the weekends.

They ride the elevator to the top floor and then climb a flight of stairs up to the roof. Some workers are already sitting on the roof's ledge and eating; even in the fresh air, the smell of garlic and raw onion from their sandwiches is strong. Mary is about to take out of her purse the hardboiled egg and two pieces of bread wrapped in a newspaper that she's brought for her lunch, but a knot of people have gathered on one side of the roof, and Selma says, "Let's go see what they're looking at."

They're watching two bottle-blond girls banter with a couple of men who are on the roof of the neighboring building, which is six or seven feet lower. "Come on girls, you can do it," a broad-shouldered chap with a big black mustache urges. He spreads his legs for balance and stretches his arms up, poised to catch the giddier and smaller of the two girls.

"Oh, Fannie, we better not," her companion squeaks.

"Come on, dollie, you, too," the other man says to the plumper and more prudent one, and he flexes like the strongman at the circus before he bursts into song. *Oh, you beautiful doll, you great big beautiful doll.* Some of the girls who watch are giggling and the men are cheering and egging the two blondes on.

"Don't do it!" Mary yells. All eyes turn to her, but she doesn't stop. "You can break your neck. Don't be a damn fool!"

Fannie pays no attention. She sits on the ledge, closes her eyes, and with a piglet's squeal, shoves off and drops into the man's arms.

"Now you, baby girl, come on," the singer encourages the zaftig blonde as he stations himself where his friend had been. He strips to a sleeveless white undershirt and extends his muscled arms. *Let me put my arms around you. I can never live without you . . .* He belts out his song, and the girl, as though hypnotized by his mock-lyrical call, sits down on the ledge and shoves herself off. Though the girl lands like a sack of flour in the man's big arms and the other watchers cheer them, Mary's stomach flip-flops and she groans. She has to fight being sick.

Back at work, she tries to figure out why the incident has upset her so much. (Did she tell me this story too, as a cautionary tale during my own reckless and rowdy youth?) She and Goldie (Goldie, who's been dead since 1918, the flu epidemic) once engaged in such an antic—an even worse one, in a shop where they worked on the Lower East Side. They were eating lunch on the roof with the other workers, and there were a couple of boys on the neighboring roof who called to the girls to jump over. The two buildings were on the same level, but a space of three or four feet separated them. "Come on, sweetie, I won't let you fall," a boy who looked like a Jewish Wallace Reid shouted at Mary. Goldie jumped first, and when she landed safely in the arms of the burly fellow next to him, Mary jumped. Her leap over to the other roof took only an instant, but in that instant a world of images went through her head. She saw herself as a charming scamp, hair flying fetchingly in the wind, throwing the dice of life with breathtaking abandon. She saw herself splattered on the pavement six flights below. She saw Hirschel wailing and di mameh's face distorted in pain as she pulled sheets over the mirror.

Everyone cheered when Mary landed in the arms of Joey, the Jewish Wallace Reid. But what a fool, she tells herself now, to play with death like it's a game, just to show off for some boy. He became her first real boyfriend, Joey. He was true to his promise and didn't let her fall that day; he waited about ten months, when the wife and little boy he never told her he had arrived at Ellis Island. Oh, how gullible she used to be. And always, always, falling for the wrong fellas—the handsome ones, the good dancers, the sharp dressers. A boyfriend she had a few years back, a real looker, called her his good-time gal. She was insulted though he swore he didn't mean anything bad by it—a compliment, he said, because she liked to have fun and didn't lay traps for guys like a lot of girls did.

But what he said rankles still. These days, when she looks back on her eighteen years in America, she thinks she's wasted her life being a good-time gal—never figuring out how to fulfill her dream of being a dancer, always passing up good chances, like Dominick, an Italian fella who made a very fine living and wanted to marry her. (But he was a goy. Her mother would have sat shiva if she'd married a goy.) There were quite a few other men, too, who proposed to her; but there was always something about them that bothered her . . . a goy, a pear-shaped behind, a grating voice that sounded like a burp, a cheapskate . . .

Her sister Buna Rivka (who was brought to America by Sarah and Sam in 1923 and is now called Ray) is always telling her, "You're just too choosy." Maybe Ray is right that Mary is too choosy, because now she has nobody, and other girls—all her girlfriends from the past, Mazie, Bessie, Sophie—all of them ended up at least with a husband and a family. Even Selma now. It's been like the American game of musical chairs, where everyone goes round and round a circle of chairs, and when the music stops you're supposed to grab one and sit down. Only she has been left standing with no chair.

Her mind keeps coming back to such disturbing thoughts for the rest of the afternoon, like a finger that can't help poking through a hole in a pocket.

Saturday. My mother, who won't be my mother for many years yet, sits down on a bench beneath a newly leafed-out tree in Crotona Park. She takes off her woolen coat because it's warm and drapes it on the back of the bench. On the lake in front of her there's a ruckus of loud squawks and beating wings— four mallards, three with iridescent blue-green feathers, the fourth drab. She watches the drab duck writhe and thrash as one drake dunks her head and another nips at her wing. The third floats about her in circles and waits his turn. The drab duck struggles to free herself, but the two who are upon her join forces to keep her down, and she sputters and sinks. They don't mean her harm. They're only following an imperative that is their nature before they mount her and mate. My mother has seen it all before and doesn't want to see it again.

She turns her eyes to the path. She can make out that a sauntering speck in the distance is a man, but she cannot yet discern what sort. . . . Someday I will have this man's eyes and his chin. When I'm a teenager I'll saunter just the way he does, hands in pockets and cigarette dangling from my lips, tough-girl style. From what she's told me and what I know of her—of them—I can envision what happens next: in a minute or two he's close enough for her to see that he's nicely dressed, beige overcoat (camel hair, she's sure) with the collar up, brown pants and a brown hat. He looks a little bit like a gangster, the way he wears his hat, raked at an angle, tipped to almost cover an eye—or like an actor playing a gangster in the movies. He stops at a water fountain, and my mother idly watches as he takes a long drink. He's carrying a fat book under his arm.

Then he sits down on a bench not too far from her, and he takes off his coat, folds it so that only the shiny lining shows, and places it next to him. He opens the book and starts reading, but his mind is not in it, and he looks around restlessly. He lights up a cigarette, takes a couple of puffs, then lets it dangle at the side of his mouth. After a few minutes, he gets up, slings the coat casually over one shoulder, and begins walking again, hands in his pockets, a tough-guy swagger. My mother is still idly watching. He stops, takes the cigarette from his mouth, throws it to the ground, and extinguishes it with a heel. When he glances in her direction she quickly looks away so he won't think she's staring, and she fixes her gaze on the sparrows that are pecking at crumbs on the walk in front of her.

Then he's standing only a few feet away. She can see out of the corner of her eye that he lifts his hat. The weather is much too warm for wool. She expects him to take out a handkerchief and start wiping his brow, but he stands there, and she realizes he's lifting his hat to her. "Mind if I sit?" he asks. His starched white shirt gleams in the sunlight.

"Oh, sure." She'd been occupying the middle of the bench, under the shadiest part of the tree. Now she slides herself into the glaring sun. He sits in the shade. She gets a whiff of Sen-Sen on his breath, a sweet licorice smell.

She stares straight ahead but she can see he's crossed one of his legs over the other, and he's shaking a foot as though impatient, like he's waiting for someone or something. Even under his fine trousers, his calf looks powerfully muscled.

In a few minutes she feels herself sweating in the unseasonably hot sun. Maybe she should go back to her room, she tells herself. But what will she do there? The whole day and evening and the next day too stretch out before her like a vast and barren desert; and she doesn't move. Instead, she finds a handkerchief in her purse and dabs delicately at her upper lip.

"You from here?" His voice startles her.

She glances over at him. Up close, with his hat off, he doesn't look at all like a gangster. He's young. Of course now that she's thirty-five, anyone under thirty looks like a child to her. "Yeah, the Bronx," she says.

"Me, too, now—over on the other side of the Grand Concourse." He gestures with his chin. "But I go to the gym on Southern Boulevard, and I just met up with a buddy from there for a couple beers." He looks straight at her; he's suddenly voluble. "Yeah, I used to live downtown but the pop lost his job, so I figured that rather than make the whole family move to a cheaper place, I'd move back with them and help pay the rent till he's working again." His voice has a good-boy earnestness now that belies her first impression of him.

"Oh, that's such a nice thing for a son to do," Mary says.

"Well, it's not permanent, of course." He keeps looking at her. His dark eyes make her strangely nervous. Something has switched in his expression and again he looks like a tough guy. It's as though he hasn't yet decided who he wants to be.

Then they're both silent. He stares off in space and begins shaking a foot impatiently like he did before. She steals another glance at him. Fine cut lips, a beauty mark just above his mouth on the left side, even a little cleft in his chin. Not one gray hair on his head, of course. She's had quite a few already; whenever she sees one she pulls it out. This boy's hair is dark and shiny like blackbird feathers. He probably isn't much over twenty.

"By the way," he says and suddenly turns to her, "my name's Morris." She can smell Sen-Sen again, mixed with cigarette and a little whiff of alcohol. "Well, the name is really Moishe, though I've hardly used that since I was fifteen, when we came here from Poland."

"I'm Mary. Please to meet you," she says. She's surprised by the little nervous quiver in her voice. She and this sort of boy—handsome, a little dangerous looking—used to attract each other like iron magnets. But she's already seen that movie, sat through it a dozen times, and knows how it always ends. I don't have to sit through that one again, she tells herself.

"I'm very pleased to meet you, Mary," Moishe says and extends his hand, which engulfs hers when she gives it to him. He keeps it for so long that she feels she should pull her hand away. I gotta go, she tells herself. But she makes no move to rise.

He fumbles in his jacket pocket and takes out a pack of cigarettes. Lucky Strike. He taps the pack until one cigarette extends above the others. "Smoke?"

"Oh, yes, thank you." She takes the cigarette and puts it between her lips; he lights a match and brings it toward her mouth. "Thanks," she says, inhaling. She glances up at him, and their eyes lock. It's like she's touched an open electrical outlet, except the charge is all down there. She has to look away. She feels herself blushing, wondering if her face betrayed what she felt. Did he feel the charge, too?

They both smoke intently, staring out at the lake. He blows out a long plume of smoke, then Mary does the same. She must look like a middle-aged woman to him, she thinks, but the strong sensation down there hasn't gone away. I should just go, she tells herself again and doesn't move. Her eye lights on his book. It's in English. She silently sounds out the words. Ad-ven-tures in Gen-i-us. Finally she asks, "What are you reading?"

For a moment, he looks puzzled, as though he'd forgotten he had a book with him. "Oh, this . . . It's by a philosopher. He says that the real history of man is about the contributions that geniuses make to human civilization—you know, Plato, Darwin, Flaubert [he pronounces the name "Flowbert"], people like that."

She's heard of none of those people. She's never read a book in English. He's a lot better educated than she is, she thinks. Silence settles itself like a third person that's sat down between them. But when she glances over at him again, she sees he's staring at her, and again their eyes lock for a moment and again the charge zaps her before she looks away, embarrassed.

"Oh!" he says. She cuts her eyes back to him. He's looking at his watch. "I'm going to be late." He rises. "It was nice to talk to you."

"Oh, yes," Mary says. She's relieved actually. He's just a boy, at least ten years younger than she is. What would be the point in starting up with a kid like that? But she's disappointed too; she would have liked to taste his mouth, to touch his strong-looking legs. Well, that's that, she thinks.

"Say." He sits down again, on the edge of the bench. "I enjoyed meeting you. You think maybe we can go out sometime, to a movie or something?"

Nothing can come of it, says the same voice in my mother's head that's been telling her for a while now that it's high time she started acting like a more serious person. But what slips from her mouth is, "Oh, I'd like that very much."

"Good. How's about tomorrow? I can pick you up about two o'clock. Okay?" He pats his pockets until he finds a pencil stub and a matchbook, which he opens up, poised to write her address on a blank spot.

My mother could have stayed home that day. She could have gone to another park, or to a movie. He could have strolled in the direction of the big fountain instead of toward the lake. In the old country they would have said it was *beshert*, destined, that they should go to the same park, on the same day, at the same hour, and she should sit down on a bench that was directly in his path, and he should glance up from his book and see her. I'm not sure that I believe in *beshert*, but I am sure that, like her untimely ejection from Sarah and Sam's home, this moment, too, led inexorably to what she would pay for to her last rattling breath.

"Six-thirty-five Fox Street," she tells him.

"Two o'clock, okay?" he repeats.

My mother has been sleeping in on Sunday mornings since she and Selma stopped going to matinees. She sometimes stays in bed until one o'clock or even later. When she wakes up too early on Sundays, she pulls the blanket over her head to block out the light that will soon pour through the ripped window shade, and she huddles like a snail in its shell until she drifts off again. She can be totally oblivious to Sunday-morning noises, such as the two young daughters of her missus practicing their piano lessons on the upright in the living room. This Sunday, though, their clamorous banging wakes her, and she can't fall asleep again.

She lies in bed ignoring the cacophony of sound. She's thinking that in a few hours she will see him again. Yesterday, when she got back to her room and thought about it, she was disgusted with herself for making a date with this fella. He's so young, and there's something unformed-looking about him: one minute he's like a soft boy and the next like a tough gangster, like he isn't even sure himself who he is yet. A Goldie expression popped into her head: Well, he ain't gonna learn on me. But in the course of her lonely evening she asked herself, Why make up your mind so fast? You can't go on first impressions, and anyway you never know what unexpected things are possible between two people. Her heart leapt up at the memory of his raising his hat to her, his handsome face and gleaming white shirt, the look he gave her when he lit her cigarette. He's such a contrast to her shabby surroundings, this furnished room in which she's lived for two years now.

My mother has lived in nothing but furnished rooms since Sarah and Sam kicked her out. This room is actually better than most. It's pretty spacious. The mattress isn't bad—no lumps and no bedbugs. There's a window that looks out on Fox Street and when she's home she can get the afternoon sun. There's even a little table radio in the room, so when she's lying in bed after a hard day's work, she can turn on the radio and listen to music. She's tried to make the place as homey as she knows how. At Woolworth's she bought a lace runner to put on the dresser and lace doilies for the arms of the old overstuffed chair that sits in the corner. On the dresser she's also placed a red glass vase and a plaster statue of the Venus de Milo, which she won at Bingo Night at the movies. But the only dear thing in the room is the photograph that sits on the nightstand near her bed—Hirschel, ten years old, his hair looking as though he slept on it wrong and his big eyes sad. She's kept it all these years, still in the fancy gilt frame she bought with her first pay from the pinafore factory. Though Hirschel is a man now, working in the big city of Riga and with a life of his own, when she kisses this picture she can feel his soft boy's cheek under her lips.

She misses him still, and she misses di mameh and her sisters Chana and Hinda. Yet she thinks she'd rather disappear from the earth than go back to where she came from. Sometimes she has nightmares, or maybe she's half-awake and they're horror fantasies. She's in the shtetl again, in the house in which she was born, with its hard-packed dirt floor and musty smells of un-washed clothes and too many bodies. She's selling vegetables like di mameh used to in the dark little hole in the wall attached to their living quarters; or she's married to the fish peddler or the man who sweeps the synagogue, a half-dozen hungry children pulling at her apron, nowhere to go for diversion but the outdoor market, nothing to do but take care of kids and serve a grumpy husband.

And yet how is she better off in a lonely furnished room, slaving in the shop day in and day out? She's not sure. She tells herself, I'm still so hungry for a little happiness. Why can't I get it? She doesn't ask too much of life anymore. But at least a nice home, a husband, a baby. She's given up on the big dream that she'd be a dancer and that she'd bring the whole family to America. Anyway, they don't need to come here anymore. They've made their own lives in Latvia by now and have no reason to come to a country where millions of people are out of work and everyone is suffering from the Depression.

Mary checks the little clock near her bed. It's ten twenty. Moishe won't be coming around for more than three and a half hours . . . but just the thought of the way he looked at her, and the fragrance of his breath, and his muscled calf—and she feels that strong, embarrassing zap like she did in the park. *Moishe.* That's the name she calls him in her mind, a name that seems so much more intimate to her than Morris. She jumps up, puts on her old silk wrapper, and goes to get her jar of cold cream from her shelf in the bathroom medicine cabinet. Her skin will be soft and smooth if she lets the cream sit on it for a few hours. This is what she's always done when she's had a date. She applies the cold cream back in her room, looking in the hand mirror that she keeps in a drawer beside her bed. Not too ugly yet, she tells herself. Her green eyes are still flecked with gold, and they're still large and clear. Her auburn hair is still thick and has nice natural highlights. People tell her she has a Joan Crawford mouth. Mary turns her head so that it will be in profile in the mirror and then flicks her eyes to the reflection. No, no sags under her chin yet, that she can detect. But she's as pale as an underdone roll. She hasn't eaten since she made herself a dish of farmer cheese with sour cream yesterday afternoon when she returned from the park.

She goes to the kitchen, where she takes her jar of herring out of the refrigerator and her loaf of sliced rye bread out of the breadbox. When Mary first rented her room, Mrs. Potesh asked if she'd like board too. Mary said no because she'd boarded before, and she knew that eating together with a husband and wife and all their children only reminded her how lonely she was, an alien presence in the midst of a family. So instead of boarding, Mary took kitchen privileges. Now, standing at the sink and eating, she can hear the Poteshes in the living room. "Stop your bellyaching!" Mr. Potesh snaps at his two daughters, who are whining about how they have nothing to do. Mary knows from the rustling sound of paper that he's reading his *Freiheit* and doesn't want to be disturbed. Of the many things Mary has always hated about living in furnished rooms, among the worst is having to listen to the squabbles of strangers.

"Shaaa! That's enough!" Mrs. Potesh yells at her daughters. "If you're bored go out and play in the sunshine."

After Mary finishes her morning snack, she's at loose ends. It's barely eleven o'clock. She goes back to her room and turns on the radio, but she finds she's too excited about her date to listen to Rudy Vallee's mellow croon. She snaps the radio off. She tries to calm herself by thinking that she'll go out with this guy once and it will come to nothing. Even if she's wrong about how young and unformed he is, he's much too educated for her . . . that book he was reading whose title she could barely understand and the names he mentioned she'd never heard of. He'd find out right away what an ignoramus she was. She's wasted enough time in her life with things that weren't going to work out, and a boy like that is definitely not for her. "I just can't afford to do it anymore," she declares aloud to herself.

But she feels as though her nerves are buzzing. What can calm her until 2:00 p.m.? She takes out of her drawer a thin beige envelope on which three red stamps have been pasted. It's the letter she received from di mameh yesterday morning. Mrs. Potesh had slipped it under her door, knocking and calling, as she always did when there was mail for Mary: "Hello? You got a letter." Mary was relieved to receive it because it had been more than six weeks since she or her sister Ray have had any word. Mary always has anxieties between letters from the family, which take so long to come. Di mameh or one of Mary's sisters or her brother could write, *We are all well and healthy,* and by the time the letter had arrived on the freighter, they could all be sick or dead. "God forbid, ptu, ptu, ptu!" Mary says aloud whenever she has such a thought.

Now she takes the letter with its spidery Yiddish handwriting out of its envelope again, sits down on her bed, and rereads it. *Mayn tayere tochter, mayn ershte trayst . . . My dear daughter, my first comfort.* That's the way di mameh always starts her letters to Mary, her eldest. *We thank you very much for the postal order for 10 rubles from you and Buna Rivka. It got here safe, and now Hinda and I can buy new shoes and a new hat for Pesach.* Hinda often writes the letters for di mameh, who is close to seventy now and has a very shaky hand; but this thank-you letter di mameh has written herself, a newsy letter telling Mary that Chana came to visit from Dvinsk with her three boys. The oldest, Dovid, is ten and at the top of his class in school; the middle one, Lev, though he's only seven, plays the violin like an angel; and the little one, Shlomo, can say *bubeh* very clear. Hirschel is still living in Riga and he writes he is keeping company with a nice young lady.

Mary holds the letter to her lips and kisses the paper again, as she did yesterday morning. Her mother's letters always make her teary, even if there's nothing sad in them. When Mary last saw her, di mameh's hair was dark; now it's surely gray. Mary fears she may never see her mother or any of them again in this world. Sometimes, when she's feeling very lonely or gloomy, she says things to di mameh in her thoughts she would never write in a letter. I was too young when I left you, Mameh. How could a girl who wasn't completely grown up yet, seventeen years old—how could she cross the ocean to such a new world, all by herself, and figure out what to do and how to live? I just was not able to do it. Mameh, I still don't know how.

Mary puts the letter back in the drawer and checks her watch. It's only 11:25, but she opens her closet door. When she remembers Moishe's elegance, everything she owns seems so ugly. Finally she takes out a dress of light-blue crepe that buttons down the front with little silver buttons. She got it for 50 percent off because there were pulled threads on the collar, but if there's anything she's still really good at, it's sewing. She'd sewed material of navy-blue sateen over the old collar and covered the cuffs, too, with navy-blue sateen. Now it looks like something you'd buy at Saks Fifth Avenue for a hundred dollars. That's the dress she'll wear today.

In the bathroom, she has to scrub the gray soap and dirt rings left in the tub by the two Potesh girls, who bathe on Saturday nights, and then she runs her bath. She washes herself with a rough cloth, then shaves her legs. She rubs a sweet-smelling lotion she bought at Woolworth's on her arms and legs and breasts and belly. It takes her forever to style her hair and put on her makeup and find the right costume jewelry to go with her dress—blue-topaz-colored earrings and a matching necklace. She hurries because she's sure it must be late. But when she stops to look at the alarm clock by her bed she sees it's only ten minutes after one. She finds her watch and puts it on. It says the same thing the clock says. She still has fifty minutes to wait before he comes.

Time passes as slowly as an old mule dragging a boulder. She sits in the armchair and lectures herself. You're still a damn fool, to get so excited by a boy you don't even know, like you're sixteen years old. He's much too young for you, and how does somebody like you come to an educated boy like that anyway? But it doesn't matter what she recites to calm herself down, because when she remembers his shiny black hair and his heavy-lidded eyes—bedroom eyes, the girls call it—every nerve jangles worse than if she'd swallowed a gallon of coffee.

She looks at her watch every few minutes. Finally, it's ten minutes to two. She goes to stand at the window so that she might see him as he rounds the corner and climbs the stoop of her house.

Two o'clock comes, and it goes, and there's no Moishe rounding the corner. Mary looks at her watch again and again. Could it be that when she wound it last night the stem came loose without her noticing and she'd set it ahead? She checks the watch against the little clock, but they both say the same thing, just as they did before. Maybe she misremembered the time he said he'd come for her. No, she can still hear his voice after he wrote her address down on the inside of the matchbook: "Two o'clock, okay?"

Suddenly she has a terrible thought. He probably rang the bell and she didn't hear it, and Mrs. Potesh answered the door and didn't know Mary was in her room. "She's gone out for the day," Mrs. Potesh must have told him. Or maybe Mrs. Potesh wasn't in and one of her bratty daughters answered the door. Just for a spiteful prank, the girl could have told Moishe, "She moved out this morning," or "We don't have no Mary living here."

Mary flies out of the room and down the hallway, her heart banging like a lid on a boiling-over kettle. "Mrs. Potesh!" she's yelling before she even gets to the living room, "Mrs. Potesh, did somebody ring the bell for me?"

Mr. Potesh has been snoozing on the couch and Mrs. Potesh knitting a mitten in the armchair next to him. Mr. Potesh sits up quickly, startled by the frenzy in Mary's voice. The ball of yarn drops from Mrs. Potesh's lap. "No . . . Nobody at all rang the bell," Mrs. Potesh says. "We've both been right here since after lunch and there's been nobody. Is something the matter?" She stares at Mary.

"No, nothing. Sorry." Mary is ashamed now. "I just thought a friend might come by." She slinks back into her room to wait some more.

She hears them talking. Mr. Potesh says, "That woman gets stranger all the time. It's not normal, a woman her age never to have a husband. What did she do with her whole life before she moved in here?"

Three o'clock comes and goes, and then four. My mother tells herself she never really believed he would come see her anyway. Even while she was dreaming of him and dressing up for him, she really knew he wouldn't come. It's happened to her several times that she's had a sense of things before they occurred. Like she'd be walking along the street and something inside would tell her, Look on the sidewalk, to your right, and there would be a dollar bill. That had happened at least two or three times.

But those were times she'd found something, and this was a time she lost something. He'd made a fool of her. Maybe he guessed she was a lot older than he, and he wanted to teach an old maid a lesson, so she'd never again think she could trick a young man. She's numb now. If he came, she would not care. She would tell him to go to hell and roast there like a goy's pig. She doesn't let herself cry because this is only one more disappointment in a long series of them. At five o'clock she puts on her hat. She will go to the movies.

2

The rest of 1932

TIME ON THE MARCH

GERMANY. Predictions are that Hindenburg will win by eight million in this week's vote . . . The reelection of Paul von Hindenburg for the presidency of the Reich is viewed by most Germans as a foregone conclusion. In the initial balloting, President Hindenburg led Herr Hitler by more than seven million votes but failed to obtain the absolute majority needed for election. Yet even if Herr Hitler repeats his previous performance, in view of the momentum accumulated by Hindenburg sentiment in the past week, the educated guess is that the fascist leader will fall behind by at least a million votes.

THE UNITED STATES. Between ten and twelve million unemployed men and women are searching the garbage cans, especially in more prosperous neighborhoods, for food that has been left—men competing with rats and stray cats of the street . . .

M y mother goes back to the same movie, with even the same newsreels, that she saw a few evenings ago. The movie is about a redheaded woman who takes a French chauffeur as her lover. My mother always goes to the movies when she's sad. She goes when she's not sad too. She goes as often as she can, even if she has to go alone. She loves the movies even more than she did in the old days because now the actors are speaking and a lot of movie theaters look like palaces built for a czar—white marble staircases, plush red carpets, glass canopies brilliant with thousands of electric lights. At the movies, she loses herself in the actors and forgets everything she doesn't like about her life.

Her sister Ray has never understood her fascination with the movies; but Ray, who's younger than Mary, was already an old lady when she stepped off the boat nine years ago, so frumpy that Mary, who'd left a girl behind in Preil, hardly recognized her. They're opposites—Ray short and roly-poly; Mary tall, slim, with a flat stomach and shapely breasts. "Say, you two can't be sisters—a Saks Fifth Avenue model and a flat-footed policeman!" Mary's old friend Estella, who didn't like Ray at all, once remarked. Maybe Estella exaggerated, but people still can't believe they're related. "We're like night and day," Mary and Ray complain of each other, though they're often together because they're the only two of their mother's children in America.

Through most of *Red-Headed Woman* Mary is restless because she already knows the movie's plot, and because the chauffeur doesn't appear until almost the end. When he comes on the screen again, she's enchanted—he's the most beautiful man she's ever seen. Charles Boyer, his name is. She'd thought that boy she met in the park, who stood her up and made her feel like a damn fool, looked like him; but he doesn't at all. At the memory of that fiasco she's disgusted with herself again, until she forces her eyes back to the screen and is caught up in the charm of the young actor's seductive eyes.

The girls in the garment trade call the first day of the workweek Blue Monday, because after the freedom of Saturday and Sunday it's not easy to begin a long week in harness. But my mother has just had a blue Sunday too. On the crowded subway train she takes to work, she hangs on to the overhead strap, and to distract herself she studies the ad just above her. The brightly colored placard doesn't help her gloom at all—Mmm Mmm Good, a smiley family at a kitchen table spooning soup into their happy mouths. . . . She's so tired of her thoughts, so tired of the stupid hopes she keeps having, about what she doesn't know—this time about a creep who was as suited for her as a baboon's skin. She can't snap out of her feelings. He made a damn fool of her—that rotten scoundrel who out of nowhere crossed her path and hoodwinked her. He could see she was just a working woman, and he thought he was too good for her. But it was her fault, too, for being as dumb and giddy as the day she got off the boat. When the hell will she wise up?

She drags through her workday automatically, like a donkey going round and round a mill. She can't get her mind off what happened, and she castigates herself as she does so often of late for not being a more serious person. She's thirty-five years old, for godsakes. How could she let herself get hoodwinked?

After nine hours, her arms and legs aching like they're ready to fall off, she takes the subway home. She gets off in the Bronx and then must walk for two blocks. She turns the corner on Fox Street. There on the stoop of the house where she lives, a man is sitting. Even before her conscious mind can register who it is, the breath flies out of her like the breath of a newborn when the doctor slaps it into life. Oh, God, run, she tells herself, but her legs feel weak as a newborn's, too, and she knows no more than a newborn whether she wants to run from him or to him.

Moishe rises the moment he see her. "Hey, Mary, sorry about yesterday. Couldn't be helped." He says it with tight lips, out of the corner of his mouth, like a gangster. Then he pulls the homburg from his head and clears his throat. "I would've called but I never got your telephone number. I had to take my mother to the doctor, and he kept us there for hours. Bleeding ulcers . . ." He shrugs awkwardly. "Well, I just came by to see if you'd accept my apology and maybe go out with me next Saturday. Do you like the boat rides in Crotona Park?" The tough-guy expression with which he started has slipped into boyish eagerness. "We could do that, and I thought that maybe after we could go to dinner at this Italian restaurant I know . . . or any place at all you'd like to go."

Years later, she will tell me of their first date—the lake on which they rowed, the restaurant in which they ate, the stories he told. And what she didn't say, I can imagine from what I knew of her, of him. They've made up to meet at the big wooden Indian that stands in front of the cigar store next to the subway station. "Two o'clock," he'd said again. My mother leaves her room twenty minutes before two, though it only takes six or seven minutes to walk to the station. She intends to stroll and enjoy the fine April weather. But her legs have a mind of their own and hurry her down the street. Don't be a damn fool, she warns herself, and she hears the warning repeated in the staccato tap her heels make on the sidewalk: don't be a damn fool, don't be a damn fool. She arrives, breathless, at the street where the wooden Indian stands. It's fifteen minutes to two—and he's already there. She sees him before he sees her. He's pacing back and forth with long, powerful, impatient strides, like the male lion in the Bronx Zoo. He wears a cream-colored suit and a panama hat with a beige ribbon at the base of the crown, and his face looks tanner than it did the week before—a smooth buttery bronze. Oh, his beauty hurts her heart.

When he sees her, he stops and smiles a radiant smile, his teeth a lovely white. He pulls her to himself, as though they're already lovers. "Hey, I haven't been able to get you out of my mind all week long," he says huskily. She stiffens an instant. He's too quick, she thinks, this same guy who stood her up and made her feel ridiculous, who's too young for her, and too fancy and too educated for her—but she doesn't break from his tight embrace.

He takes her hand and leads her down the subway stairs. In the train, he sits very close to her. He hasn't relinquished her hand. He gazes at it and caresses her palm with a thumb that looks stout compared to hers. "How small and fine your hands are. That's one of the first things I noticed about you last week," he tells her.

She steals a glance at her hand that remains cradled in his. It's as though she's seeing it for the first time. It is small and fine, just as he said. Who would think that hand is used day in and day out to pin dress parts on a dummy? All the way to Crotona Park, he doesn't let go of her hand, which she renders up to him, bemused but blissful too.

In the park, he rows their rented boat with athletic grace. He's taken off his jacket and tie, and she watches the work of his firm muscles that are only half-hidden under his short-sleeved shirt. The shiny dark hairs on his fore-arms are manly and to her exquisitely beautiful. She'd like to touch them—the thick black curls on his head too. She'd like to reach out and touch him everywhere. But she also likes sitting across from him in the boat and just looking at him.

The sun is bright but not hot, and the slight wind is fragrant with the newly mown park grass. She throws her head back, half-closes her eyes (though she can still see him), and feels herself relaxing, like floating in a warm bath. Right now all her recent resolves have flown from her head like a flock of pigeons, and she can think of nothing else to want from life but this moment.

He chats boyishly as he rows. He tells her that back in the old country his family lived near Nowy Korczyn, not far from Krakow, on a huge estate with a turreted watchtower, many servants, a very big farm. Twenty, thirty people worked for his family, picking wheat, barley, potatoes, sugar beets, taking care of cows, sheep, horses. The boat floats along, and Mary loves dip-ping her fingers in the water of the sapphire-blue lake and creating a gentle ripple around them. Mama ducks and their sweet babies trail the boat and circle it charmingly whenever Moishe stops rowing. She loves listening to his life story, his voice like warm amber to her. He tells her that before he came to America in 1921, he'd been sent to a gymnasium in Krakow, where he got the top prize for writing an essay on the glorious and tragic history of the motherland. (She doesn't tell him that she's been to school for less than a year altogether, nine months in Preil, where she learned to read the Hebrew alphabet; and in America, night school for a couple of months, until she fell asleep in class because she was tired from working in the shop all day; and when the teacher woke her up and the other students laughed, she never went back.) He says he was twenty-five years old in February and asks her age. "Twenty-six," she says without a pause. "An older woman," she adds with a wink, and he laughs.

For supper he takes her on the subway to Manhattan, to Angelo's Restaurant on Forty-Fourth Street, with waiters in black jackets and bow ties; and wine-bottle candleholders, plump with drippings of red and green wax; and a mandolin-and-accordion orchestra. "Ever had osso bucco? How about Sangiovese for the wine? Tiramisu for dessert?" He orders it all for her, things she's never heard of that are more delicious than anything she's ever tasted. He seems neither a boy nor a tough guy now. It's like in a dream where a person keeps transforming into someone new—he's a sophisticated upperclass gentleman . . . the young actor Cary Grant. His sophistication makes her feel like a girl. She's disoriented but so intrigued too. He tells her about a book he's been reading, in German, by an Austrian Jew, Stefan Zweig, about a man two hundred years ago who could just touch a person and they'd be cured of any illness by the power of his animal magnetism. "You could turn the world upside down with power like that," he says. He tells her he knows six languages—Polish, German, English, Hebrew (to read), quite a bit of Russian, and of course Yiddish.

He hasn't put his tie back on since he took it off at the lake, and his collar is open. Just under his neck she can see swirls of curly hairs, black and shiny as coal, as heavy as her dear tateh's had been. She's sad for a moment, remembering summertimes when she was a little girl and her tateh had come back from bathing in the river, how she'd loved to rest her cheek on the warm pelt of his chest . . . "So when we arrived here," Moishe says, cutting into her revery, "I thought I'd be able to go right to an American gymnasium. I already knew a lot of English and would've done just fine in school here." His

expression changes, boyish again and undefended. "But my mother's brothers cheated her out of a lot of money when she left Poland." He pauses to get
a pack of cigarettes from his jacket pocket. He offers Mary one before he
takes one himself. When he lights her up—that intimate gesture of bringing
the flame of the match toward her mouth—their eyes meet, and again, just
like that first time on the bench in Crotona Park, a powerful charge courses
through her down there. She inhales deeply and blows the smoke through
her nose, playing the sophisticated older woman now. She feels all his different selves calling out the different selves in her.

"Yeah, they gave my mother a lump sum that was just enough to furnish
our apartment here and invest a little bit for some tiny income every month.
The pop works every once in a while doing translations, but he's never gotten out of the habit of his Talmud study, and that's mostly what he does, day
and night. I've got a sister three years younger than me, but my mother never
wanted her to hold a job, so guess who's left to hustle," he says with a shrug.
His fingers clutch his wine goblet. Mary reaches out and touches them. He
looks like a boy now. He puts the goblet down and turns his hand up to receive hers, and they sit holding hands for many minutes.

In the street, on the way to the subway station, he stops and pulls her into
a dark doorway. The gangster is back. He lifts her chin with gruff fingers and
brings his mouth down hard on hers. She can smell the red wine and cigarettes on his breath, and it's strangely exciting to her. His hands wander her
body. She doesn't want to stop what is so lovely, but she can't let him do what
he's doing. Their hands perform a brief ballet of struggle, until he lets her
win and embraces her gently. "Come to bed with me," he whispers huskily.

She shakes her head no.

"Why?" he asks doggedly.

What can she say? The truth is, she really wants to. But she knows the
game young men play. If she says yes now, she'll have this night with him, but
that will probably be the end of it. "We hardly know each other," she answers
softly. She chooses those words because they will tell him she's not loose, not
a game girl who will sleep with any man who asks her—but they hold out a
promise for what she may give when they do know each other.

He's made a date with her for the next Saturday. All week my mother floats
on the breathtaking memory of him. He's Moishe the Magician who's pulled

her out of sadness like a magician pulls a rabbit out of a hat. He's as far above any man she's ever gone out with as the sky is from the ground. The girls at work have already noticed that there's something different about her. "Where are you, Mary? A million miles away," Selma says when they walk to the subway station together on Monday evening. When Paula, an old maid of almost forty with a limp and a brace on her leg, asks if she'd like to go see *Shanghai Express* with Marlene Dietrich next Friday, Mary declines, though she doesn't tell her she must stay home Friday evening and get her beauty sleep so she'll look well rested on Saturday. Paula knows something is up. "So who's your Prince Charming you don't come out with any of us no more?" she asks.

My mother only shrugs at all such questions, though her lips turn up in an involuntary smile. She can't tell them about what has happened to her. She thinks that to put it in words would be like picking apart a rose—you'd end up with a heap of finger-smudged petals in place of an exquisite blossom.

By Thursday she's begun to worry. What if he's decided she's acting too hard to get and it's not worth the effort for him? Oh, she was never good at this! She always knew how to stop the fresh ones she didn't care for. But with those she did care for, she couldn't figure out the right time and the wrong time to say yes. Maybe that's why she's reached the age of thirty-five with nothing. The next Saturday night, she holds out again. And all during the week she has misgivings and regrets.

Because I was not so much her child as her intimate, from whom she kept few secrets, and she told me all through my growing-up years that she'd been crazy wild about him; because when we sometimes played music on the radio and I watched her dancing alone, I understood through the movements of her breasts and hips and open arms how she could offer up her whole being lavishly, heedlessly, vulnerably; because sensual joys brought her wonder surpassing temples (though she had few such joys during my childhood. "Oh, take it all in, Lilly," she breathed ecstatically when, having sold my first book, I treated her to a restaurant as fine as a palace)—because of all that, this I imagine as plainly as if I'd been there: how for him she flung aside what she'd believed the years had taught her, becoming again a roof jumper; how she gave every bit of herself, stinting nothing; how she let herself be carried away like she'd boarded the train she'd been waiting for forever.

One Saturday night—she's known him perhaps four weeks by now—they go to a movie theater not far from Fox Street because Moishe wants to see Edward G. Robinson in *The Hatchet Man*, the kind of movie he gets a big kick out of, he says. After, they stop to buy ice cream, and they walk down the street holding hands and licking on their cones like they're a couple of kids. When they reach the house where Mary lives, Moishe asks if he can come in. Of course he can't because she has no place to take him in the apartment. She can see from the light in the front window that the Poteshes are home and are sitting in the living room.

"How's about if we go up to your roof," he says. "It's such a gorgeous night."

Since she'd moved in with the Poteshes, she's never yet been up to the roof; but she says yes, because it would be lovely to look at the stars with Moishe. They climb the five flights of stairs and open the door to the rooftop. There's no one around, not on that roof or the neighboring roofs which she can see by the light of the moon . . . No, there is someone! She jumps guiltily, startled at the movement of a body in white. But it's only a shirt, big and ghostly looking, hanging on the clothesline that crosses the roof. Except for its flapping and fluttering in the breeze, everything is absolutely still. It's like she and Moishe are alone in the world. The stars are so close that it seems she could reach her hand up and she would be burnt by them. Someone has put two pots of jasmine on the ledge, and the heady perfume of the flowers makes her pleasantly dizzy, as though she's just drunk a glass of strong wine.

Moishe stands behind her at the roof's edge, his arms tight at her waist. She can feel his warm breath on her hair. She can feel him hard against the small of her back. When he turns her toward him, he tilts her face with a firm hand; and they kiss, for hours it seems. She has never in her life been so present to a kiss. His grip on her is so tight it occurs to her that she might suffocate; but the thought passes in her mind as indifferently as if she were watching a trolley pass on the tracks. The only thing that matters in the whole universe is his tongue probing her mouth.

He loosens his hold on her so that he can take off his jacket, which he spreads, lining down, on the roof's tarred floor; then gently he pulls her down with him. She is sure that if she resists, if she relinquishes the splendor of this moment, she will be sorry for the rest of her days.

———

That night on the rooftop didn't lead directly to me. But it was a beginning. Saturdays, Sundays, and also Wednesdays (a big date night in the Bronx), this woman who will be my mother and this man who will be my father are always together. They go to movies or stroll on Southern Boulevard or they take the train all the way across the city to go to the Coney Island amusement parks or walk arm-in-arm on the boardwalk. They end most evenings by making love.

Sometimes Moishe's parents and sister go to Philadelphia to visit the home of his mother's girlhood friend, who was the daughter of Nowy Korczyn's mayor, and they stay overnight. On those nights, Moishe takes Mary to the West Bronx, to the apartment in which he lives with his family. He leads her through the living room, with its old-country porcelain knickknacks and little tables and big chairs, straight to his own books-and-papers-strewn bedroom. He shoves the latest book or magazine he's been reading from his bed and pulls Mary down with him.

But usually his family is home and he and Mary must make other arrangements. If Mary is certain that the Poteshes have gone out to a double feature, she takes Moishe to the narrow bed in her own room. If they can't go to his place or hers, they might go to the cluttered bachelor apartment of Moishe's buddy Seymour. Moishe tells Mary that Seymour is an older guy, a numbers runner he met at the gym on Southern Boulevard, where he likes to hang out with all the colorful and shady characters, boxers and gamblers and general hoodlums who frequent the place, though of course he's never been any of those things himself. Mary never meets Seymour, but she often lies with Moishe on Seymour's lumpy bed.

Moishe makes love to her all the ways she's always dreamed of being made love to. Sometimes he's tender, like a sweet boy. She loves that, how he kisses her eyes, her cheeks, her throat, her earlobes, how he slowly moves down her body with long kisses before he finally mounts and enters her; and later he lies on his back and she loves to do to him what he did to her, in the same slow and tender way. Sometimes the way he makes love to her is scary, like he's one of the hoods from his gym. He might seize a clump of her hair while he's inside her and wrap it hard around his fist; if she reaches up to loosen his grip he tugs harder, so hard she fears her scalp will tear; and if she tries to push his head away he raises a hand as though to slap her. Her scalp hurts for a little while after, but when the pain fades, she admits to herself that his fierceness thrills her, pleasures her.

When Moishe gets out of bed and goes to the bathroom to take a shower, Mary puts her lips on the pillow where he's lain and breathes in the lemony scent of his pomade. She caresses the wrinkles that his body made on the sheet. She misses him. She listens for the instant the water stops. Then, still naked, she paddles down the hall and knocks softly on the bathroom door. "A wet kiss?" she implores. She fears he'll think her too clingy, but she can't help herself.

"Hold on," he calls, and a few seconds later he opens the door, his back or legs still dripping. "Hey, doll face," he says in a husky voice. He takes her in his arms and covers her face and neck with kisses. Sometimes, his belly pressing against her, she feels him grow big again. He moves her in a backward dance to the sink, where he holds her firm by the buttocks and boosts her on to it. The porcelain is hard and cold, but she opens herself to him and barely notices the discomfort. After, they shower together, mouths still sucking greedily on one another under the harsh spray of water.

When she's away from him, she replays their lovemaking over and over in her mind's eye. She's seldom out of bed with him. He is making love to her while she pins bodices to skirt waists on her dummy or rides the subway to work, even while she eats lunch with Selma and her other friends in the shop. Selma nudges her and says, "Mereleh, you're a million miles away again."

"Mary, watcha thinking with that cat-who-swallowed-the-canary expression on your mug?" Paula teases. Mary is thinking, He's the pleasure of my eyes, of my heart, of my whole self.

Sometimes she tells herself, This is all I'll ever need. I won't ask anything more of the world. But sometimes, because this ardor for him feels like the main event of all her years, she's sure there's a larger significance to it. Why had she been sitting on that bench that Saturday afternoon in Crotona Park? —Any other Saturday she would probably have been at a movie. And why was Moishe in Crotona Park on just that day that she was there, when he lives in the West Bronx and had never before gone walking in a park in the East Bronx? What was it that put her in his path if not providence? *Beshert*— destined. He is her *besherter*. She imagines a life with him, their own apartment, making their supper as she waits for him to come from work, their baby on her knee—a miniature Moishe whom she loves already with such fierceness. She imagines herself on Fridays, *bentching licht* like her mother did, her head covered with a kerchief, her eyes closed beatifically. All her years in America, she's been drifting aimlessly, but with him that will change.

———

Though Moishe doesn't earn high wages at Cohn's Fine Suits, he's nevertheless a big spender, as Goldie used to call boys who lavished gifts. He gives my mother a tortoiseshell comb with an embossed silver-plated handle, a black-beaded evening purse, a red silk scarf. She's ecstatic to get them, though she'd be happy even if he never gave her a thing. She takes the presents to work to show Selma, because she knows Selma will be thrilled for her. "Oh my God, how beautiful!" Selma exclaims at every gift Mary shows her.

Mary's favorite gift is a multistrand necklace of polished green stones that Moishe says is the color of her eyes. When she opens the leatherette box that holds the necklace, she gives a yelp of pleasure, and Moishe tells her slyly, "Say, you'd look adorable wearing nothing but that." He says it with a half-concealed smile of mischief, like a kid who asks for more cookies than he believes he'll be given.

She'll deny him no pleasure, not even that one. They're in his room because his family has gone to Philadelphia for the weekend to visit Tamara, the daughter of the old mayor of Nowy Korczyn. Mary excuses herself and goes down the dark hallway of the apartment, to the bathroom. There she takes off every bit of clothes she's wearing, and she twists her hair in a pile atop her head because that will make her look even more naked. Then she walks back to Moishe's room, totally nude except for the green stone necklace. When she catches a glimpse of herself in the hall mirror, she feels funny, like his parents can see her. Her cheeks are flushed with excitement, but she's afraid that despite what he said, he'll think her too brazen. She thinks maybe she ought to run back to the bathroom and at least put on her panties and brassiere; but she keeps going and enters his bedroom again. He gives a long, low whistle, throws himself on her, and pulls her down to the floor. "Yeah, that's what I want," he grunts in his tough-guy voice that thrills her. They make love right there, the red-and-white flower design of his mother's carpet, which she sneaked from their estate in Poland, beneath them.

Then they lie together on the floor, holding one another. "Dance for me," he growls softly into her hair, which has come down around her shoulders again. She's not sure if she's heard him right. "Dance for me, just as you are, with only the necklace," he orders.

She rises to her feet and dances a slow, sinuous shimmy, the green stone beads swaying with her breasts. She lets him gaze at every part of her. She keeps an enticing smile on her lips, though she worries a little about what he might be thinking of her. When she's finished her dance, he lifts her in his arms and throws her on his bed. He lets her know very soon what he's thinking.

She loves their lovemaking, but what she loves the very best are those times when Moishe is sure his family will be spending the weekend in Philly, and she doesn't have to leave his bed to go home. They sleep together like two spoons in a drawer, her lips pressed to his back, her fingers curled in the hair of his chest. She's never in her life slept as well as she does with him.

Mayn tayere, geliebte shvester . . . My dear, beloved sister, Hirschel writes my mother from Latvia, summoning her briefly out of the sweet new dream that's become her life. He addresses her by her shtetl name, Gita Mereh, which only those back home still call her. *Yesterday di mameh and our sisters Hinda and Chana, and Chana's little ones and husband Mendel all came to Riga. Why? To see me and my darling Dweira stand beneath the canopy! What do you think of this, my dear Gita Mereh? Now your little brother is a married man! The only way my joy could have been more complete would be if you and our Buna Rivka had been here, too, to see it.*

She's so relieved he's happy, especially at this time when she's caught up in her own joy. He's never blamed her for not keeping her long-ago promise to him, and now he's settled. Oh, how can he be a married man of almost thirty? She recalls as though it were yesterday how she promised her little brother, while the cart driver waited, impatient to start on the long trip to Vilna, "You'll be the first." And she recalls the time he was very little, and what she did to him, which was the worst thing that has ever happened in her life. Di mameh had sent her to buy a herring for the family's lunch, and she took with her Hirschel, who wasn't even two years old. She was di mameh's eldest, so it was her job to take care of him, and she almost never put him down because she loved him so much. On this day, she carried him into the dark little grocery store, and they peered together into the big herring barrel with its swarming fishes. "Which one should we buy, Hirscheleh?" she asked. He pointed to the one he wanted her to choose, and the grocer pulled the squirming herring out of the barrel with wooden tongs, banged it hard against the counter twice, and wrapped it in a piece of old newspaper.

She was so hungry, she'd had hardly anything to eat that day; so as she walked along holding Hirschel in her arms, with her teeth she unwrapped the herring's head and sucked it. The salt tasted so good, and it filled her mouth almost like a meal. But Hirschel was squirming, and he fell from her arms . . . She will never forgive herself. She could kill the idiot that she was, tear that stupid girl apart like a herring. He fell from her arms onto the cobbled stones and bawled so hard that his little face turned fiery red, and no matter how much she kissed him and told him he'd be all right and sang little songs to him to try to make him forget he fell, still he didn't stop bawling. So she had to confess to di mameh that she dropped her baby brother on the hard ground. Di mameh didn't scold her, but she looked so upset that to Mary it was worse than the worst scolding. And when Hirschel started walking, he limped. Der tateh took him to a specialist in Riga who declared that Hirschel would be a cripple his whole life. Mary knew then that it was because she dropped him on the cobblestone street when he was a baby, and that she would never forgive herself, even if she lived to be a hundred.

But now he is a happily married man, and she need have no more worry for him.

3

Winter and spring, 1933

TIME ON THE MARCH

This week, on every eminence along Germany's borders, including the Polish Corridor, bonfires flamed to signalize the Nazi ideal of an awakening nation. In every city and every town, uniformed Nazis marched to the center, where, amid the blare of brass bands playing patriotic songs in which the whole assemblage joined, Nazi orators proclaimed the dawning of a new day.

President Franklin Delano Roosevelt delivers his inaugural address: Let me assert my firm belief that the only thing we have to fear is fear itself—nameless, unreasoning, unjustified terror.

The world was rocking and would soon tip over. There were signs everywhere, but almost everyone was distracted and paid no attention—my mother, too, of course. Just as she dreamed away 1932, she would dream away 1933. It would take some time before her eyes would open, though her early years in Europe should certainly have taught her to be an insomniac.

When she was thirteen, her father was beaten up by the Kristaps brothers, three half-wits who specialized in the sport of waylaying elderly Jews whom they caught walking alone at night. One Kristaps would drag the Jew by his hair, another by an arm (which he more than once separated from a Jew's socket), and a third would clap a filthy hand around the Jew's mouth to muffle his cries. They'd lug him to a field where it was unlikely anyone might come along to interrupt their fun, and there they'd pummel and kick until he'd mercifully pass out, their crazy cackles and sneers of "dirty Yid" echoing in his bloodied ears. They'd empty his pockets too, though that wasn't more than an afterthought because they knew they'd usually find only a few kopeks. Anyway, robbery interested them less than the pleasure of roughing up Jews.

The night it happened to der tateh, he'd just put the finishing touches on a wedding dress that was needed by a bride the next day, and he'd wrapped it carefully in paper and gone out to deliver it to her. After the Kristaps brothers finished with him, he lay in the snowy field so long that when di mameh found him, bits of ice were clotted in his beard and eyebrows and around his nostrils. The stars were leaving the sky by then, and he'd regained consciousness, but his legs wouldn't hold him up and his back felt like it was being cut by broken glass. The paper in which he'd wrapped the white wedding dress was torn to shreds and the dress was a stiff brown rag of dried blood and mud.

Di mameh covered him with her coat to keep him warm and ran to get help. She pounded on the door of a house where she saw a mezuzah hanging on the doorframe, the old shoemaker's house. He answered the door in his nightgown and nightcap. He could guess what happened from the look on her face. "It's already the third time in a couple months we had to help carry someone," he said, and he told her to sit while he went next door and got his grown son to help him carry her husband home. He lit a candle so she'd have more light while she waited for him among piles of old boots and shoes and scraps of leather and his three-legged carpenter's stool. "Please, mister, hurry," di mameh urged the old man. She was sick with worry for her poor broken husband lying in the cold field.

It seemed forever before the shoemaker returned with his son, who was dressed in a scroungy fur hat and a big muffler. "You better bundle up, too, Papa. It's freezing out there," the son told his father. Di mameh waited some more while the shoemaker rushed to put on a jacket and coat over his night-clothes. "The last guy we carried, old Mr. Gelman, told us a couple weeks later that he went to the police station," the shoemaker's son said, "but they laughed at him like he was a mouse complaining the cat hurt his head when she chomped it."

"Yes, no use going to the police," di mameh agreed. She only cared now about rushing the father and son out to the cold field where her poor husband lay waiting.

"Yeah, best to just forget it," the shoemaker said as they all ran to der tateh.

But the family couldn't forget it. He wasn't the same person anymore. An hour or so bent over a garment and wolves' teeth gnawed his back; and in his mind he kept replaying the scare and shock of that night. Mary had been working as an apprentice to a tailor in Rezhitse, a shtetl thirty kilometers from Preil, when der tateh was attacked, but when she came home she saw how he'd changed, not just physically but his mind too. He'd always been a kissing, hugging father, and he still managed loving words when his children came to him, but his features settled into a mask of misery . . .

Der tateh has been dead for almost eighteen years, but sometimes Mary tells herself he watches over her from the other world. Tateleh, help me, she cries when life gets to be too much, because she knows he wouldn't want his little girl to suffer. And yet it's a mystery to her how he could have let her cross the ocean all alone when she was only seventeen years old, how he could have let her go out of his life forever. Was it because the crazy Kristaps reminded him that Europe was dangerous for Jews? *Antisemiten,* anti-Semites—she thinks she heard that word even before she heard the words *mameh* or *tateh.* Antisemiten were seared into her earliest memories. In 1903—the pogrom in Kishinev, the frenzied mobs emptying out of churches on Orthodox Easter, led by priests, marching through the towns crying, "Kill the Jews!" She saw the illustrations in a Yiddish newspaper—she was seven years old and it was her first image of horrors—Jewish babies torn to pieces by bloodthirsty mobs, the corpses of Jews strewn on the streets. She had nightmares of mutilation and murder for weeks but was ashamed to tell anyone how the pictures had terrified her.

The 1905 pogroms, too: hundreds of them that year, thousands of Jews killed, in the Ukraine, Odessa, Makariev, Kerch, Yekaterinoslav, which was near Kiev. The newspaper picture of the Yekaterinoslav pogrom sent her into enduring panic. The dead, mostly children, were lined up neatly in a row, as though they were sleeping, except you could see their bashed-in heads and bloodied bodies. For a long time she was afraid to be alone in the dark because the image of those small bodies, some that looked just her size, would appear before her eyes; she'd have to suck her lips between her teeth so she wouldn't scream . . . In Latvia, too, that year. Mary remembers one night, der tateh and di mameh sitting at the little table in the kitchen, a flickering kerosene lamp lighting their faces and the page of *Riga Avize.* She'd been asleep, but the creaking of the wobbly wooden chairs woke her. She lay with her sisters atop the tiled stove where the four of them always slept. Der tateh must have thought they were all sleeping. He read to di mameh from the newspaper, his voice a low whisper, but Mary heard. She covered Hinda's ears so her youngest sister wouldn't wake up and get scared at the words.

A pogrom led by the Riga Black Hundreds—there were really thousands of them, not hundreds; not just riffraff but landowners, rich peasants, clergy, policemen. They ransacked Jewish shops, attacked the customers, attacked anybody who looked Jewish. They roamed the streets brandishing guns, clubs, stones, shouting, "Death to the rich communist traitor Jews who ruin our motherland!" They burst into the Riga Jewish Hospice for the Aged and beat up the elderly . . .

He let me go away to keep me safe from such things, Mary sometimes thinks.

Monday, before the 8:00 a.m. bell goes off in the shop to signal it's time to put noses to grindstones, Selma, her pretty round face flushed, hurries over to my mother's station. When Selma is talking to someone, she's in the habit of standing with her hands behind her back, which makes her crooked spine less noticeable. But this time she's holding only her left hand behind her back. "Mary, darling" she says, pausing dramatically, "I want you to be the first one here to see." She slowly brings the hand forward and presents it with a flourish. On her ring finger is a little gold band with a minuscule diamond that sits on top like a tiny pebble.

"Oh, Selma, sweetheart!" Mary cries and grasps her friend to her heart. "Oh, mazel tov, mazel tov!" Now Selma won't have to keep working. She's been working for more than ten years, since her father died when she was fourteen, and though shop work is hard for everybody, Selma's scoliosis can make bending over the machine excruciating.

Some of the other girls drift over to see what the commotion is about before they settle down to work for the day. "Oh, you lucky dog! When are you quitting here?" Paula the draper cries to Selma before kissing her on both cheeks.

"Free from prison! Are we all invited to the wedding? What are you gonna wear?" Bertha the finisher wants to know.

"I don't know yet what I'll wear . . . Maybe I'll make something myself," Selma says, and Mary sees a shadow pass over her face. She knows what Selma is thinking. She'll be walking down the aisle, all eyes on her, and what everyone will see is her disfiguring hump.

"Selma, listen, I'll help," Mary says. "This Sunday, we'll make the dress together, okay?" When Mary worked for the tailor in Rezhitse she'd learned to make a dress from beginning to end—cut material according to a pattern, baste lining onto sleeves, make buttonholes and collars and cuffs, even do the fitting on the customer when the dress was almost finished. Of course, she hasn't done it in a long time because America has no use for workers who can do it all. In America, she has only to fit parts of a dress on a stuffed dummy and pin the pieces together before she hands the garment over to a baster who does the next step. But she still remembers how to do everything. She once even made a wedding dress all by herself for a hunchbacked bride. She designed it with a straight skirt, which brought people's eyes to the girl's nice slim hips and long legs, and she made a beautiful shawl, puffy like a white cloud, that not only covered the girl's shoulders but also masked her deformed back. You'd never think, This is a bride with a hunchback, if you hadn't seen her before. The girl and her mother were so thrilled they gave Mary an extra ruble for her work. "We'll make you look beautiful like Sylvia Sidney," Mary promises Selma.

Sunday afternoon, when Mary arrives at the apartment in which Selma lives, it's redolent with the smell of *Poilishe kichelach,* little Polish cookies, which her old mother baked just that morning for them to eat while they sew Selma's wedding gown. "Thank you for helping to make my beautiful Selma a beautiful bride," she tells Mary in Yiddish. She brings out a bottle of schnapps and three glasses because she wants to toast l'chaim and mazel tov to Selma before Mary begins work. Selma's mother is stooped over with the deformity they both share, but she's a jolly little person, bustling about, bringing pins and scissors and whatever they'll need for Mary to fashion the wedding dress. "When you finish, I'm going to sew pearl decorations all over the bodice. Won't that look nice?" the mother asks. She's overjoyed that the daughter she's been worried about her whole life is getting married. Mary can't help a flash of envy . . . about which she feels guilty . . . But why isn't she lucky enough to have her own mameh here in America, who would also be joyful at her daughter's wedding? She's a dozen years older than Selma. Why isn't she the one who's getting married, whose wedding dress they'll be making?

But she is happy helping Selma make her wedding dress—not just because she likes Selma, but also because sewing is the one thing Mary is sure she still does very well. Selma's brother-in-law, who's a cutter but doesn't have a job right now, has followed the specifications Mary gave Selma. From two small bolts of material they'd bought in the shop at a worker's discount, he's cut out strips of taffeta for the skirt, the bodice, and the long sleeves of the dress, and a long wide strip of satin for the shawl. As Mary arranges her materials, Selma pours them two more glasses of schnapps and they toast one another; then two more glasses, which they down giggling like young girls. Selma says, "You'll be the next one, Mary, darling. And then I'm gonna do the same thing for you. You'll see what a wonderful dress I'll make you to celebrate."

"From your mouth to God's ears," Mary says lightly, though it's her solemn prayer too.

She's a tiny bit tipsy, but her concentration when she works on the dress is as focused as a ballerina executing twirls, because she knows she mustn't make unsightly pucks in the material by pinning in the wrong places. She measures, then she drapes the white taffeta panels over Selma's breasts and waist and hips as Selma, in her petticoat and brassiere, obligingly stands still, or turns round and round, or walks up and down whenever Mary orders her to. Selma drifts in ecstasy, exclaiming every few minutes, "Mary darling, you're so wonderful to do this for me!" Then Mary snips, measures again, fits again, and deftly pins the taffeta, her hands sure and steady, despite the l'chaims.

Finally, Mary stands over Selma as Selma stitches on her sewing machine all the places where Mary has put pins. It's dark outside when they've finished; Selma's mother, who brought them chicken noodle soup for their hasty supper, has long since gone to bed. Now Selma stands, arms raised, and Mary pulls the dress over her head. Exquisite, except for Selma's crooked spine.

"Okay, stand still now, head up," Mary says, holding her breath as she drapes the wide satin shawl she's already hemmed over Selma's shoulders, smoothing and puffing and pinning where they'll sew. "Let me see, sweetie. Walk. Turn around." It's just as she hoped. Selma's hump has vanished like in a fairy tale, and she's a lovely, slim-hipped bride, surrounded by a sweet puffy white cloud of satin. "You're gorgeous," Mary tells her.

"Oh, let me see," Selma cries, and lifting the dress so she won't trip, she grabs Mary's hand and they run to the bathroom where there's a long mirror on the door. Selma scrutinizes herself in her wedding dress with its clever shawl. "Oh, Mary, darling, you've made me look . . ." Selma is crying because, Mary knows, she looks so beautiful.

"You'll be next, Mary. You'll see," Selma says again.

Sometimes my mother thinks that the reason her tateh let her go away all those years ago was not because it was dangerous to be a Jew in Latvia; it was because he took a close look at her, a grown girl, and said to himself, She's ready to marry. And who could she marry there? —another tailor, the man who opens the synagogue doors and sweeps up after the Sabbath, a baker if she's lucky. Where would her poor tateh get dowries for her, then Buna Rivka, then Chana, then Hinda? Maybe he thought, I'll send her to my eldest daughter and my son-in-law in America, where dowries aren't necessary, and they'll find a husband for her . . . Well, she didn't turn out to be the kind of girl for whom Sarah and Sam were disposed to find a husband.

Yet maybe she's wrong in believing der tateh wanted her to go to America so she might marry a man who wouldn't ask for a dowry. It was so long ago, she can't recall what really happened . . . Sometimes she thinks she remembers der tateh didn't want her to leave, that he warned her, "You're too young to cross the ocean all by yourself." She had to struggle with him to let her go. "I'll be okay, Tateleh. I can find good work there," she told him, though she hadn't dared to say she hoped to become a dancer on the American stage. Yes, the more she thinks about it, the surer she is that that's the way it happened: she'd heard such fairy tales about America and envisioned herself riding in a carriage pulled by a beautiful horse that wore red plumes. When der tateh tried to discourage her from going, she was headstrong and wouldn't listen. And then her first year in America, he died in a cholera epidemic.

Tateleh. God didn't grant her enough time to be his daughter. Mary misses him now even more than the day she received the terrible black-bordered envelope from Preil and she knew even before she tore it open that of those she loved, there was one she would never again see on earth. Sometimes she's so afraid she'll never see any of them again, di mameh, Hinda, Chana, her baby brother. Sometimes she's sorry all over again she ever came to America, where she labors like a slave, worse than in Europe. By the end of the day her arms feel like they're weighed down by lead because she's had to stretch them out for so many hours; her back is a field of misery; and her fingertips are torn and rough with pinpricks. She envies the women who get to prance into the shop to pick up a last pay envelope and call out, "Toodeloo, everyone! I just got married!" There's no escape for a woman but marriage.

But now she may be the next one to toodeloo. She has very good reason to hope, though her sister Ray thinks it will never happen with Moishe. "He's using you up! *Mishugeneh*, crazy one! Don't you know that's all he wants from you?" Ray has been yelling at Mary in that foghorn voice of hers ever since Mary let slip that she's in love, and that, yes, of course she's been going to bed with the man. Ray doesn't have a single ounce of romance in her whole body, Mary thinks, and that's why it was so easy for her not to disappoint Sarah and Sam after they brought her to America. Ray was a dried-up old lady from the day she was born Buna Rivka. It gives Mary absolutely no happiness to be with her. (Yet who else does she have in America who knows or remembers or cares about der tateh, di mameh, Hinda, Chana, Hirschel?) "Leave him and find somebody that's gonna marry you!" Ray bellows every time she sees Mary.

"Shut up! You don't know nothing!" Mary yells back each time. What the hell does Ray know? How can anyone know what goes on between two people who are in love? And then, like a miracle, Moishe justifies her faith. They're sitting in a booth at Kirschman's delicatessen, eating corned beef sandwiches. He grins at her.

"What?" she asks. His grin always makes her smile.

"Listen, doll, I had a little fight with my mother. You know, her lady friend—Tamara, the one she goes to visit in Philly, whose father was the mayor of Nowy Korczyn?—well, Tamara has a niece who's about twenty-two years old now . . ."

Mary puts her own sandwich down on her plate. Her hand is as trembly as if a doctor just told her she has a serious disease. "Your mother wants you to meet this girl?"

"Yeah, she got it into her head that it was time to make a *shiddach* with me and the mayor's grandniece. So I figure now's just the time to set her straight. 'I'm not going to Philly to meet anyone,' I told her, ''cause I've got my girl right here in the Bronx.' You know, it's really all my fault, sweetheart. I should've told her and the pop months ago. But now she knows," he says, tearing off a huge bite of corned beef sandwich, "and that's that."

Oh, God, please, yes! Mary thinks. He wouldn't tell his mother about us if he wasn't sure.

"So then my mother says, 'Okay, congratulations. And when am I going to meet this marvelous person?' . . . So, how about it, sweetheart? I promised she'd get to meet you very soon. What do you think?"

"Oh . . . But what if she doesn't like me?" It hits her like a stone's blow. His mother would have no reason to like her. No big estate owners in her family, no mayors, no Talmud scholars. Only tailors, nobodies. She's worried sick. She pushes her sandwich plate away from her.

"Dontcha like your cornbeef, hon?" the waitress comes over to their table and asks.

"Oh, yes, it's fine," she says.

The waitress gives her a wink and ambles off with Moishe's empty plate.

"Ah, Mama will love you," Moishe says. "Look, the first Saturday of next month we're taking her to the Yiddish Art Theatre. They're opening *Mirele Efros,* Mama's favorite, starring Berta Gerson. She loves Berta Gerson."

"Your father, too?" A man might understand Moishe's feelings for her better, might be an ally against the mother.

"Naw, he meets with his Torah group Saturday nights. And anyway, he has no interest in the theater."

Is Moishe such a kid, so blinded by the wonderful thing between them, that he doesn't know what his mother will surely think the minute Mary opens her mouth? "Maybe we should meet some time when your father will be there, too, Morris."

"No, sweetheart, I already told Mama we'll take her to the opening of *Mirele Efros,*" he insists. He tells Mary that at the appointed time he and his mother will meet her at the Freeman Street station, and there they'll catch the Second Avenue El, so they can all go together to the theater. And after the play they'll go to the Delancey Grill, where his mother always goes with Tamara when she comes to New York. "Mama says they like it because it's not too noisy there, and people can hear each other when they talk."

The week before the date with Moishe's mother, Mary has to run to the bathroom so often that finally the forelady cracks, "What's going on? You got a boyfriend hidden away in the toilet?"

By Saturday morning, she's a wreck. She knows she'd better eat some breakfast. She waits until she hears the Poteshes leaving the kitchen, then she goes in and takes a slice of her American cheese from the refrigerator and a piece of her rye bread from the breadbox. She eats standing at the sink, warning herself that if she keeps being so tense, by the evening she'll look like a wrung-out rag. Leaning against the sink, she drinks a glass of water.

She wants his mother to like her; she wants his mother to tell him, "Moishe, a year of going out with this girl is enough already. If you love her so much, marry her and give us a grandchild from you." "Oh, God, I've got to make her like me!" Mary says aloud, then glances at the door worried that Mrs. Potesh will come in and say, "Who are you talking to?"

She goes back to her room, takes her best dress out of her closet, and spreads it on her bed. A black rayon with a low V-cut at the neck. Whenever Moishe sees her in this dress, he makes a long wolf whistle because it shows off the firm roundness of her bust; but she doubts Moishe's mother would like that. No, the dress is not at all suitable! She returns it to the closet and takes out her green taffeta. She holds it up to herself. It has a pointy collar that buttons almost to the chin. That's good. But she bought it six or seven years ago, when hemlines were so short. The skirt barely covers her knees! Back into the closet it goes, and she pulls out her only other dressy dress, a red woolen sheath. That one is just right in both the neck and the skirt . . . But a form-fitting red dress is not what you wear when you're meeting for the first time the lady who you hope will be your mother-in-law!

She can't afford to go out and buy a new dress because today she must give Mrs. Potesh rent money, more than a whole week's salary. She sits on her bed, hugging herself, rocking back and forth. What should she do? She pulls the green taffeta out of her closet again and examines the hem. Yes, it would be nothing for her to lower the hemline. But she's worked a lot on taffeta, and she knows that wherever a needle has gone through the fabric there are unsightly pricks when the thread is pulled out. Still . . . the pricks would be near the bottom of the skirt, and maybe at night no one would even see they were there.

She rips the old hem out, re-sews a much smaller hem, heats her iron— just a little so that the material won't scorch; and then, spreading the dress out on the bed again, she irons back and forth with a heavy hand until every trace of the crease of the old hem has totally disappeared. But she was right— a neat line of pricks still clearly recalls the old hem. It can never be ironed out! She tears at her hair in despair. She studies the dress again. Well, it will have to do. She has no other choice.

By the time the clock says 6:45 and she leaves the house to walk to the train station, she's more exhausted than if she'd put in a fourteen-hour workday.

At the Freeman Street station they're already waiting for her, Moishe so tall beside his mother, a plump little woman wrapped in a mink stole and wearing a small hat with a veil that comes down to the tip of her nose. Mary rushes toward them, and the moment she's close enough to greet them, it's as though a wicked elf is hovering in the air: a sudden gust of wind blows Mary's black felt hat off her head and rolls it like a wheel down the street. "Oh, no!" she cries.

"I'll get it!" Moishe shouts.

Mary watches him hop and stoop and reach for the hat, which blows away again the instant he's about to pick it up; and there he goes hopping and stooping and reaching again. Poor Moishe looks as comical as a Keystone Kop in pursuit of a hooligan, and Mary tries to stifle a nervous giggle that wants to bubble out of her mouth. She cannot stop it. It blasts out in a high-pitched squeal. Oh my God, just like a lunatic! she thinks.

"Oh, dear," Moishe's mother says as he hops off after the rolling wheel of black felt once more. The hat is halfway down the block before he catches it.

Mary is mortified by her imbecilic nervous giggle. She stands opposite his mother, and they stare at each other for an uncomfortable moment. His mother gives her a stiff little smile. "Well, you must be Miss Lifton," she says. Her Yiddish accent is much less pronounced than Mary's.

"Yes, very please to meet you, Mrs. Federman." The voice that comes out of Mary's mouth is unfamiliar to her, an octave higher than her normal voice. She sounds nervous even to herself. And she's unsure whether or not to offer to shake hands. She decides she'll wait for Moishe's mother to make the first move. But Moishe's mother clutches the mink around her shoulders and doesn't offer her hand.

Moishe returns with her hat and hands it to her. "So, my two favorite ladies in the whole world have met already," he says. He looks different some-how, a little sheepish; the tough-guy swagger she's come to find so attractive has vanished in the presence of his mother. He ushers them onto the elevated train.

"Here, Mary, you sit here," he says, and she takes the seat he indicates. "And you sit here, Mama." He points to a seat just in front of Mary. He slides in beside his mother, turning toward Mary as he positions himself, giving her a quick, encouraging smile.

The train lurches and starts. As they zoom toward Second Avenue, Mary gazes at the back of their two heads—one with the thick black curls she knows so well and loves so much and has run her fingers through so many times; the other with dyed-blond hair, a neat, tight hairdo peeking out from under the hard-shell beige hat. Mary feels abandoned, sitting behind the man she loves and his mother.

At the Yiddish Art Theatre, the usher shows them to the aisle where their seats are, and Moishe says to Mary, "Go on, darling, you go in first." She hopes he'll follow and they'll sit together and perhaps secretly hold hands. That would help her a lot.

But she hears him say, "Now you, Mama," because it would not be gentlemanly for him to be seated before his mother sits. Mary understands, though she despairs. His mother has barely said a word to her since they met, and now she is sitting next to her. What will she talk to this woman about until the curtain rises?

Moishe arranges his mother's fur stole on the back of her chair. "No, no, Morris, it's not comfortable like that," she tells him. "We should have checked it. It's too late now. Let me just hold it on my lap."

"I don't mind holding it for you on my lap," Mary offers, but Moishe's mother doesn't seem to hear her and arranges the stole on her own lap; then she pushes her veil back over her little hat. There's a tragic expression on her face, as if someone has just died.

Now all three of them look straight ahead at the stage, expecting the play to start, but it doesn't, and finally Moishe's mother turns to him and begins a conversation. "Mrs. Rosen—you know, that nice neighbor upstairs—asked me if you feel all right, because you look so pale. Are you getting headaches again, Morris?" He assures her he feels fine and has had no headaches for a very long time. She changes the subject to her daughter, Moishe's sister Fay, who just that afternoon was stopped on a Manhattan street by a man who's the president of a top modeling agency. "He gave her his card and said please call him because he can place her right away."

"Uh-huh, she's a very beautiful girl," Moishe says. Mary knows him so well that she can tell from the sound of his voice he's uncomfortable.

"Well, Fay would never lower herself like that, to be a model," his mother huffs, and then there's silence again and all three of them look straight ahead at the unraised curtain.

Mary is hurt that Moishe's mother doesn't try to include her in a conversation. She's angry too. How rude this woman is! What nerve to act like I'm not here and not even say boo to me. She clenches her teeth in vexation

. . . But mostly she's worried that she's made a bad impression, and that his mother will try to push Mary out of her son's heart because she'll think that Mary isn't good enough for him.

Finally the house gets dark and the curtain goes up. The play onstage is a moral melodrama, about a bossy widow who chooses a wife for one of her sons and gets the tables turned on her because the wife is even bossier than she is. Mary has trouble concentrating on the story. I made a fool of myself with my stupid laughing over the hat, she thinks . . . Or maybe his mother isn't friendly because she's already guessed my age. Of course, that's it! . . . Women see things right away about other women that men don't see . . . Mary can't keep her mind on the action.

After the play, Moishe helps his mother arrange her stole on her shoulders, then helps Mary into her coat. They walk to the Delancey Grill three abreast, Moishe holding each woman by an arm. Mary has never had trouble matching her gait to his when the two of them walk together; but now she feels she's hobbling and stumbling like a drunkard.

"So what did you think of the play, darling?" he asks Mary.

"Well . . ." What should she say? "I was very happy that Mirele's grandson made peace between them all at the end," she finally manages to declare, because that much she'd paid attention to.

"The point is that she's a Queen Lear," Moishe's mother says. "She's as foolish as Shakespeare's king because she gives away all her power to her children, just hands it over to them."

"But in the end her sons are much nicer than Goneril and Regan ever were," Moishe says, "and even her daughter-in-law is redeemed."

Mary is lost. She feels stupid and ashamed and annoyed with herself and everyone else.

At the Delancey Grill, they wait for a man Moishe calls the maitre d' to show them to their booth. The paneling on the walls is dark polished wood. The booths are red leather, with seat cushions accented by golden buttons. The gleaming white linen napkin in front of Mary is starched stiff as cardboard. The maitre d' wears a black bow tie and has a snobby voice like Basil Rathbone. "May I recommend the porterhouse? It's excellent tonight," he says before leaving them with three menus. When she's seen elegant restaurants such as this one in the movies, she's longed to be in them; but she can't take pleasure now because she's so afraid this night will not have a happy movie ending.

Moishe and his mother have already deposited their napkins on their laps, and quickly Mary does the same. Her face feels as stiff as the napkin because she tries to keep a pleasant, interested expression pasted on it. She doesn't trust herself to relax her face muscles because she might cry like a two-year-old or snarl at Moishe's mother like a mad dog.

"I'll have the baby lamb chops, Morris. That's what Tamara and I always have when we come here," Moishe's mother says.

"Yes, you have the baby lamb chops, too, darling," Moishe tells Mary. "They're very good. I'm having them, too."

"Okay," she says. Mary has made baby lamb chops for herself a few times. She likes to pick them up by the bone and gnaw them, but she's pretty sure that's not what you're supposed to do in a fancy restaurant. Yet baby lamb chops are so small . . . How do you cut the meat off the bone without making a terrible mess? She decides she'll wait to see if Moishe and his mother will cut their lamb chops with the sharp knife that sits at each place setting or pick them up by the bone. She wants to show Moishe's mother that she knows how to comport herself in a nice restaurant at least.

"So what do you do, Miss Lifton?" Moishe's mother asks after another black-bow-tied waiter has taken their orders. Her lips smile but her eyes are as expressionless and cold as a dead person's.

"I told you, Mama. Mary works in the garment industry," Moishe says. He's sitting beside Mary, and he reaches for her hand under the cover of the tablecloth. He squeezes it and she gratefully squeezes back.

"Oh, are you a dress model? You're pretty enough to be one." Moishe's mother gives her another stiff smile.

"No, I'm a draper."

"What's that?"

"Mary does sewing," Moishe says. "Say, I forgot to order wine. Who wants wine?"

The waiter brings the bottle Moishe orders, and when he pours a few drops, Moishe lifts the glass and makes a solemn show of examining the color and then rolling the wine around in his mouth. "Very good," he tells the waiter, and the waiter pours them all a glass.

Moishe downs his wine in a few minutes and then pours himself another glass. Moishe's mother fiddles with the stem of her glass but doesn't drink. Mary takes a few sips from her own glass. They sit silent as stones.

Mary has been seeing in the newsreels that terrible things are happening in Germany. That's an important subject to talk about, she thinks. She ignores her nervousness and forces the words out. "What do you think Hitler would do if—" But Mrs. Federman doesn't hear her and begins her own sentence. "Fay would like to go to the Catskills for a week. It would be good for you, too, Morris. When you get your vacation in June, I think we should go together. Tomorrow I'll write for a reservation at Grossinger's."

After dinner Moishe's mother pays the check, and Moishe excuses himself to go to the men's room. "Too much wine," he says shamefacedly. Mary watches him as he makes his way to the men's room. His walk is a little unsteady. He drank so much because he was nervous, she thinks; he really wanted his mother to like me.

"Do you have parents living here, Miss Lifton?" Moishe's mother asks pleasantly.

"My father died in Latvia . . ." She's about to say in 1915, but thinks, I better not mention the date because she might ask whether I was already in America and how old I was then. She takes a gulp from her wineglass. "And my mother still lives there. I hope someday she'll come to America."

"It must be very lonely for you, without parents here." The woman's voice is gentle, but Mary senses danger. "What did your father do before he died?"

"A tailor . . ." She wanted to find out if I have any *yicchus*, family status, and now she knows the truth, Mary thinks. It doesn't count for anything that tateh was such a gentle, honest man . . . Mary is angry again because Moishe's mother makes her feel she's such a nobody—no good family, no riches, nothing.

"We had an estate in the old country with a big farm, but I never wanted Moishe to be a farmer. You know, he can read in six languages, and he went to the gymnasium in Krakow. He got prizes for being the best student." Mary sees Moishe coming from the men's room and is relieved. "Here, unfortunately, he's had to go out to work because we've had some reverses. He'd like very much to go to school, but he can't do both. He's not so healthy and hardy, you know," his mother continues because she doesn't know Moishe is standing behind her. "He has bronchitis every winter . . ."

"What are you talking about, Mama?" he laughs. "Are you talking about some invalid?"

In the street, Moishe whistles for a taxi, and they all pile into the backseat, Mary first. She finds herself uncomfortably squeezed by his mother and her fur stole. When the driver finally stops in front of Mary's house, Moishe hops out of the cab. Mary turns to his mother before she exits the cab on her side. "I was very please to meet you, Mrs. Federman," she says, hearing the shake in her own voice.

"Likewise, dear," Moishe's mother tosses off.

Moishe comes around to give Mary his hand to help her out. She clutches at it like a drowning person, but he doesn't seem to notice. He walks her to the door of the apartment house and pecks her quickly on the cheek. "I'm sure Mama's watching," he explains.

She doesn't care. Why should he pretend to be like a little boy in front of his mother when he's a man of twenty-six already? She throws her arms around him and tries to give him a real kiss, but they bump awkwardly as he pecks her other cheek. "Sweetheart, I guess I better get back to the cab right now," he says. "I'll come by tomorrow. Two o'clock, okay?"

She watches him as he walks off; she wants him to look back at least and give her some signal, something warmer than the peck, but he doesn't.

Mary is too tired even to wash her face. She slips out of her dress and lets it fall to the floor in a stiff taffeta heap. Her girdle and stockings follow, and she gets under the blanket in her panties and brassiere. Her feet are freezing cold. She's cold all over. She's very mad at Moishe for not sitting next to her at the play and in the cab, for not kissing her goodnight the way he should because he thought his mother might see. She's even madder at his mother. She thinks, That damn woman will tell him I'm stupid and worthless and he needs to find a young girl from a good family with a lot of money so he can quit the job he hates and maybe go to school to make something of himself, like he's always wanted. She'll take him to Philadelphia to meet the grand-niece of the mayor of Nowy Korczyn.

In the middle of the night, only half-awake, she gets up like a sleepwalker and goes to the window. She's sure she heard his footsteps on the pavement. She pulls the window shade up. The pavement is lit up by a street lamp that burns all night. The street is absolutely empty, as still as a cemetery. She sits on the window ledge watching the sky change from black to dark turquoise to pale blue-gray. She broods about the years that have flown by since she came to America—passed almost as quickly, it seems, as the colors have just passed in the sky. She asks herself what she could have done differently in those years so that she wouldn't be sitting in this spot now. If only someone had come along to show her how to use her dancing talents to break into show business, or even how to use her sewing talents to open her own tailor shop. But no one came along because nobody does when you're poor and a nothing in a strange country, she tells herself, and she was too young and ignorant to figure out by herself how to do things. She creeps back into bed and pulls the blanket over her eyes, but she doesn't sleep. She's sure Moishe's mother is butting into their business right this very minute. That busybody! She bites her fist, and though no sound comes from her mouth, she weeps because he's her little bit of happiness in a wasted life and her big hope for the future, and she's so scared that she's lost him.

Moishe rings the doorbell at two o'clock sharp on Sunday afternoon. All that morning she'd been sure his heartless mother was filling his ears about Mary's faults and he would stand her up. But miraculously, there he is on the stoop, holding out to her a little newspaper-wrapped bouquet of pink carnations. He's an angel to her eyes, dressed so handsomely in his three-piece tan suit and a brown hat raked over an eye gangster-style again. She throws her arms around him so hard that he stumbles backward.

"Oops!" he cries, seizing the iron railing. "Hey, doll, you almost knocked us both off balance." He laughs and again he offers her the flowers, though now they're crushed.

4

TIME ON THE MARCH

All of Germany's Jews are in terror . . . Not even in czarist Russia with its pale have Jews been subject to a more violent campaign of murderous agitation. An indeterminate number of Jews have been killed. Hundreds of Jews have been beaten or tortured. Thousands of Jews have fled. Thousands of Jews have been or will be deprived of their livelihoods.

Years later she would blame herself. Never, to the day she died, would she forgive herself. But how could she have known in 1933 that it was a matter of life and death? No one in America seemed to know it. How could she have paid attention where it needed to be paid when she had so much else to worry about—not just Moishe's mother, not just holding on to her young lover, not just hoping he'd make an honest woman of her, but also keeping body and soul together when that was no simple matter—keeping a job, making enough money to eat and pay the rent on her furnished room, surviving?

One Monday morning my mother gets off the subway train and dashes to West Thirty-Sixth Street, to Reisman Brothers, where she's been working this season because Seidman and Sons had too much stock left over from the previous spring season and wasn't hiring. It's a little after eight o'clock, so she's hurrying because she has the same forelady she used to work under at the Seidmans, and she doesn't want to hear that sarcastic "Good afternoon!" the forelady always says whenever somebody is a little late. Mary is out of breath from running. When she's a half block from the building, she sees her coworkers pouring out the big glass doors. Oh, my God, a fire! she thinks and runs faster to see if Paula, the draper who wears a heavy brace on her leg and beside whom Mary has worked in many jobs, has gotten out okay. But when she's close enough to see the workers' faces, they don't look like they're escaping a fire; they look angry. "Minnie, what's the matter?" she cries to the closest one.

"The louses, Mary! Can you believe what they did?" Minnie's face is splotchy with rage, but her lip trembles as though she will cry. "We get up to the fifteenth floor, and we see the shop door is padlocked, and there's a big sign on it that says 'Closed Until Further Notice.' How am I gonna pay my rent on Friday?"

The presser they call Red Shlomo spits out, "They should grow radishes in their nose, those miserable cowards! No damn Reisman anywhere around. Not a single 'Oh, we're so sorry to do this to you all of a sudden.' Not even a 'Kiss my ass.'"

"But it's still the busy season. Slack season doesn't start till the end of June," Mary tells them, because that's the way it's been since she began working in America.

"What kind of busy season if nobody has money to buy something?" one of the cutters says. "*Nu*, so, how do you like your messiah now?" This he directs to Minnie, who'd worn an FDR button pinned to her work dress every day up to the new president's inauguration.

"Hell, nobody can work miracles," another cutter says. "The guy barely took office. Why don't you give him a chance?"

"And in the meantime we'll all starve to death," Shlomo says. A verbal tussle erupts, while Mary and Minnie and a bunch of others stand on the street, disoriented as lost puppies, trying to figure out what they must do next. The whole country is in a mess. How will they find another job if no one is hiring?

One by one, everybody drifts away to mull their fate. Mary takes the train back to the Bronx, because she's not sure where else to go. She calms herself, thinking, I don't have to be so upset. I have a little money saved up in the bank and I won't starve. She'd heard President Roosevelt announce on the radio just a few weeks ago that he was making the banks safe for all depositors. It wasn't like the winter of 1930 anymore, when the Bank of the United States failed: it had been owned by an immigrant from Lithuania who used to work in the garment industry himself, so she'd trusted it. She put all her money in the Southern Boulevard branch of the Bank of the United States— everything she'd saved up for slack season, every cent she'd managed to put away through the years so she could someday send for Hirschel. When she heard there was a run on the Bank of the United States, she ran, too. For three hours, she stood waiting in a line, hoping to get her money out—she and hundreds of other frantic Bank of the United States depositors. Finally some lowly official emerged and shouted through a bullhorn so that even those at the end of the long line would hear, "Go home, everybody. We're closing down. The Bank of the United States has no more money left."

"He's putting a big lock on the door!" the people who were close enough to see yelled out. "*Gonif!*"—thief—they screamed. "May Satan burn him in oil, that Joseph Marcus!" an elderly woman who was standing near Mary cursed the bank's dead founder. The woman's husband was banging his head on the side of the bank's brick building till blood gushed down his face. It puddled on the pavement before his wife ran to him and made him stop.

"Murderers!" Mary yelled and shook her fist along with the others. The 1929 stock market crash had affected her no more than the drop of a snowflake on her cheek, but the 1930 bank failure wiped her out.

She feels so ignorant about how banks work, but after hearing President Roosevelt, his voice so distinguished and confident, promise that no bank depositor would ever again lose a penny, she reached under her mattress where she kept an old stocking in which she'd wadded up a single five-dollar bill and many one-dollar bills. She pulled another bulging stocking with a bunch of one-dollar bills from the pocket of a tattered coat she never wore that hung in the back of her closet. For a while she'd also kept three five-dollar bills in an envelope she hid between her girdle and her skin; but that had been uncomfortable, so she sent one of the bills to di mameh and added the other two to the stocking in her old coat pocket. The money in the stockings was the sum total of her savings since 1930. The day after the president's radio speech, she'd deposited every dollar of it in the Bronx Savings Bank . . . So if she doesn't keep on believing in Mr. FDR, she'll go crazy with worry.

Mary gets off the subway train at the Bronx Park stop. It will help make the morning's shock go away, she thinks, if she can relax for a bit under a tree. She seeks out a bench on which she and Moishe had sat a couple of weeks ago, not far from the merry-go-round. She sits listening to the calliope playing "A Bicycle Built for Two," and she wishes Moishe were with her right now. She wishes she were his wife and she wouldn't have to worry anymore about where to find work. She watches mothers clasping their toddlers as they go up and down and round and round on the ornate wooden horses, and she feels so alone in the world. She longs to be one of those mothers, or even one of those toddlers. She calculates just how much money she has in the bank. If she's careful there's enough for a couple of months, and surely she'll find something before the money runs out. She was going to send Hirschel a little something because he and his wife moved into a new apartment and they have to buy more furniture. But that will have to wait . . . She'll go looking for a job to-morrow. But, oh, how much easier and better it would be if Moishe would just say to her, "Don't worry about anything. We'll get married. You'll stay home and take care of the house and our babies . . ."

She'd had a little fight with him a couple of nights before. They were in Seymour's bed and they'd made love and it was wonderful as always. But after, thinking of how much hope he'd given her that evening in Kirschman's delicatessen when he'd said he told his mother, "I've got my girl," she impul-sively leaned over him and asked, "Moishe, we love each other so much, why can't we just get married?"

Ice froze her veins because she saw a fleeting expression of annoyance on his face that never used to be there. He sat up and grasped her hard, his fingers digging into her shoulders, shaking her a little. "Sweetheart, listen to me, listen good. You know there's nothing I'd like better than that, don't you? Don't you know that? But I'm already working my ass off at Cohn's Fine Suits, and I'm barely able to feed the four mouths I've already gotta feed. You know I have to help my family, at least till my sister Fay gets married. But how can I know when that'll be? How the hell can I know?" He said it with an almost menacing expression and gave her shoulders another shake.

She wanted to shrug his hands off her and tell him, Damn you, don't use that tone of voice to me. She wanted to yell, Why can't your sister, who's twenty-three years old, for godsakes, get off her tush and go out and get a job and help support the family—or why can't your father put his Torah down and go to work for a change? . . . She would have been within her rights to say that. But she didn't have the guts. She'd been so terrified that she lost him after that lousy evening with his mother.

"And anyway," Moishe added, "there's a depression going on. How can anybody get married at a time like this? Who knows how long they'll have their job even."

Well, my mother thinks now, he was right about that anyway—two days after he said it, she loses her job! That thought actually makes her feel a little better: he'd marry her if there wasn't such uncertainty. She tosses her head back and faces the sky. She tries to imagine bright rays radiating from the pale spring sun and warming her; but a gust of wind reminds her that it's cold and she pulls her coat more closely around her neck.

It's not easy to find a new job in the middle of the season during a depression. My mother walks from factory to factory, asking if they need a draper, and the answer is always, "Not hiring." Finally she sees an ad in the Yiddish newspaper *Forverts*: "Experienced draper wanted." The shop is on Grand Street, though most of the garment industry has long since moved from the Lower East Side. Outside, it's warm and the midday sun is bright, but the dark lobby of the dilapidated building is as cold as a tomb. There's no elevator boy, so she must take the ancient cage elevator by herself up to the top floor. It shakes and clangs and bangs and stalls. She thinks, It will feel like I'm taking my life in my hands twice a day if I work here. But she needs a job, so she can't turn back.

A tough-looking man with boxer's ears and a bent nose comes over to her when she gets out on the shop's floor. "Yeah, can I help you?" he asks above the din of the machines.

She tells him she's come to inquire about the draper job.

"Okay. I'm the foreman," he says. "You married?"

She shakes her head no.

"Sorry. I'm looking to hire a married lady with kids to support and a husband outta work," he tells her.

"And so what am I supposed to do?" she says because she's too tired to appreciate his social consciousness.

"You're a good-looking girl. Find a man to support you," he answers and turns his back on her.

But that's not as bad as the foreman of a shop in a nice, new-looking building on Seventh Avenue who answers her inquiry, "Do you need any drapers?" with a leer and a "Maybe" and a big pinch on her seat. When she clenches her teeth and hisses, "Watch your stinking hands!" he snickers, "Okay, sister, and you get lost."

A couple of weeks later as she's walking over to a diner on Southern Boulevard to get a five-cent cup of soup for her lunch, she runs into an old shopfriend, Yetta, who tells her she heard they're hiring over at Alexander and Schwartz, and Mary again rushes to the subway station to catch a train, this time to Thirty-Eighth Street.

The foreman reeks of stale cigarette smoke and cracks his gum loudly as he listens to her tell him she's a draper with years of experience. "Sure, I'll hire you," he says. "Our drapers get twelve dollars a week."

In the spring of 1929, Mary was earning twenty-seven dollars a week. Of course, she doesn't expect to get paid that much now; but even in her last job, for Reisman Brothers, every Friday evening she found eighteen dollars in her pay envelope. "I can't work for less than sixteen," she says doggedly.

"Yeah, I guess you gotta pay your rent on Riverside Drive, huh? Sorry, dollie, but twelve dollars is what we're offering. Take it or leave it." He punctuates each statement with a loud gum crack.

"I'll take it," she says as he's turning to walk off, because she's afraid she can get nothing better right now.

Alexander and Schwartz is a non-union shop, but that's okay with Mary. Though she has a union book, she's resented shelling out dues, a dollar every week from wages she slaves for. Now she'll save the dollar. She's never been sure, anyway, what good the union does. It's true that garment workers usually have to work only five days a week now, and not six like when she first came to America; but in other ways shop owners still get away with murder. For instance, the union rules say shops have to provide high stools for the drapers, yet there are still foreladies like the one she had at Seidman and Sons and Reisman Brothers who make them stand on their feet all day long, right next to their stools.

But Mary soon sees big differences between a union shop and Alexander and Schwartz. At Alexander and Schwartz you get twenty-five minutes for lunch and no other breaks all day. You work a twelve-hour day even though for years garment workers in union shops have had eight- or nine-hour days. The lighting is bad and your eyes water and burn because they're so strained. There's one filthy towel and a common cup in the ladies' bathroom. There's only one toilet stall, so you have to use up part of your little lunchtime standing in line. And the toilet overflows to the floor with paper and pee and worse for a week before the gum-cracking foreman, Mr. Berg, calls in a plumber.

Judith, a young baster, is mad that he waited so long. "They treat us worse than beasts in a barnyard. Wouldn't you clean out a pig's pen sooner than a whole week?" Her nostrils flare like a pugilist's. Some of the workers call Judith *di vilde*, the wild one, because she's always talking fiery socialism, and she looks wild too, with her black hair, coarse as a horse's tail, escaping the red ribbon with which she ties it up. Mary likes her, though, because Judith always has a big friendly wink for her, and even in the dingy shop, she struts her stuff, head up and breasts forward, like she knows she's worth a lot more than twelve lousy dollars a week.

The next Monday, before the 7:00 a.m. bell rings, Judith walks over to every girl on the floor and hands her a slip of paper with Yiddish, English, and Italian writing on it. It says, in block capital letters, HOW LONG WILL WE TOLERATE THE DEPLORABLE CONDITIONS AT ALEXANDER AND SCHWARTZ? EVERYONE INTERESTED IN CHANGING THESE UNFAIR LABOR CONDITIONS MEET ME IN THE LADIES' ROOM AT LUNCH!!!! The paper is ripped at the exclamation points where the angry writer pressed her pencil down too hard. "I wouldn't go with her if they paid me," the draper who works next to Mary says. "Don't you go either, Mereleh. She'll lose her job and make everyone who listens to her get fired, too. Look how her hair flies in all directions like the wind. She's a crazy person, a troublemaker."

"Yeah, I'm not wasting my little twenty-five minutes for lunch on her," the draper who works across from Mary says. "I bet that's why the bosses didn't want to fix the toilet—they don't want the radicals meeting in the ladies' room."

At lunchtime, Mary looks around the room and sees that only a few seats are empty. She sits hunched over her sardine sandwich. She's been at Alexander and Schwartz's for little more than two weeks and isn't sure what to do. Just before the back-to-work bell rings, Judith comes out of the ladies' room with five or six other girls. Mary thinks Judith must be disappointed that so few showed up for her meeting, but Judith wears a beaming smile, and as she passes Mary's workstation she catches her eye and gives her a wink, as though to say, "We're still friends even though you stayed away."

Judith settles herself at her workstation, lifts a garment from the little heap in front of her, and begins basting. But in a minute she complains loudly, "*Gottenu,* you can go blind in this place because they're too stingy to put in some overhead lights. I swear I never worked for a company that deserved a strike more than these jerks."

"Hey, pipe down! Be happy you got a job," the cutter Larry tells her.

"Judeleh, everyone knows you're a agitator for the union," another cutter says and laughs.

"Sameleh, everyone knows you're an ignorant good-for-nothing slave who lets himself be exploited by fat-cat bosses," she retorts.

"It could be a lot worse than at Alexander and Schwartz, believe me, I know," Larry says, his head bent to his work. Mary says nothing but thinks that though she's worked in some pretty bad places, she hasn't seen a worse one since she came to America.

A couple more days go by, and Shirley, one of the basters, a girl of seventeen or eighteen with a child's clear skin and big blue innocent eyes, comes out of Mr. Alexander's office a few minutes after 7:00 a.m. She goes to her workstation, disconnects the little lamp she brought herself to make her workspace brighter, and winds the cord around the base. Her eyelids are swollen, as though she's been crying.

"Leaving already? You just got here," Judith quips before she gets a look at Shirley.

"I'm fired," Shirley says with tight lips.

At lunchtime, Judith tries to call all the workers together right there on the shop floor. Most stay in their seats, eating their sandwiches or sipping soup from thermos cups; they ignore her. Mary leaves her lunch at her workplace and goes to join the little knot that gathers around Judith, who tells them the story Shirley told her: The evening before, Shirley left the shop with everyone else; but when she was almost at the subway, she remembered that her good sweater was still hanging over her chair, so she ran all the way back to the building and went up to get it. The place was empty except for Berg, the foreman. "Say, fancy meeting you here," he told her, jovial like he was thinking about some joke. Then he came up close to her and slid his hand between her legs.

"That pig of a capitalist puppet! The girl is working here to earn money for her wedding!" Judith yells. "You can bet she shoved him off as hard as she could and ran for dear life. So this morning she goes to Alexander's office to complain, and he says to her, 'I don't want to hear no stories. All my people have got to get along.' The guy didn't even bother to look up. Shirley says all she could see of him was that checkered motoring cap he's always wearing. He was bent over some shipment report or something, something that showed him how much money he was making off our backs. So Shirley says to the button on top of his cap, 'Well, I can't let anybody disrespect me like that, and I hope you'll do something about it.' He jerks his head up, his face so splotchy red he looks like he's having apoplexy, and he yells, 'I don't have time for this! Get your damn things and leave the shop!'

"Just like that, just as though she hasn't been losing her health and self-respect by working in this lousy pigpen twelve hours a day for starvation wages, while he goes tootling around in his LeBaron convertible roadster." Judith gives the table a couple of furious whacks with the wooden measuring stick the basters use, like she's whacking a capitalist's head. "Let's do work stoppage!" she yells between gritted teeth, just as the bell rings telling everyone it's time to get back to work. The other workers hurry off, but all five of the remaining basters agree that Shirley must be avenged. They sit down at their station, fold their arms, and remain idle.

The drapers are supposed to carry the dresses they've finished pinning over to the basters, who then do their part. The drapers don't know what to do with the garments now except bring them to the basters' station as usual and lay them in a heap. Soon the garments that await the basters' needles are piling up so high that the basters' heads can't be seen. When Berg finally notices the garment mountains, he storms out to fetch the boss, who marches into the shop with such a furious stride that the floor shakes. Berg, cracking his gum in a nervous staccato, tails him like a hound.

Judith rises. She ignores Berg as though he's not there. "Mr. Alexander," she says, "if you want us to sew another stitch, you gotta fire your nauseous-making foreman and reinstate Shirley." Yes! Mary thinks, exhilarated just hearing Judith's daring. When she first came to this country, ignorant about the cuts and lashes the world had in store for her, she was plucky like Judith, too, she tells herself.

The clack and whoosh of the machines have stopped, and no one breathes. Mr. Alexander's lips twist savagely though no words come out. His motoring cap rides so low over his eyes that they're hidden, which makes his silent, moving mouth look even more sinister. Finally, he yells loud enough to be heard in the street nine flights below, "Who the hell wants you to do anything but get your asses out of here! I don't need to put up with mutiny when workers are a dime a dozen. You got five minutes to clear the fuck out."

A few workers gasp. Most are silent. A couple of finishers walk out in sympathy with the basters. Mary thinks, I'm walking with them, and she gets up. But she can't walk out. Right after she started at Alexander and Schwartz, she and Ray sent a chunk of money to di mameh to help get the roof patched because di mameh had written that the spring rains were as bad as the days of Noah's ark and she and Hinda had to put all their pots under the leaks to keep from floating away.

The next day, everyone but the fired basters and the two finishers who left with them are back at the shop. It's as Mr. Alexander said. Workers are a dime a dozen. Eight new girls are sitting in their chairs, and everything has returned to normal.

But only for a while. The following week, the International Ladies Garment Workers Union sends two or three dozen people every day to picket the Alexander and Schwartz Company. They demand that it become a union shop, that the foreman be fired, and that the six basters and two finishers be reinstated. The picketers march up and down in front of the building carrying signs. THE EXPLOITATION OF WORKERS IS BAD FOR AMERICA! WOULD YOU WANT TO WORK IN FILTH? THAT'S WHAT ALEXANDER AND SCHWARTZ MAKES US DO!! SUPPORT WORKERS' RIGHT TO UNIONIZE!!! They bellow an old union song with tuneless gusto. *Solidarity forever, Solidarity forever, Solidarity forever, For the union makes us strong!* They beat the air with clenched fists like they're beating on the heads of Messieurs Alexander and Schwartz and every other capitalist who sweated them and cheated them from the day they stepped off the boat.

"Stay here with us. You belong out here. Don't be a strikebreaker!" Mary hears the picketers yelling at the workers who pass the line. She takes the elevator up to the ninth floor and resumes her place at the dummy. She tells herself, All those girls probably have mothers and fathers or husbands to support them, and who do I have? And what do I know about politics, anyway? I'm just a working person who needs a job.

But she's never crossed a picket line before and it bothers her a lot. She wants to join the strikers; yet if she does, it means she probably won't be making any more money for what's left of the busy season, and when the slack season starts there's seldom work, even in the best of times. So from now until September she'll almost certainly have no money coming in; and in these hard times, who knows if she'll find anything even in the fall. Her savings are half gone because she didn't want di mameh and Hinda living under a leaky roof; and she's been hoping that after she gets a few more paychecks she and Ray can send Hirschel just a little something at least, for his first anniversary that'll be coming up soon . . . But when she thinks of the twelve miserable dollars a week in wages, the twenty-five minutes for lunch, the twelve-hour workday, the overflowing toilet that made her gag every time she had to go in there and pee, and how a worker got fired because the foreman thought it was his right to get fresh with her, then she knows what she's got to do.

Saturday afternoon, my mother is sitting on a blanket with Moishe at Orchard Beach, where they've gone for relief from the unseasonably hot spring weather. She's working up to telling him she's gone on strike, though she's a little worried about how he'll react. When they go out for breakfast on Sunday mornings, he always looks through the *New York Times* while they're waiting for the waiter to bring their order. He sometimes reads things to her, and if it's an article about unions or Reds, it's predictable he'll remark, "If they don't like the system here, there's a boat leaving for Russia in the morning." But she really agonized before she decided she'd join the strikers, and she needs to tell him about her decision, which feels so important to her.

He's rubbing suntan oil on his legs, an unlit cigarette dangling from his lips. She's just about to spit out her news about being on a picket line when he says, "I'm sick and tired of working for peanuts, selling suits to assholes for that Cohn, who's the fucking king of the assholes." He informs her he's got some deal going with this guy, Katz his name is, whom he met at the Southern Boulevard gym. She knows, because he's told her, that the gym is full of gamblers and numbers runners and all sorts of types that sound unsavory to her. "What kind of a deal?" she asks, alarmed.

He shrugs. "I don't want to go into it. It's too complicated to explain right now." Then he tosses the cigarette aside and stretches out on the blanket. "Sun's nice," he says.

"But what will you be doing, Morris?" He doesn't answer her. He closes his eyes and turns his face up to the sky.

"Who is this guy?" she persists.

He bolts up, snapping, "Damn it, what the hell's the diff?" and suddenly he grabs her shoulders and shakes her hard, like he did when she asked why they couldn't get married. "Morris, stop!" Mary yells through juddering teeth. An old lady on the neighboring blanket is tsk-tsking loudly. Moishe drops his hands, but he glares at Mary and she glares back. "Look," he says out of the side of his mouth, "when I'm goddam ready maybe I'll tell you, okay?" Then they turn away from each other and stare out at the ocean, both nursing wounds. They're silent for a long time, like they're each alone on the blanket. "Boy, that sun's really hot. I'm going for a swim," he remarks under his breath to no one, and walks off.

My mother watches his shapely calves scissor across the sand. She misses his tenderness so much—the way he used to be with her. But mostly she's worried, because if he's not her future, then she has none. She's so afraid she's losing him, and it seems to her that he's changing into a different person by leaps and bounds, and she doesn't know how to change him back. He never used to be so short-tempered and violent, and now maybe he's getting himself into something dangerous and won't even explain what's going on. It's like he's on a boat that's pulling out to sea while she's immobilized like a pebble on the shore.

The first day my mother marches on the picket line, she feels exhilarated, like she used to on the dance floor when she was with a perfect partner and they never missed a step. She joins the other picketers in shouting out lusty labor songs—"The Union Makes Us Strong," "Hold the Fort for We Are Coming," "The Internationale." She parades up and down Thirty-Eighth Street, waving her ILGWU picket sign. DID YOU KNOW THAT SWEATSHOPS STILL EXIST? WE ARE STRIKING AGAINST INTEROLERABLE WORKING CONDITIONS AT ALEXANDER AND SCHWARTZ! The number of picketers increases every day, and whenever a new face appears, she cries with the others, "Welcome, Comrade!" She wants to help bring even more workers to the strike, because she's disgusted by the humiliation of her days at Alexander and Schwartz. When Fania, one of the sewing-machine operators, crosses the picket line, Mary shouts, "Fania, don't be a scab! Don't shame yourself. Stay out here with us!"

Fania, heavy and arthritic from sitting for almost forty years behind a sewing machine, waddles and limps into the building, as though she hasn't heard Mary; but before the door closes behind her, she shouts back, "So how am I gonna pay my rent?"

"With the lousy wages they give you, you can hardly pay your rent anyway!" Mary yells hoarsely. She's dizzy with elation when the other picketers cheer, and Judith shouts, "If we had a dozen like this Mary, Alexander and Schwartz would disappear from the face of the earth!"

The union gives each of the striking workers a little bit of money every week, so that they can stay on the picket line and won't have to go looking for work. She still hasn't told Moishe she's striking, because she knows he'll say something like, "I guess you guys were better off in the old country making a ruble a week." Ass, she thinks (though it doesn't stop her from loving him, and she can't surrender hope that someday, when things get better, they'll be married).

She's been counting how many picketers show up each morning, but now there are so many it's impossible to count them—two hundred at least, on some days maybe three or four hundred—workers from Alexander and

Schwartz who walked out of the shop when they heard the union will give them a few dollars to live on, ILGWU members who come to help their fellow laborers, passersby who are moved to join the strikers by the leaflet that's handed to them or by the litany of abuses they hear from those who worked at the company. But not all the passersby are friendly. Mary holds a leaflet out to a pugnacious blond fellow who sneers at her, "Ah, you're just a bunch of commie Jews."

"At least read it and don't talk from ignorance," she tells him. He spits on her before he walks away.

"You bastard!" one of Mary's draper friends shouts at his back. But Mary calmly wipes the spittle off her shoulder. Jackasses like that can't dampen her passion.

Another day, an old union organizer, Pauline Newman, comes to talk to the picketers. Mary squeezes up front with Judith, whose hair still sticks out like it's been electrified despite the red bandana meant to contain it. Judith tells her that Miss Newman is a close friend of Eleanor Roosevelt's and even advises FDR because she knows everything about the special problems of women workers. She worked at the Triangle Shirtwaist Factory in 1901, when she was only eleven years old, and though she left long before the fire, she never forgot the women who were killed there and she's devoted her whole life to women workers. After Judith's gushing description of Pauline Newman, Mary is disappointed when she sees the person who finally mounts the soapbox—her hair cut short and severe like a man's; her tailored tweed jacket like a man's too. She wears ugly wire-rimmed glasses that make her look as plain as a boiled potato. Mary has worn shoes with high heels even to work ever since Goldie told her that high-heels flatter the legs; but she sees that Pauline Newman isn't the kind of woman who cares about such things. She wears lace-up shoes. Mary never could understand women like that who do nothing at all to try to improve their appearance.

But when Pauline Newman starts to speak, the hundreds of strikers who are gathered up and down the sidewalks of Thirty-Eighth Street and even spill over into the street are as spellbound as if Greta Garbo were standing on the soapbox. And Mary is as spellbound as any of them. Pauline Newman has a Yiddish accent, but her voice is rich and musical. She talks about a strike she led in 1909, when she was only nineteen years old, and how it grew to twenty thousand working women, and how together they made the garment industry safe for organized labor, which got rid of the sweatshops—for good, they'd hoped and dreamed. "But now, dear friends, there are scoundrels like Alexander and Schwartz"—Pauline Newman's throaty voice becomes tremulous—"who try to turn the terrible tragedy of the Depression to their own advantage, who think desperate workers must put up with any abuse, any injustice—starvation wages, unsanitary conditions, corruption of innocents. But, dear friends," Pauline Newman's voice rises to a shout, and Mary feels herself rising up on her toes, so transported is she. "We're telling Mr. Alexander and Mr. Schwartz that if they think we're going to let them drag us back to the dark ages, they have another think coming!"

A roar goes up from the crowd. "Union! Union! Union!" My mother's throat grows raw with shouting. She tries to hold back tears, but they come spilling out anyway, and she wipes them surreptitiously, a little embarrassed by how carried away she feels. She envies Pauline Newman, who knows what's really important and has been able to put everything into the fight for it and hasn't wasted her life drifting rudderless and without purpose.

Then the stench of manure reaches her, and she looks into the street and sees three mounted horses. "Break it up! This is an illegal gathering! You strikers are stopping traffic!" the policemen shout. The horses move relentlessly toward the crowd, and people scream and scatter. The approach of the horses seems to Mary like a dream, and she remains as still as a sleeper, but only for a moment. "You go to hell, you jackasses!" she screams at the uniformed men.

One of them pulls on the reins and his horse trots toward her. The horse halts so close that Mary can see the gleaming drops of sweat on its black coat. It snorts, and moisture from its nostrils spatters on her lip. "Pardon me?" the policeman asks Mary softly. "What was that you said?" His eyes shine with pleasure.

Judith pulls on Mary's sleeve. "Let's get outta here," she breathes. But there's no place to move, and Mary won't be deterred anyway. "Jackass bastard!" she yells again, and the cop's billy club comes crashing down on her forehead. Lights flash under her lids and she crumples to the ground.

"You lousy bully," Judith screams, dropping to her knees beside Mary, shaking her fist at the cop, who looks on from the Promethean height of his saddle atop the stallion.

"Fucking kikes!" he sneers, and again swings his billy club, glancing it off Judith's shoulder as he turns his horse toward other strikers who haven't had the good sense to scatter. The whack isn't hard enough to fell Judith. "Mary! Are you okay?" she cries, because Mary hasn't moved.

"Miserable bastards," Mary whispers, and her eyelids flutter before she sits up.

"Oh, sweetie, you're bleeding," Judith says weakly.

Mary touches her forehead and feels a swell of flesh. Her fingers come away red.

She doesn't wipe the blood away, not even in the subway when she sees people looking at her. "Mommy, what happened to that lady?" a child asks, and the mother says, "Shhh, that's not polite."

"That's okay," Mary says. She touches her forehead. The swelling is bigger than a tablespoon now, and she can feel the clotted blood. To her it's a badge of honor.

She goes home and cleans herself up because it's Wednesday night and Moishe is coming to take her out to dinner. She feels really good about herself. Strong and sure. Don't exaggerate, you're no Pauline Newman, she chides herself. But still, she can't remember how long it's been since she's felt so good about herself.

"My God, what happened?" Moishe exclaims when she opens the door to him.

"Oh, I fell when I was getting out of the bathtub."

"Hey, you ought to be more careful, sweetheart."

"Yeah . . . Lemme go get my sweater," she says quickly, and goes back to her room for a minute; she's afraid he might guess from the expression on her face that she lied.

"That dumb joker, that Katz, just got arrested," Moishe tells her between clenched teeth when they walk down the steps together. "Looking at a two-year sentence, the putz."

"Who? The guy from the gym? He wanted you to do something against the law?" So she was right. Moishe could've been in jail now. "Oh, Morris!" she cries.

He drops her arm and puts his hands in his pockets. "Look, just mind your own business," he says sullenly, and they walk to the subway in silence. She'd like to give him what for; yet how can she complain about whatever he's hiding when she's hiding, too? She'll never tell him about the strike, how wondrous it's been for her, how much she's loved being part of it—even the blow she sustained for it, which makes her love it all the more.

———

The strike has become almost like my mother's secret lover. In the mornings, she rushes from the subway to the picket line as eagerly as she's rushed to trysts. In the evenings, when she's not with Moishe, she thinks about the strike almost as much as she thinks about him, and she replays in her head all the things the picketers did and said that day. I'd rather starve before I work at another place like Alexander and Schwartz, she vows breathlessly. I'll never take a job at a non-union shop again. Before she falls asleep at night, she sees herself at the head of a huge parade of picketers—a champion of working-class struggle, a ferocious and fearless firebrand. Obsessed! she thinks, and laughs at herself. She really likes it that Moishe doesn't suspect a thing about his clandestine rival. It feels good to have this little secret from him. Isn't it the only piece of her that she's kept back, the only part of herself she's denied him, since that first night on the roof?

I cheer her on. Much better, for so simple a soul, to be obsessed by simple slogans than by a lover who's as cloudy as a muddy river. Much safer, despite even the baton's blow, to think day and night about unions and comrades and struggles for justice than about a love as insubstantial as the ether: that's what I'd like to shout to her across the eight decades. But she would hear such selfless nattering like a deaf person hears the shouting of a mute—which is just as well, for if she'd chosen better and safer, how could I come to be?

5

Spring and summer, 1934

TIME ON THE MARCH

August Hoppe, Hitler Youth leader, addressed a rally of goosestepping youngsters in Munich this week: German Youth! Throw from you the last remnants of your Christian education, which destroys the character of Nordic man. Hurl from you the Jewish-Christian ideas of sinfulness, pity, and love for your enemies. Carry before you the conquering symbol of the swastika. We must be hard if we would conquer. A curse upon sympathy and mercy! Praised be that which makes us hard and cold, so that we may unmoved see the destruction of the evil sons of sound fathers.

The world slumbered and dreamt on, to each his or her own private little dream or nightmare. And most of the time, my mother slumbered and dreamt along with them. Only once in a while did she hear the voice that boomed in the distance—but how could she be sure it said what she thought it said, since no one else seemed even to hear it? And so she closed her eyes and slumbered again.

She comes home from the Saturday-afternoon meeting of her union local, her face still flaming. Judith had nominated her for the local's secretary, jumping up and announcing, though everyone knew it already, "At the Alexander and Schwartz strike last year, this Mary here even fought a fat-pig cop who charged her with a horse and knocked her flat!" A lot of the girls she'd marched with on that picket and some others before she went back to work at Seidman and Sons shouted, "Mary, yes! Second the nomination!" Then right away someone moved that nominations be closed. "No, no, I can't," she told them adamantly. "I just can't do it." She was too ashamed to say she couldn't do it because she knew that a local secretary had to take notes and write letters to union headquarters, and she couldn't write in English. On the subway ride home with Yetta, who lives a block away, she confessed the truth.

"Mary, just go to night school," Yetta urged. "You know how to write in Yiddish, and you know already how to speak English, so it'll be nothing for you to learning English writing." But Mary remembers how years ago she fell asleep in night school, and when the teacher woke her up everyone was laughing at her. She's almost twenty years older now; it would be even harder to sit at a desk at night after a whole day at work and struggle to form letters in English as though she was six years old. Impossible. But for the rest of the afternoon she can't stop chiding herself for her shameful ignorance.

And there's more to upset her too, she thinks as she starts dressing for her evening date with Moishe. She stands by the window in her room to get more light and peers into a little hand mirror as she applies mascara to her eyes. She's been calculating how many Saturdays she's dressed for him. And Sundays. Wednesday evenings also. They met in 1932, and now it's 1934. —That means they've had over three hundred dates, and they've slept together almost three hundred times. Her sister Ray who, as far as Mary knows, has never gone to bed with a man in her life and doesn't have a sexy centimeter in her whole fat little body, won't stop nagging, which hurts worse on days like today when Mary is feeling small: "What does he need to buy a cow for if he gets all the milk he wants for free?" "What kind of devil dances in you to be like that?" "Di mameh would be ashamed to death if she knew what's become of you." That one is the worst of all. It pains her like a thousand slaps to think di mameh would be ashamed of her.

That's why this evening in Seymour's room, while Moishe is taking off his tie, she screws up her courage and, trying to sound lighthearted, says again, "Moishe, darling, we're so crazy about each other. Why don't we just . . . elope together—run off and get married?"

He tosses the tie onto a chair. Mary watches it slide to the floor where it lies in a little brown heap like a dead bird. He walks over to her and lifts her chin with his fingers. His exaggerated sigh says, We've been through this already. She hates it when he's patronizing like that; she shakes her head away from his hand, but he grasps her chin again. "I want you to look at me, sweetheart. You know I love you. Don't I show you I love you? You know damn well I tried last year to do something that would bring in more than a pocketful of peanuts, and then my idiot partner ends up in the slammer for two years. So what the hell else can I do in the middle of a depression? Huh? This week I sold six suits." His voice gets louder with each breath. "You know what kind of lousy commission you get on six suits? You think we can live on air? I'm supporting four people already!"

She doesn't want a fight with him, but she's got to make her point. "Moishe, listen to me. If we were both earning . . . My wages aren't so bad since I'm back to Seidman and Sons . . ." She'd rather quit work and have his babies and cook his meals—but a piece of happiness is so much better than none at all.

"Yeah, what do you make now, eighteen bucks a week? You can barely live on that by yourself, you gonna help support me and my family, too? Look, doll, I've had a hard week. Can we have a nice time tonight or not?"

That testy edge in his voice still has the power to unnerve her. She thinks, It's not like those strikes, where we screamed and carried on till we made Alexander and Schwartz and all those other places into union shops . . . Anyway, what good would it do to scream my head off at him if I'm the one who loses when he's unhappy? He's worn her down. She unfastens her garters.

I want to crawl inside her ear and shout, Oh, Mama, Mama, what do you see in this bellyaching sack of bile, this failed movie-gangster? Where's the unflappability of that Mary on the picket lines? I want to poke her and yell, You ignore what's rotten about this creep for the sake of his bedroom eyes, his hairy chest, his organ of generation that refuses to generate. Beware! Here's a white-livered coward. Take heed! Here's a black-hearted deceiver. But if he doesn't cooperate, this *besherter,* this destined one, I can have no more substance than her gauzy fantasies; I float forever.

Next Saturday. "Mary, ya goin' out tonight?" It's Mrs. Potesh standing at the closed door of my mother's room.

She puts down her hand mirror and opens the door to her frowning missus, whose face is made up with lipstick and rouge though her hair is still rolled in big curlers.

"Yes, I'm just getting ready to go out," Mary tells her.

"Well, don't forget to make sure the front door is locked good before you leave. There's lots of burglars around these days. We're going to a double feature and who knows what time we'll be home." Mrs. Potesh always has a complaining tone in her voice. It makes Mary feel like she's done something wrong, though she hasn't left her dishes in the sink since Mrs. Potesh admonished her about it; and she makes sure to turn out the light in her room, even if she's only going down the hall to pee, so she won't waste electricity. "Be sure to double-lock the door with your key," Mrs. Potesh tells her again.

Mary hates living by a missus. Moishe could rescue her from that too, if only he would. She can't help feeling resentful that he won't. But there's no use thinking about it and ruining the evening.

A half hour later, Moishe rings the doorbell, and Mary runs to the door shouting, "Coming!" She ushers him into an empty front room and throws her arms around his neck even before he can take off his coat and new fedora. "Oh, *boychikel*, I missed you since Wednesday," she tells him, because she really did.

"I missed you too, sweetheart. Say, where's the sourpuss family?"

"At a double feature. Let's go to a movie, too. The Loew's State has Cary Grant and Irene Dunne."

"So they'll be gone maybe four hours." He drapes his coat over the living room sofa, where Mary never sits, and tosses his hat down on it. "Why don't we go to the movies later?" he says, and presses her close against his starched white shirt. "We can't go to Seymour's tonight. He called me right before I left to tell me something's come up and he's going to be using the place himself. I was just thinking I don't know where we could go."

She feels him hard already. It still stuns and excites her how quickly it happens when they're together. "Yes, okay," she whispers, and leads him by the hand to her room and her bed.

Later, he lights a cigarette for her and one for himself, and they lie on her little bed, smoking and listening to the *Rudy Vallée Show* on her radio. Her head is nestled on Moishe's chest. I don't have a lot in life, she tells herself, but at least I have this. These are the moments that enchant her still, that she still thinks about when her back is killing her and her arms feel like they'll drop off as she stands at the dummy all day long and pins.

Not more than an hour has passed, but she hears the front door slam and Mr. Potesh yelling, "Couldn't you wait two minutes until we got into the house before you threw up again?"

"Simon, the child couldn't help herself. She's sick."

"She made a mess all over the upholstery of the car."

Moishe jumps from the bed. He and Mary look at each other like two burglars caught in mid-heist.

"Tsk, that girl didn't even lock the door," Mary hears Mrs. Potesh grumble. "Rutheleh, let's go to the bathroom and I'll wash you up. Come," she says to her younger daughter. "Pearl, go find the thermometer so I can take your sister's temperature. I told that girl to double-lock the door and she didn't even lock it once."

"She didn't go out yet. She's still in her room," Mr. Potesh says. "She's smoking in her room. Can't you smell it? I thought you told her not to smoke in this apartment. And what the hell is this? Whose coat and hat is this on the sofa?" Mr. Potesh yells.

"Pearl, take Rutheleh to the bathroom. I'll go see why she's smoking," Mrs. Potesh says.

Moishe, still naked, glances around the room, but there's no place to hide. Mary drops the sheet she's pulled to her chin and jumps from the bed to fasten the chain on her door. She's not quick enough. The door opens, and in two seconds Mrs. Potesh takes in the scene.

"I have to ask you to move," she says. "I have young daughters. I don't want them to see such things." She closes the door quietly.

Mary presses her lips together hard. She feels like she will throw up, too. It's awful to have such a witness to her shame.

My mother and Moishe are sitting in their usual booth at Kirschman's delicatessen. He doesn't seem at all upset that Mrs. Potesh saw him naked, or that as he and Mary were slipping out the front door, Mr. Potesh yelled to her back, "We expect you out of here for good no later than Monday!" Moishe finishes a bowl of matzo ball soup, while Mary tries to sip a cup of coffee. Her hand is shaking so hard that the coffee puddles on the table. She watches him. They don't speak. How can he eat and enjoy his food after such a terrible thing has happened? The waitress brings Moishe the pastrami sandwich he ordered, and he takes a big U-shaped bite out of it and chews thoughtfully. Finally he says, "You oughta get a little apartment by yourself, so this won't happen again."

She slams her cup down on the saucer. "Morris, you know damn well I don't have money to get my own apartment. I live where I live because that's what I can afford," she hisses. She's burning up with rage. She's been so humiliated, and to him it's nothing. He obviously doesn't care how the hell she feels. Suddenly she's like a nearsighted person who's just put on glasses and can finally see what's farther than three feet from her nose. It makes no sense to her that after two years she still has to sneak around with him from bed to bed, like they're a couple of sixteen-year-olds. It makes no sense that if he really loves her he would have so little regard for what she wants and needs. In a few months she'll be thirty-eight years old (though, of course, he doesn't know that), and women can't have babies forever. With all her heart she wants a baby before it's too late, her own baby to hold in her arms. Just the other day Gertie at work read to them from the newspaper about a lady in Canada who gave birth to five babies—five in one swoop—and she can't even have *one* because he won't marry her. But what does he care?

And now she has to move, and she doesn't even know where to begin looking, and what does he care?

"Look, Mary, I've got a proposition for you."

"What?" she asks suspiciously.

He leans over, takes her hand, peers at her solemnly. "If you get a little apartment, I'll help out with the rent. You pay what you've been paying, and I'll pay the rest of it. How about that, sweetheart?" She moves her fingers as if to pull away, but his grasp is firm. His eyes fasten hers and she can't look away. "We could be together any time we want if you had your own place. I could come up after work . . . Any night we wanted to sleep together the whole night we wouldn't have to wait for my family to go see Tamara in Philly. How's about it?" he asks again, eagerly, boyish, like he used to be at the beginning.

She's about to point out to him that if he doesn't have the money to get married, how come he has the money to help pay her rent? And she can just hear what Ray would say, she can just see the sour grump on Ray's face as she said it: He'll never marry her if he can sleep with her any night he likes . . .

But how delicious it would be—to have the regular comfort of him all night long. To be held in his arms, to feel his soft breath on her hair as she fell asleep, to wake in the morning and find him there still and kiss his eyelids until he woke up. These are things she cherishes even more than sex. And now he's saying she can have them, regularly, not in some distant future when they might marry, but right away.

No. She's wearing the glasses that let her see farther than three feet from her nose. "If you can help me pay the rent when we're not married, you can do it when we're married," she says quietly. She doesn't look at him. She stares at her fingers, which she's loosed from his grip. She waits for him to say something, but he's silent.

"I'm so mortified that Mrs. Potesh knows. I feel sick in my guts about it. So how could I bear it, living in a little apartment with neighbors always watching you come and go and everybody knowing we aren't husband and wife?" She doesn't care if she sounds shrill or if the man and woman in the next booth are staring. "How could you even ask me to do that!"

"We will be husband and wife, sweetheart, I promise you," he says in a whisper, and grasps her hand again, so firmly that she couldn't escape even if she wanted to. "But I can't do it yet. You know why, don't you? You know it's not just the money problem."

"Then what? It's your mother, isn't it?" She really wanted to believe it was only money that stood in their way, but deep down she always knew it wasn't just that. His mother thinks she isn't good enough for him. Mary is furious that his damn mother should butt into business that wasn't hers . . . But he just said someday they will be husband and wife.

"Mama is very set in her ideas, sweetheart. I didn't want to talk about it, but you knew yourself that night we went to the play last year. Listen, don't hate her, Mary. She's an old lady, and how long does she have in this world? You know, she's my mother and I love her, but one of these days she'll be gone and then we can do what we like."

He actually promised that someday they will be husband and wife. That's all she can hear now. A wild animal is thumping inside her chest.

They find a rear apartment in a redbrick building on Charlotte Street—two rooms, furnished, for twenty-five dollars a month. To spare my mother embarrassment, Moishe tells the landlord that they are Mr. and Mrs. Morris Federman, and that he's a traveling salesman, which means of course he won't be home every night.

The apartment is much shabbier than the Poteshes'. The mattress on the bed sags. The headboard is made of some sort of tin that was long ago painted purple, but the paint has flaked off, revealing black splotches beneath. The first thing she does to unpack is place on the chipped plywood dresser the gilt-framed photograph of Hirschel as a boy, which she's carried with her to every furnished room for twenty years. In the small kitchen there's a rickety icebox and an old stove with missing knobs. The only window in the kitchen faces the apartment house in back, which is so close that you and your neighbor could shake if you both stuck a hand out. But none of that bothers Mary. Nothing can dim her happiness, because this is the first time she's had her own apartment, and Moishe promises he'll come to her often.

And it makes her so happy that Moishe acts like this is his home, too. The table of the dinette set in the kitchen wobbles, so he neatly folds up a little piece of a paper bag and places it under the shorter leg. Next, he fishes a matchbook out of his pants pocket and cuts a piece of it to a size and shape that will fit the name slot on the mailbox. He finds a pen in his jacket pocket. "Look, sweetheart," he says, and Mary watches over his shoulder as he writes on the blank side of the matchbook cover, *Mr. and Mrs. Federman.*

To her, it signifies more clearly than an announcement in the newspaper that his intentions are true; and she's so moved that tears roll down her cheeks. They both laugh at her as Moishe gets up, shakes out the gleaming white handkerchief from his breast pocket, and gently brushes at her teardrops. They go downstairs together, arm-in-arm, to fit the nametag into the little slot on the mailbox. In Mary's heart, it's a ceremony almost like a wedding.

Their first evening in the apartment is their virtual honeymoon. In the bedroom/living room there's a loveseat (Mary loves that word), and that's where they initiate their new life together: Moishe turns off the harsh ceiling light, turns on the soft light of the little table lamp, pulls her onto his lap, and they make love on the loveseat. It's not at all like some act they've done together three hundred times and more. It's so intense and tender that she feels like a girl. It's like a first time.

She wants him to feel always that the little apartment is his haven. With her next pay envelope tucked in her coat pocket, she rushes to Gimbels to buy a smoking jacket such as men in the movies wear when they loll around their drawing rooms. A gorgeous burgundy smoking jacket with a black satin collar and satin piping. She's high with happiness. Looking for the cash register, she spies a handsome pair of men's black leather slippers in a size that looks just right for Moishe (on sale for half price, yet!), and then a glass ashtray of dark amber, just the shade of his eyes. By the time she leaves Gimbels, the envelope in her coat pocket feels very thin; but she doesn't worry because Moishe insisted on paying the landlord the entire first month's rent by himself. She hangs the smoking jacket in the little bedroom closet and sets the slippers underneath it, where they await him whenever he comes to her. I have this, she tells herself. This is all my mother lets herself think about for now.

She makes sure there are always enough Lucky Strikes in the cigarette box she placed next to the loveseat. He brings an extra shirt and pair of pants to keep in the closet so he'll have a change of clothes when he's spent the night. She likes to wash and iron the shirt and press the pants that he leaves; she loves to touch and smooth and care for what he's worn and will wear again. She feels as content as a little girl playing house (except for the times when she remembers with some resentment that she's too old to be playing, that she should be living the real thing). When he isn't there and she's lonely for him, she looks at his clothes that hang in her closet and rubs her cheek against them, and she feels better. She knows he'll return. Whenever the landlord addresses her as Mrs. Federman she answers as easily as though it were true. In her heart, it is true.

The first time she gets ready to cook for him, she examines the battered forks and knives she's taken with her from one furnished room to the next, and she runs down to the nearby boulevard where there's a Woolworth's. She buys cheap but shiny utensils and new plates too, and napkins and two wine-glasses. But her cooking isn't very good. For twenty years, since coming to America, she's never cooked for anyone; she seldom cooks for herself. When you live by a missus, even if you have kitchen privileges, they don't like it if you're in the kitchen very much, and though they pretend not to, they watch you as though they think you're stealing their food; so her usual supper has been something like tuna fish eaten right from the can, standing up at the sink. Sometimes, when she feels too anxious about cooking for Moishe, she goes to the delicatessen and buys wonderful things to take home for their suppers—smoked cod or lox or whitefish with golden skin. She brings home for him huge corned beef or pastrami sandwiches on Russian rye bread with the fat sour pickles he loves, or even *gedempte fleysh mit apricoten* in a big tin she pays Kirschman's a five-cent deposit on. She loves to watch him eat when he's enjoying his food. Once in a while he gives her a few dollars to buy something for their suppers, but she never asks him for money.

She's never in her life been as happy as she is during the first months in the apartment. He comes to see her four or five times a week and he stays all night. Even on the mornings they must both go to work, she loves having a cup of coffee and a buttered *seml* with him before they both rush to the subway and their jobs. She can't believe her good fortune to have so much of him. Sometimes she simply forgets the end goal and thinks, Oh, if only this were every night, then I'd be the happiest woman in the world.

My mother's biggest problem is her sister Ray, of course. She hasn't told Ray about the apartment because she knows already what Ray would say, and she doesn't want to hear it.

"I'm living with a girlfriend from work now," she says when she brings Ray a letter from di mameh.

"So how can I reach you if I need you?" Ray asks.

"What do you need me for?" Mary answers. She must shield herself from Ray, who can't understand a thing about a woman's love for a man. Mary wonders again and again how they could have been born from the same mother and father. Even the people they each like are as different as pajamas from a ball gown. Mary's best friend in her whole life was Goldie, so sophisticated, like Mae West; and who is Ray's best friend? That Molly the yenta, who's been in America for almost as long as Mary has but still looks like a greenhorn, sagging *tsetses,* big belly; doesn't even know about wearing a good brassiere to lift her up or a girdle to slim her down. And Ray is just like Molly. Mary is ashamed even to go places with her. Yet it's still true—who else but Ray knows or cares about the family they left behind? Though Ray nags and they often fight, it eases Mary's heart to sit near her sister while they read the letters from back home. It's like the family is together again.

My most darling sister, Hirschel writes to Mary in early September, 1934, giving news that di mameh and Hinda came by train to Riga for a visit, Hinda reports she's keeping company with a widower in Preil, di mameh has bad arthritis and sometimes she complains of stomach pains but is otherwise fine. *Our Hinda says married life must agree very well with me because I have put on many kilos. You certainly wouldn't recognize the skinny little boy you left twenty years ago.* Mary and Ray sit balanced on the edge of Ray's bed as they read. When they sit like this, Mary forgets that Ray calls her *a shandeh un a charpeh,* a shame and a disgrace, because she's sleeping with a man who doesn't marry her. She forgets that Ray said their mother would die if she knew—and that Ray makes her so angry she sometimes feels she could shake her until her teeth clinked like a tambourine. They snuggle as close as lovers, each with two fingers clasping an edge of the letter, their heads touching, their arms hugging one another's waist, just like when they were little girls in Preil.

There's seldom a letter from Hirschel without some political news, because he subscribes to three Yiddish papers and a Latvian paper and is very interested in politics. In this letter he writes about hooligan students from the University of Riga who call themselves Perkonkrusts, which means "thunder cross." They wear black berets and dark gray shirts and trousers, which they tuck into their knee-high boots. *You'd think educated people who are lucky enough to go to the university wouldn't run around in a herd like sheep;*

you'd think they'd have a little bit of humanitarian feeling too—but you'd be wrong. They look and sound like that lunatic wind-up doll in Germany with the black toothbrush pasted above his lip. They go around shouting "Jobs and Bread for Latvians" and "Latvia for Latvians." And I don't have to tell you, because I'm sure you can guess, what they say about the Jews.

"Nothing new, the lousy antisemiten," Ray grumbles. She's not interested in politics. Because she doesn't go to movies, she doesn't see the newsreels; and she reads the *Forverts* only for dark dramas—stories about immigrant girls being led into white slavery, immigrant men taking wives in America and forgetting the wives they left behind in Europe.

But my mother does see movie newsreels, all the time. And since she became active in the union and union people are always talking about politics, she pays a lot more attention than she used to; she pays attention to the political news in the *Forverts* too. In the last months, when she's seen or read about what's happening overseas, she's thanked God that Germany is very far away from Latvia. But now, what Hirschel says about the hooligans in Riga . . . she remembers der tateh's face, chalky as death, and his hollow eyes when she saw him after the Kristaps brothers finished with him. A shiver of fear goes through her because suddenly in her mind's eye she sees Hirschel looking like der tateh looked.

I imagine this was the first time—late summer, 1934—that my mother thought, Maybe there is something to be very worried about. But who else was thinking that in America? The Depression was using up most of the worry-energy people had; almost no one was paying attention to the threats of a madman and his copycats overseas, and who could guess that in a few years the world would witness inconceivable horrors? Why do you always have to scare yourself about nothing? my mother might have admonished herself in 1934 whenever she thought that perhaps her family was, or would soon be, in dire trouble.

"Who do you think is the widower that Hinda is keeping company with?" Ray wonders, because that's what struck her the most about Hirschel's letter, and how happy di mameh would be if her youngest daughter, who's not so young anymore, got married. "I bet it's that Yossel the butcher with the big head of blond curls who had the sick little wife from Dvinsk. He used to give soup bones for free when Hinda shopped by him."

My mother doesn't hear her because she has her own thoughts. She's scaring herself again. "Maybe we should try to bring them all here," she tells her sister . . . though how could they bring the whole family to America? Where would they even get the money?

"All? Who? Here? That's all di mameh needs to see!" Ray says, and Mary knows that she's back on the subject of Moishe and her sinful life with him, though Ray hasn't guessed the half of it. For the rest of her visit Mary keeps her mouth shut on the subject of bringing the family to America.

But that night she has a terrible dream that Hirschel, ten years old, wearing the same short pants he wore twenty years before, is kicked into a little heap by the knee-high boots of jeering Perkonkrusts. He can't run away from them because he's been a cripple since she dropped him out of her arms when she was busy sucking on the herring head. He writhes and thrashes, his skinny legs bloody. His shrieks become her whimpers and she wakes herself. She reaches her arms out to Moishe for comfort, but it's a night he hasn't come to her. She sits up, lies down again, sits up again, struggling to erase the images she dreamt. She can't fall back to sleep. She lies there lonely in the dark room, hearing nothing but her own breathing. She curses herself for what she didn't do twenty years before . . . when she'd planned to ask Sarah and Sam to bring Hirschel to America, and instead like a damn fool she went out dancing with a bad cold and got double pneumonia and Sarah and Sam kicked her out.

She jumps out of bed. She'll throw on her clothes and run over to Ray's place right away and tell her she must go to Sarah and Sam and beg them to help bring the family to America. No, she'll go, too, as much as it will pain her! She'll take Hirschel's letter to them, and she'll say that she feels in her bones that terrible times are coming . . . But Ray is right. Di mameh would be so unhappy if she knew of Moishe. Ray said it would kill her. And how could Mary keep him a secret if they were all in America? No, she can't send for them until Moishe marries her.

She lies down again. You can give him up, she tells herself. "I can't! What else do I have?" she cries out loud. She sits up in bed and turns on the light because she's frightened in the dark . . . She'll send for them the minute he marries her. She envisions herself standing arm-in-arm with Moishe at the edge of the water, watching the arrival of a big ship, Hirschel and all of them waving to her from the deck.

6

Fall and early winter, 1934

TIME ON THE MARCH

Armories shelter thousands in the cold . . . In New York City, the cold snap has doubled attendance in government armories now used as daytime shelters for the homeless. Sleeping is not permitted in the armories, which are cleared of so-called guests by 5 PM; however, women, but not men, will be permitted to spend as much of the day as they wish at the Municipal Lodging Houses.

Dr. John H. Becker has been arrested in New York City in connection with the death of Loretta Wilson, nineteen years old, whose body was found in a clump of scrub oak near Port Jefferson, Long Island. The woman's death followed an illegal operation . . .

My mother had plenty of things to scare her in the fall and early winter of 1934, and she couldn't afford to be worrying about things that didn't yet need worrying about: that's what she told herself. America had plenty of things to scare it, too. So the country couldn't afford to be worrying about things that didn't yet need worrying about, either. Nobody, anywhere, could afford to be worrying about things that didn't yet need worrying about. And just about nobody did.

There's a public telephone down the hall on my mother's floor. The young girl who lives in the apartment across from the phone seems always to be on it, cracking gum as she chatters away, fiddling with her hair, digging a toe of her brown-and-white saddle shoes into the worn carpet. Usually my mother doesn't care if the girl is on the telephone because she doesn't have many occasions to use it herself; but sometimes when Moishe is late, she hopes he'll call to tell her when she can expect him.

"Excuse me, but would you mind leaving the line open for a little while?" she asks the girl one Wednesday evening. She's made spaghetti for Moishe, who always comes on Wednesdays, but he hasn't shown up, though it's already after eight. She's sure that something must have happened and that he's been trying to call her. She's been out to the hall a dozen times already, imagining she heard the phone ring, but the girl is always chatting into the receiver.

The girl holds the phone tucked between her shoulder and chin as she examines the bright red fingernails on both her hands. She's giggling at something the person at the other end of the line has just said, and she doesn't hear Mary. But the woman who lives in the apartment next to the phone hears because her door is cracked open for air, and she comes out into the hall.

"For godsakes, you're always hogging that telephone like you're the only person on this floor," she scolds. "It doesn't belong just to you. Why don't you hang up and give somebody else a chance."

Mary has run into the woman many times in the hallway, but they've only nodded at one another and said hello. Mary knows through the Negro super with whom she sometimes chats that the woman is a beauty operator in Sol's Beauty Parlor, which is just down the street. She's about forty, pretty in a large-woman sort of way, with blond hair that she wears in ringlets piled atop her head, just as Goldie sometimes used to do.

The girl's giggles have become guffaws and she's oblivious to everything but the voice on the other end of the phone, even though the blond woman is standing right behind her now. The woman huffs indignantly and taps the girl on the shoulder with a firm finger. "Hey, did you hear what I just said?"

The girl looks at her, startled, then languidly says into the receiver, "I gotta go, Bertie. There are some very rude people here." She hangs up with a bang, then saunters across the hall and slams the door to her apartment behind her.

The woman stands hand on hip, glaring after the girl. "Tut, tut, did you ever see such a brat?" she asks Mary. She's wearing a flowered silk kimono over her full figure, and her perfume smells musky. Mary likes it very much. "Say, it's about time we met. I'm Ruchel, but everyone calls me Ricki," the woman tells her and extends a hand. When she smiles, there's a gap between her front teeth, but it doesn't make her look unattractive. "I hear your husband's a traveling salesman. Say, let's go to the movies sometime when he's on the road, or maybe we can have a glass of wine together."

Her vivacious manner too reminds Mary of Goldie. "Oh, yes, I'd like that," Mary says. It would be nice to have a friend who lives in the building, so she won't be so alone and have so much time to worry when Moishe isn't there. On the evenings he doesn't come to her the little apartment feels like a huge box, and she's a tiny stone rolling about aimlessly. When she finally does lie down, she can't sleep. His absence feels worse than it did when she lived with the Poteshes because then she knew exactly the days she would see him and the days she would not, and she grew used to the routine. Now, she expects him always, and when he doesn't show up, not only is she lonely for him, but she's sick with panic: What if that hoodlum he wanted to do business with is out of jail and getting him into trouble? Or even worse, what if he's coming less and less because he's tired of her?

"Swell!" Ricki says and extends a hand again.

So some evenings when she and Ricki are both manless, they go to a movie, or Ricki brings over a bottle of sauterne and she and Mary share a glass and a cigarette. Mary admires Ricki's tough-girl independence and likes her salty stories and her talk about boyfriends who can "stick their heads up their you-know-whatsits if they act like a jerk." Ricki says she was a sucker once and got married, but now "Freedom" is her middle name. She has two boyfriends at the moment, one ten years older than she is and the other ten years younger, and her present arrangement is much better than being stuck with some sap who thinks he's the king over you.

"Hey, why can't your husband get a job in New York instead of leaving his pretty wife alone so much? Ain't he afraid of the wolves?" Ricki asks one Sunday afternoon when she sees that Mary is blue. Moishe had come to her only twice that week.

Mary has never yet told anyone the whole truth about Moishe and herself, but she knows Ricki would not judge her like Ray does. "He's not a traveling salesman. He's not my husband," she says, and the cry of her heart comes spilling out: She's sure his intentions are good and he'll marry her when his mother is no longer around, though she's not educated or from a good family like he is. She'd do anything for him, anything at all, all he has to do is ask her. She's never loved a man as much as she loves him.

Ricki clicks her tongue and shakes her head. "Oh, hon, don't you know you've always got to keep a bit of you back? You can't give them everything or it'll kill you."

"Ain't that the truth," Mary agrees and sighs. It's almost killed her already, all her worry that he'll stop loving her, that he'll never marry her.

———————

On the Saturday my mother turns thirty-eight, she awakens alone in her little apartment and thinks, How did I get to be so old? Only yesterday she was seventeen, mounting the cart that would take her away from Preil. How can years fly by so quickly? In the bathroom, she peers into the medicine-cabinet mirror. She turns on the light so she can see herself more clearly and peers into the mirror again. She doesn't like what she sees anymore. "The face is a clock," she says out loud. There are two lines etched from the sides of her nose down to the sides of her mouth. The corners of her eyes look as though a bird has been dancing there. It seems like every day now she has to pluck another gray hair from her head. At this rate she'll be bald soon. Moishe must see how much she's aged. These thoughts shake her.

It shakes her too to think she's not had a period for more than two months. Every time she goes to the toilet and pulls down her underpants, she expects to see the little russet streaks that have always preceded her periods, but they don't come. She's heard the change of life can sometimes happen to women when they aren't even forty. Can that really be true?

Later that morning, Ricki brings over a glossy little store-bought cake with pink icing and one candle. "I didn't put more on because at our age it's not such a happy reminder," she says. She takes a matchbook from under the cellophane of her pack of Chesterfields and lights the candle. "So where's the jerk on your birthday when he oughtta be here?" she asks, because Mary has complained to her a lot lately about Moishe's neglect, and Ricki has told her many times already, "Hon, just cut him loose and take your fishing pole back to the sea."

"He's coming this evening and we're going out to celebrate," Mary is happy to be able to tell her. "He already made a reservation at a Chinese restaurant."

Before she blows out the candle, she closes her eyes. Her wish is that he'll marry her soon, that she'll have a real home with him—and babies before it's too late. She prays it's not too late. But most of all she wishes that he will always love her.

Ricki slices them each a piece of cake, and Mary goes to the cupboard and gets two plates and two forks. Ricki puts the slices on the plates and slides one of them in front of Mary.

"Say, can I ask you something, Ricki?" Mary says. She's embarrassed to talk about it, but she's worried and she wants to know Ricki's opinion. "I haven't had my visitor for about two months. Do you think maybe it's possible I can be going through the change already?"

"Thirty-eight, huh? Yeah, it's possible. I had a girlfriend who stopped her periods when she was thirty-six, but she was such a skinny little thing . . . Are you sure it can't be something else?"

"Yeah, I'm sure. He's always very careful about the rubbers," Mary says. (But as she's saying it, she feels her blood pounding. How she wants a baby! She didn't dare let herself think what Ricki is suggesting—but maybe it's true.)

"I wouldn't be too sure if I were you," Ricki says, and tells her about a customer at Sol's Beauty Parlor who just got out of the hospital, still sick as a dog, after a botched abortion. "Just like you, she always said the guy she was with was careful about the rubbers, and it happened anyway. Everybody knows those little suckers are always breaking."

"Well, I think Morris would have told me if one of them broke on him," Mary says. She gets up from the table and goes to make coffee for them. She's excited because of what Ricki said. The thought makes her light-headed. Would he marry her now if she told him she was going to have a baby? Maybe that would be the way to get his mother to accept her—to present her with a grandchild. But, no . . . something like that would be too wonderful. She's not that lucky. She stands at the stove, waiting for the water to boil, and she sighs. "I'm probably going through the change," she says.

But a few days later she's at work, pinning a bodice on her dummy, when she feels a tingling sensation around both her nipples. She's never felt such a thing before, but she has no doubt about what it is. Her mind runs wild while her fingers automatically stick the pins where they need to go. If it's a boy she'll name him Avrom, after her father. If it's a girl she'll name her Lilly, after her mother's sister whom Mary doesn't remember because she went off to England when Mary was only four years old; but for Mary's fifth birthday she sent her a little doll with red trousers and a tall furry black hat. It was the only doll Mary ever owned, and she kept it until she left for America. Lilly. Mary likes the name. She grins to herself. She wants to stand on the stool and shout out to the whole shop what she knows for certain.

Her mind whirls round and round. She's elated, but scared too. What if Moishe is unhappy that she's going to have a baby? The more she thinks about it, the more she's sure he won't be happy . . . and how can she go through with it if he doesn't want to help her? If he won't marry her, Ray will make her feel like a piece of dirt. And if things get worse for the Jews in Latvia and the family has to come here and she has a baby and isn't married . . . But the child is already so real to her that she can smell its fresh-apple breath and feel its sweet weight in her arms even as she pins the unfinished dresses on the dummy. She can't give it up. She remembers when she lived on Orchard Street, the tree in front of her window, a robin's nest. A nasty blackbird got into the nest. She banged loudly on the window to shoo it off, but it didn't budge until it broke every egg and gobbled the insides, scraped them clean; and then it flew away. How the mother robin keened for her lost babies, all night long. Her pitiful screeching. I will fight to death first, Mary vows to herself and clenches her teeth.

But by the time she gets out of the subway station that evening, she knows it's impossible. She can't do it alone. How would she even support a baby? And he'll make the same litany of excuses: he can't marry her because he has to support his family, at least until his sister marries; and anyway, the country's in the midst of a depression and he can't even be sure from one day to the next that he won't be laid off; and most of all there's his mother . . . No, Mary won't even tell him. It would be pointless.

She walks home from the subway station, chilled by the cold bitter wind and her cold bitter life. She tries to remember stories she's heard at the shop about how girls get rid of it. —That's the phrase, and it nauseates her worse than whiffing rotten meat. She remembers one girl years ago, Eva was her name, who worked right next to her at Goldman's. She said the boy gave her a brown pill that smelled like pee and made her throw up everything inside her. She felt like she was vomiting up the baby too; but still she didn't come around. The boy ended up marrying her after she threatened to report him to the police for giving her the pill. Mary calculates that the child must be eight years old by now . . . No, she won't stoop to threatening Moishe about anything.

She remembers hearing girls talk of other ways too—that you can get fixed up if you take hot baths, hot douches, hot drinks; if you jump rope, jump off a chair, roll down the stairs, roll from the bed to the floor; if you put a hot mustard plaster on your belly, if you take two tablespoons of castor oil and put hot rags on your belly—but she never heard of a single case where it worked. And what if she tried something that didn't make her come around but just damaged the baby? The thought makes her slip her hand under her coat and caress her belly, caress what's inside. But when she arrives at her house, she goes straight to Ricki's apartment because there's no doubt about what she must do.

"What happened?" Ricki says when she opens the door and sees the pale wreck that Mary is. "My God, you look like a corpse."

"Who did the abortion for that lady you were telling me about?" Mary says.

Ricki looks surprised only for an instant. "That's what I thought," she says somberly. "Well, you don't want that guy. He put her in the hospital. She's been subpoenaed to go to court to testify against him, and if she doesn't do it she'll go to jail herself." Ricki puts her arms around Mary and kisses her on the forehead. "Oh, you poor baby," she says.

Mary stiffens because she can't afford to give into her feelings now or she'll fall apart. "Don't you know anyone else who could do it?" she asks.

Ricki thinks for a minute. "Yeah," she says after a while. "I have this married lady who's a customer. She and her husband have three kids and they can't afford any more right now. I'll ask her who she went to. It was just a couple weeks ago. She said it cost her fifty bucks."

"Oh, God, I don't have it. I've got about thirty in the bank."

"What about Mr. Hot Shot?"

"No, I'm not even going to tell him," Mary says resolutely. But where will she get the rest of the money?

"Look, hon, don't worry about it," Ricki says and disappears for a minute. She returns with an argyle sock from which she takes a fat roll of dollar bills and counts out twenty of them. "You'll pay me back when you can."

Two days later, clutching an address printed in Ricki's childish scrawl on the margin of a page torn from the beauty parlor's copy of *Ladies' Home Journal,* my mother takes the train and then a trolley car to Dr. Peter Allensky in Brooklyn. She realizes she's not far from Ocean Parkway, where Sarah and Sam live. If they knew what she was about to do they'd say they'd been right in all their bad thoughts about her. She's even worse than they'd imagined, a murderer of an innocent soul she should hold dearer than her own life. She wants to be dead together with the baby she has to kill. To be dead and have it all over and done with. She hates that bastard Moishe for not loving her enough so that she can have this child.

The house stands on a respectable-looking tree-lined street. No one would suspect the terrible things that go on in Dr. Allensky's office, Mary thinks. She tells a bland-looking middle-aged woman behind a desk that she would like to see the doctor. "Certainly, just have a seat and we'll call you," the woman says pleasantly, as though Mary has come to have her tonsils examined.

In the waiting room there are five other women. Nobody makes a sound except for the one who nervously clears her throat every few seconds. The only words spoken are the receptionist's, when she comes to tap a woman on the shoulder and say, "You're next, dear." The tension that hangs in the air is suffocating, and Mary struggles for a breath. She watches the women out of the corner of her eye. They look into space, up at the ceiling, down at their hands, anywhere but at one another. She sees she's the only one among them who doesn't wear a wedding ring. She hides her left hand in the pocket of her dress.

Every twenty minutes or so, the receptionist taps another woman and takes her off. They must leave by a back door when they're finished, Mary thinks, because she never sees them again after the receptionist leads them away.

Finally it's Mary's shoulder that the receptionist taps. Mary rises on shaky legs and follows her through the little front office into a glaringly white examination room. "Doctor will be with you shortly," the receptionist says in a chipper voice and leaves her alone with her agony. Mary clenches her fists hard, as though that will keep the tears in check.

Dr. Allensky enters a minute later. He wears a bow tie and has a tortoise-colored beard. The eyes beneath his horn-rimmed glasses look sad. He extends his hand to Mary and asks almost tenderly, "How far advanced are you?"

"About two months." Her voice sounds odd to her, like the voice of someone else.

"Good, there should be no complications then. And you and your husband have decided for certain you can't have this child?"

"I'm here because I'm not married."

His expression shifts into cold stone, like that of a hanging judge now. "You've been misinformed then," he says. "I do this not to encourage immorality but because I have sympathy with married people who can't afford to bring children into the world while there's a depression going on."

"I can't afford to bring a child into the world," she tells him simply.

"I can't help you, miss," he says. "Please go." And turning his back on her, he leaves her alone in the examination room.

———

This she never kept from me, even in my earliest years:

That evening, my mother is lying in her bed staring up at the ceiling when she hears Moishe's key in the lock. She doesn't care that her hair is a disheveled mess; that she's in a wrinkled dress, her stockings and girdle strewn over the loveseat. She's never before let him see her this way, but she doesn't care anymore.

He comes into the room, and she sits up in bed. He looks surprised, shocked at her appearance. "What's going on?" he says. She glares at him and doesn't answer.

"Sweetheart, you look terrible. What is it?" he asks more gently. He sits down on the edge of the bed and tries to take her in his arms.

She resists. She's sure his gentleness will disappear when he hears what's inside her. "I'm pregnant."

His eyes look like that of a man facing a noose.

She glowers like she'd like to slug him. "Don't worry, Morris. I'm not expecting a goddam thing from you. And you don't have to tell me we can't have it. I already know that."

He opens his mouth and closes it again without saying a word, but the panicked look flees.

It disgusts her to look at him. She scowls at her hands. "I'm trying to find a way to make an end of it." It sickens her even to say it—that she must make an end of what she wants so much.

"Oh, sweetheart, what kind of heel do you think I am? Would I leave you alone with this mess? I'm going to help you. Of course I'll help!" The words gush from him, and he moves again to hold her. This time she doesn't resist, because she's so tired she can hardly keep her head up, and his chest is her familiar pillow, and she has nowhere else to go. "Don't you know I wouldn't shirk my responsibility at a time like this?" he whispers huskily and strokes her hair.

"Hey, listen, doll," he says after a while. "I think that Seymour knows a guy. It's somebody he had to take this girl to, just a couple months ago. I'll ask him right away—first thing in the morning—so you can get this lousy business over with."

He's as good as his word. The next afternoon he comes to take my mother to an address not far from where she lives, a shabby little fourplex with boarded-up windows on one side and drawn shades on the other. Moishe rings the only bell that isn't taped over, and a gray-looking woman with a funereal face opens the front door and ushers them up a flight of stairs into a little apartment. In an expressionless voice, she asks for thirty-five dollars.

Mary opens her purse, but Moishe stops her before she takes out the money. "No, I'm taking care of it," he says, and he fishes out an envelope from his jacket pocket and hands it to the woman. "Thirty-five dollars," he says.

She opens the envelope, counts three ten-dollar bills and a five, and nods. "You can wait for her in there," she says and points him to a small room furnished only with a sagging couch that sits in a corner. She leads Mary to another room, which looks like it might once have been a kitchen but now has only a sink and a long table draped with a white cloth. Above the table hangs an uncovered lightbulb. "You can put your clothes on the pegs over there, and then get up on the table," the woman says without looking at Mary. "He'll be with you in a minute."

The woman closes the door behind her. Mary unbuttons her blouse, then buttons it again. She wants to run away. I can have the baby on my own, she thinks. Don't they have relief for women with children and nobody to help them? Let Moishe go to hell, and Ray, too. I don't need nothing from them . . . But her brave thoughts don't last a minute. She can't raise a child all by herself, with nobody else to love it, just the two of them against the indifference of the world. And how can she have a baby and no husband when she might have to bring her relatives to this country? Impossible! She unbuttons her blouse again. She takes off all her clothes and lies down on the hard table. The light from the uncovered bulb burns down on her, like she's a criminal in a police movie. Her teeth are chattering a terrible tune. She knows she'll be cold for the rest of her life.

She doesn't even notice when a portly man in a gray-white smock opens the door and comes into the room. She jumps when she hears him say, "Nothing to worry for. This will be finish before you know." She sits up, and he tells her, "No, no young lady. You must relax. Lie down still." He has a heavy Russian accent. She lies down again, but turns her head to watch him. He takes from a cupboard a pewter-colored instrument about a foot long. "This is womb opener," he tells her. "It does not hurt too much if you relax." She doesn't want to know what the instrument is. She doesn't want to look anymore. She just wants him to do it and get it over with.

She squeezes her eyes tight and thinks of the river in the forest that was not far from her home in Preil. She wishes she were there, sitting on the green bank of the river with her little brother. She wishes she were anywhere but here, on a table with her womb held open by cold metal. Then stabs of pain, like the bites of wild dogs, begin in her womb and tear through her so sharp that her whole being is pure pain. She clenches her teeth together hard because if she lets herself scream, she will never stop. She will scream herself into hell.

When the pain subsides, she opens her eyes again. The man is holding a long spoon that is encrusted and dripping with blood. Her baby.

"See, nothing to worry for," he says in his Russian accent.

7

Winter to late summer, 1935

TIME ON THE MARCH

BERLIN. Organized gangs of youths, many in storm troopers' boots, roam the bright avenues, rush sidewalk cafés, and hurl Jewish-looking patrons into the streets. Men and women fall. Aryans kick them and spit on them. Steins and chairs hurtle. Windows crash. Mobs pursue terrified Jews down the street. Police look on calmly. At times a chant is raised: *The best Jew is a dead Jew!*

Germany passes the Nuremberg Laws . . . Acres of red swastika flags brighten Nuremberg's musty old buildings. Some five hundred thousand people march in the parade to Luitpold Hall, where Hitler announces new laws forbidding marriages or extramarital relations between Jews and German citizens on pain of imprisonment. Jews may not display the German flag or engage Aryan female domestics under forty-five years of age. The brown-shirted Reichstag members leap to their feet to approve unanimously.

Oh, Mama, Mama, Mama. So beautiful, so hungry and willing and sensual. What sad fate tied you to a roué . . . Or was he simply a man who didn't know his own mind? . . . Or a weak reed bent by his mother's stormy will? . . . Or a kid in a grownup's body, unmindful of any suffering but his own? . . . Well, whoever he was, your dreams weren't his.

Oh, Mama, how did you not find someone to love and cherish you? How did you stay asleep so long when you should have been up and doing? And how much I learned from you, even in my earliest girlhood years, when I saw your missteps and told myself, Never follow.

Moishe brings my mother a box of chocolates and a rhinestone brooch in the shape of a pretty little bird. She stands in the kitchen, refusing to turn around and look at him. He presses himself against her, lifts her hair, and kisses her tenderly on the back of her neck. "We'll just put it behind us, like it never even happened. Okay, sweetheart?" he cajoles her softly. "I know it was really hard on you, and I'm so sorry. Come on, doll, look at me."

She holds herself rigid, even with his warm breath on her. She folds her hands into angry fists, like she'll pummel him. Between clenched teeth she says, "Your lousy pity goes no deeper than the skin on boiled milk."

He tries again to turn her around to him, but she shrugs off his tug. She doesn't want to look at him. But finally she does, whirling around to face him, hissing, "Maybe you can put it behind you, but I can't, Morris—the shame of what I had to do because of you. Damn you! The loss of what I wanted more than anything!" She's so furious that her blood is racing like a wild horse.

But eventually, she gives in.

How could she? Did she justify it like a hangdog drunk—"Just a few more, till I get a little stronger"? Or maybe she held fast to the belief that after what she went through because of him, he'd certainly make an honest woman of her. Or was she still convinced that he was her only intended, her *besherter,* her destined one? What else can explain her going back to him?

Oh, Mama, Mama, Mama.

Six or seven months after the abortion. A whole week goes by and no Moishe. I'll give that louse a piece of my mind when I see him, my mother tells herself. Sunday morning, she fixes a cup of coffee and a toasted bagel and sits down at the table to have her breakfast. And in he walks.

"How you doin', doll. I just worked out at the gym and thought we could go out to breakfast, but I see I'm too late." He kisses her on the top of her head and sits.

She stands up and lets him have it, everything she's been saving all week, her voice growing sharper with each statement. "Do you know how long it's been since I laid eyes on you, Morris? If you love me like you say in bed, it's time to show me, damn it! You told me yourself you're a grown man and can do what you like. You're almost thirty years old, for godsakes!"

His jaw is set like one of the gangsters he hangs out with at his gym. He stares at her with a steely gaze. But it can't shut her up. "I have a right to expect more, Morris! I want a real home, I want a baby. I want to get married!" she shouts, pounding the table right under his nose.

He jumps up so violently that he knocks over the chair and it crashes to the floor. "Goddam you!" he yells, grabbing her shoulders, shaking her so hard and long that her teeth make castanet clicks. His eyes are bugging out and his fingers are digging into her flesh, and she's scared. He's suddenly a madman.

"Stop it, you bastard!" she screams and beats his chest with her fists.

"Bitch! You call me a bastard?" He lets loose of her shoulders and draws a hand back to slap her.

"Bastard!" she yells again through her shock. She braces herself for the blow, her lip curled in revulsion. But he turns and grabs the first thing in sight, her coffee-filled cup, and hurls it across the kitchen. It splats on the wall, and dark streaks of liquid run down and puddle on top of the broken shards of crockery. "Bitch, look what you made me do!" he shouts and glowers menacingly. Let him kill me, she thinks coolly. I don't give a damn.

But he picks the chair up from the floor and sits back down on it, his rage spent. "What the fuck do you want from my life?" he says in a low growl. "You know why we can't get married right now. If you don't accept it, then maybe we need to stop seeing each other."

She's breathing hard. She wants to kick him, scratch his face, but she sits, too, and tries to calm herself. She wants to beg him to love her more than he does . . . *No!* She's not a punching bag. She can't keep taking it and taking it forever. "Okay. Then we need to stop seeing each other," she says quietly. Her mind doesn't believe what her mouth is saying. How can she give him up when she's loved him so much for three years? She wants to pull her words back. But she doesn't. She lets them hover in the air between them.

"Mary, I told you a million times that one of these days . . . " He begins in a placating voice, but it turns into a snarl. "Damn you, if you don't trust me about us, if you don't believe I'm doing the best I can, then what the fuck am I doing here?"

Oh, good riddance to bad rubbish, is what I think.

But . . . let me see it from his side for a moment. Why would he want to marry her? She's more than ten years older than he, uneducated, poor, no rich farms, no mayors in her family. All the deficiencies for which she blames herself, true . . . But that being so, why did he take up with her and monopolize her most crucial years? . . . Oh, why should I see it from his side? May he drop dead!

But if he doesn't help make me, who will? . . . No, live, stay!

He pushes back from the table and sits with folded arms, his fingers digging into his biceps. "Ah, forget it. It's no use talking to you," he finally says with a disgusted wave of his hand, and rises and walks to the door and slams it behind him.

She jumps to her feet to run after him, but she sits down again. I gotta have some self-respect, she tells herself.

An hour passes, and still she sits at the kitchen table, damp ovals of sweat at her underarms because the airless apartment is humid already though it's only eleven o'clock. She knows his mother despises her, has known it since that one and only time they met. But why can't he love her enough to fight his damn mother? He's left her for good, she's sure, because that's what his mother always wanted him to do. She stares at the jagged lines of coffee stain that run down the wall, the broken crockery and puddle of coffee on the floor. She's exhausted, doesn't even have the energy to clean it up. Her uneaten bagel has attracted a fly that drones and buzzes from the bagel to her cheek and back again to the bagel. When it lands on her, she waves it away, hissing a *sssstt* of annoyance; but it would take more strength than she has to rise from her chair, look for an old *Forverts,* roll it into a weapon, and swat the life out of it.

Another hour passes and still she sits. She thinks, He was my hope for the future and the one bit of pleasure in my life. She watches a fat black cockroach skitter across the floor and squeeze under the door of the cupboard where she keeps spaghetti and cereal. "Nobody to live with but insects, like being in the grave," she says aloud in the empty room and snorts with self-pity. She won't even be able to stay in this apartment if he's not helping her with the rent. It's his lousy mother who's to blame, she tells herself again; if that cockroach was his mother, I'd take off my shoe and bash its head in and crush it to pieces. But she doesn't even have the energy to get up from the chair and go lie on the bed.

When Ricki knocks on the door and calls, "Yoo hoo, Mary, are you there?" Mary wishes she could hide because she's not in the mood for Ricki's cheery toughness. Ricki opens the door that Moishe left unlocked. She's in her old kimono, but her yellow ringlets are piled high in an elaborate hairdo and she wears blue eye shadow, like she's been getting ready to go out. She's carrying a cup of coffee and balancing a plate of chocolate cookies like a waitress. "Fresh from the oven," she declares. She puts the cup down on the table and waves the plate under Mary's nose. "Take some, they're great." Mary reaches for a cookie because she doesn't want to be impolite.

"Take two. They're small," Ricki nudges; then she clucks sympathetically. "Hey, I heard the fight—damn the thin walls—and then I saw him leaving, so I figured you needed company. I had a date to go out myself, to see a matinee of *Jubilee* on Broadway, but he called me up, right in the middle of my getting ready, to say he has to go to Buffalo 'cause his brother's in the hospital. I believe it like I believe five bucks will buy me the Empire State Building. Lousy men. They should all fall asleep and wake up as women."

Mary gives her a halfhearted chuckle. She doesn't want to talk about men. All she wants is to have Moishe back.

"Well, to hell with every one of 'em!" Ricki says. "Listen, sweetie, they're playing Greta Garbo and Fredric March at the Fox. Wanna go?"

"Oh, I think I'm coming down with a little cold. Anyway, I was going to stay home today and do my nails and wash out a few things." She tries to sound upbeat. But in a minute she's sobbing in Ricki's arms, tears bleeding down her cheeks, and Ricki is stroking her temple and saying, "That heel, that bastard. He's as full of meanness as a watermelon is full of seeds. He never was good enough for you, sweetie. Didn't I always tell you?"

"You know what we ought to do?" Ricki says after she opens a can of tomato soup and heats a bowl of it for Mary, who admits she hasn't had breakfast or lunch. "You're laid off for slack season and I've got vacation coming. Let's go to Steiger's for a week. I hear it's better than Grossinger's and a lot cheaper too. I got a girlfriend who just came back from there. I bet you never been to the Catskills. It's a great place to meet eligible bachelors."

"Oh, Ricki, I don't have the money. I probably won't get work again until busy season starts in September." She doesn't want to go anywhere unless it's with Moishe.

"Say, don't give me that about money," Ricki cajoles. "If you don't have enough, I'd front you. But aren't you getting that unemployment insurance now? Make a blessing on FDR's head and don't complain. Listen, all you gotta do is show up at the unemployment office on Monday morning, just like usual; then we'll go away for a week, and you'll be back in time to pick up your check the next Monday. Sweetie, it'll do you a world of good. I'm not taking no for an answer."

Ricki is right—during slack season Mary won't have to be spending what she saved up during busy season anymore, because nowadays she can get unemployment insurance. And her rent is even paid till the end of the month.

Moishe helped pay it the week before last . . . The thought of him makes a lump the size of a duck egg form in her throat. No more thinking about that louse! she admonishes herself.

What had she planned to do with the little windfall? She was going to send a bit to Hinda and di mameh. They hadn't asked for anything lately but they can always use an extra something. Yet the fight with Moishe has sunk her into a bog of despair, and if she stays in the apartment how will she be able to climb out? She's furious with him, absolutely fuming that he raised a hand to her. Yet how can she forget the good parts of all their years together? Everything in the apartment will remind her of him: the dinette table—how he used to sit there in that burgundy smoking jacket, which is still hanging in her closet; the loveseat—how they made wild love on it or, just as wonderful, cuddled there like an old married couple; the bed—how they slept together as close as two spoons in a drawer, her knees tucked into the backs of his, her groin caressing his seat . . . And now he's left her, and it wasn't meant to be after all. Oh, how will she bear it, knocking around this place when she can't hope to hear his key in the lock? She does need to get away for a while, to think about what she'll do with the rest of her life.

So on Monday morning, my mother stands in line and collects her unemployment check; then she goes home and packs the valise Ricki lends her, which is decaled with cheery pink flowers, and then she and Ricki take a subway train to the bus station. As she boards the bus she suddenly thinks, what if Moishe comes back? Maybe she shouldn't have left. He'll open the door of their apartment with an apologetic look on his face. That bastard, he should apologize! But no, he'll expect her to throw herself in his arms and beg him to forgive her. But she won't be there. Good! Maybe that'll make him miss her the way she misses him . . . No, she's sure he won't be back. She's got to stop deluding herself. He was probably waiting for any excuse to get rid of her. Now he has one, and he can blame it on her. She was the one who sent him packing.

Once the bus leaves the city, though, and follows the Hudson River, her mood lifts. To her amazement, she's enjoying the sparkle of diamonds the sunlight makes on bright water, and the little towns the bus passes through, with their quaint shops and market-day bustle, so different from the city in which she's lived since coming to America. The bus turns onto a long bridge and crosses the Hudson, then turns north and soon is lumbering up a mountain. She hasn't seen such a varied palette of greens since she was in the forest on the outskirts of Preil—pale yellow almost like straw; chartreuse bright; olive green; deep, lush, velvety green; shadow-dark green that's almost black. She's filled with sudden hope. She's not so old that she can't make a new life for herself. She's not even out of her thirties. They pass Liberty, New York, and by the time the bus driver calls out, "Steiger's Bungalows and Resort," she feels like she did when, bent so far over the railing that an alarmed fellow passenger seized her by her belt, she caught her first sight of the lady with the torch. "Oh, you were so right to bring me here, Ricki," she says when they get off the bus, and she throws her arms around Ricki's generous form.

All week at Steiger's, her depression comes and goes and comes and goes, like the rhythm of the mountain fog and the glittering sun that disappears in fog again. Some mornings she actually forgets she's mourning for Moishe. Ricki takes her blueberry picking before breakfast, and Mary can taste the sunshine in the succulence of the fresh fruit. They remind her of the berries in the Preil forest, where she used to go with Hirschel when he was a little boy, before she was sent off to work in Rezhitse. She showed him where to find the bushes and how to pluck off the wild berries (*yagdas*—she hasn't thought of that word in so long) and to place them carefully in the little tin pail she held for him. Her pleasure and her sadness, which the memory of blueberry picking brings her, are only for her dear brother now.

There's a little orchestra at Steiger's on Friday evening—accordion player, drummer, clarinetist, and fiddler, all dressed up in tuxedos, a red carnation in their lapel buttonholes, like they're playing with the Paul Whiteman orchestra. The women guests, decked out in rhinestones and cheap cocktail dresses or diaphanous summer gowns, have tried hard on working-class wages to look like the nightclub-hopping ladies they see in the movies. The men guests, fewer in number than the women, obligingly wear dark jackets and ties, though their faces are gleaming with sweat, and the summer humidity makes them swim in their clothes. Mary dances with everyone who asks her—good-looking young waiters, who are required by the management when they're not working in the restaurant to entertain the single ladies; the pressers and cutters who save up all year for a two-week escape from the stifling city; even elderly retirees who are huffing and puffing before the dance is over. It doesn't matter how they look or who they are, since she's not interested in anything except being out on the floor and moving to the music, enjoying herself. She's still light on her feet and quick to sense a fella's style. She never misses a step.

But then one of them, a coarse-looking cloakscutter in a pink shirt and red bow tie, who's asked for three dances in a row, whispers in her ear, "Whaddaya say we go out on the terrace for a little smooch?" She gives him a flat and loud no and refuses to dance with him again. She's as repelled as if he'd unzipped his fly and exposed himself right there on the floor. She can't bear even the thought of any mouth but Moishe's on hers.

"So what did you do to Max to make him go around telling all the guys you're a cold fish?" another dance partner asks with amusement. She doesn't care; it's true, anyway—she's a cold fish now. She'll be a cold fish the rest of her life if she can't have Moishe again.

Around midnight, Ricki pulls her aside between dances and says into her ear, "Sweetie, would you mind not coming back to the room for an hour or so?" Ricki nods in the direction of the exit, where the bronzed young life-guard she'd been chatting up that afternoon, dressed now in a white dinner jacket with a black bow tie, leans against the door, waiting for her.

"Sure, that's okay," Mary says, though her feet are hurting by now and she's feeling a bit bedraggled. She'd like to get out of her shoes and girdle and stretch out on her bed and close her eyes.

After Ricki leaves the hall, my mother leaves, too, and wanders over to the deserted swimming pool area where there are lawn chairs and a stack of towels. She covers a dew-wet chair with a towel, wraps another towel around her shoulders like a blanket, and tucks a third one around her legs.

Through infinities of space and years, I watch her. I long for her. I long to tell her what I know: that someday, eons away maybe but as certain as the sun, something to solace her—some small but undeniable something—will be salvaged from all that's made her suffer. Oh, Mama, would that give you comfort now?

She sits and stares into the velvet darkness. There's no way she can escape the strains of music that come from the main building . . . "Blue Moon," "Chasing Shadows," "When I Grow Too Old to Dream." Again sadness creeps up on her like the fog, and she moans into the dark. But it's not for Moishe; it's for der tateh, who's been dead for almost twenty years. He's the one she wants and misses. She'll never be his little girl again, never again sit on his lap and be rocked by him and see his eyes shiny with love for her: those thoughts are like knife slashes. One time—he'd just come in from shul, and she ran to him, buried her head in his chest—he whispered so no one else could hear, "My prettiest, my favorite one." She would give her life to hear him whisper that again. No one will ever love her as he did.

It takes about four weeks for letters to go by slow freighter, then indirect train, then plodding horse and wagon from New York to Preil, and even if the recipient answers immediately, there can be a two-month wait between writing a letter and receiving an answer. In May, Mary and Ray bought a postal order for five dollars to send di mameh, who was having pains in her stomach and needed to go to Riga where there's a stomach specialist. Now in July a letter from Hinda finally arrives.

The doctor's medicines are helping di mameh feel better, she writes. *When we got back from Riga, Irina from across the street* [Mary remembers the woman, young in those days, who wore a big silver crucifix around her neck] *brought over milk-and-potato soup, and that also helped soothe di mameh's stomach. Dear Irina, such a guteh mentch, a good human being. She's looked in on di mameh and fixed things for her all week while I was at work. But one like Irina is not easy to find among them. Yesterday I was walking home when it was just getting dark, and five boys I never saw before, not more than fourteen years old, all of them with shaved blond heads, yell out to me Dirty Jew and they gang up on me.*

Like what Mary has been seeing in the newreels and reading in the Yiddish papers about Germany. *Gottenu!* she cries, and a chill surges through her veins.

. . . They tore the sleeve on my jacket, almost ripped it out altogether, and tripped me so I fell down on the ground. One of them kept smacking me with a stick and just missed cracking my head in half. Then the devils all ran off laughing like it was nothing but a good joke.

Such incidents have happened in Preil for two hundred years; but to Mary their meaning is even more frightening now. That article from the *New York Times* that the new draper read them in the shop the other day, "Anti-Semites Firmly in the Saddle as Persecution Spreads in Reich," it was called. Maybe it's spreading all over Europe. Hirschel's last letter was a worry to her too. The Perkonkrusts were everywhere in Riga these days, saluting each other with a raised arm just like Hitler's thugs, shouting out their silly slogans, boycotting Jewish shops. *And that Karlis Ulmanis, who took over*

Latvia in a military coup last year, Hirschel wrote, *he knows he can get cheers from big crowds in any town or city here just by screaming, "A Latvian Latvia!"*

She needs to share these letters with Ray. But she feels too mortified to go see her sister, because the last time they were together, Ray was a broken record about her favorite subject again, and Mary yelled, "You stupid monkey, you don't know nothing about how it is between a man and a woman who love each other!" Now Ray will take one look at her haggard face and she'll say something mean, like, "Did that user finally find somebody else to milk?" But Mary is so afraid for Hirschel and di mameh and all of them, because Europe is becoming dangerous. The promise she made them more than twenty years ago and didn't keep—she needs to find a way to keep it now.

And now I have nothing to lose when they come, she thinks, because I have no more dark, wonderful secret life I need to protect . . . *Oy, Tateleh!* A superstitious fear makes her shudder, and she speaks to her dead father: Talk to God so he won't punish me and those I love for my sins.

My mother arrives just as Ray is about to leave. Ray is dressed in her ugly little pillbox hat and carries a big pocketbook on her arm. "Well, look who's here," she says. She tells Mary she's busy; she's going to meet her girlfriends from the shop and have supper with them at the Automat. But when she takes a closer look at Mary's face, she gets scared. "What's the matter with you?" Ray asks. Mary says nothing, only hands her the two letters, which Ray reads without taking off her hat or putting her pocketbook down. She makes distressed little grunts as she reads.

"We have to do something, we have to do something now," Mary repeats after each of Ray's grunts.

Ray has been worried, too, even before Mary brought her these letters. She hears what people in her shop are saying about what's going on in Europe. Suddenly everyone she knows is talking about it, even her closest girlfriends. And now she pays more attention to the news articles in the *Forverts,* too. They report terrible things—about little Jewish children being beaten up by German children, synagogues being burnt to the ground, Jewish shop windows being shattered and the shops being looted. Everyone is worried . . . But her sister is always so emotional about everything, so she must be the sensible one. She takes off her hat and puts her pocketbook back in the closet of her room. Her friends will have to have supper without her.

The missus has gone out for the day, so she and Mary can sit at the oilcloth-covered table in the kitchen and figure things out. "Wait, I'll make some tea for us," she offers.

My Aunt Ray stands at the sink and fills the kettle, thinking about what they can do. The terrible truth, she tells herself, is that they can't do anything. How can she and Mary help the whole family get the papers that would let them leave Latvia and cross Europe and come into America? And even if they could get papers, where would she and Mary find the money for the trains and ships and the people who must be bribed along the way? And even if they had the money for the trip, where would they all live?—di mameh, Hinda, Chana and her husband and three children, Hirschel and his wife? There were so many of them. You couldn't squeeze them all into a furnished room. And how would they all eat? Where would they get clothes to wear? It's not as simple as saying, "Well, they can get jobs." There are no jobs now in the middle of a depression. Even people who are already American citizens are having a hard time finding jobs. Impossible. It was all impossible. She's got to believe that the ugliness in Europe will pass—just like it always has before.

The kettle boils and Ray pours the hot water over a Lipton tea bag, which she's put in a glass that once contained a *yahrzeit* candle for der tateh. She dunks the bag up and down, then places it in a second yahrzeit-candle glass, and again she pours hot water over it. "It'll blow over, what's going on in Europe," she finally says, putting one of the glasses and a box of sugar lumps in front of Mary. "There've been antisemiten since the Bible. They come and they go."

"But it's getting worse. What did Hinda just go through?" Mary cries.

"Those were just stupid kids. It was worse for der tateh, remember? And yet we all managed to live there and survive." My Aunt Ray won't let my mother see how worried she is, because that will make my mother more worried. That's how, years later, she'll try to explain to me what didn't happen in 1935. "Anyway, what can we do right now? We don't have the money to bring them over this minute."

My mother shoves the sugar box and the glass of tea to the side and puts her pounding head down on the kitchen table. This is how people go crazy, she thinks. She can't bear it. "Ray, listen to me." She jumps to her feet and cries, "Just Hirschel for now! We'll beg Sarah and Sam for the money. You go to them. They like you. Please, Ray, you go and ask them to lend enough money to bring Hirschel over."

"Don't be foolish. A married man wouldn't run away without his wife."

Yes. That's true. His *beloved Dweira,* he calls her. He would never leave without her. It was the Hirschel she saw last, the boy who was ten years old, that she was remembering. A vision—clear as though it were happening this minute—of Hirschel the child writhing under a Perkonkrust's boot won't leave her head. "We'll bring the wife over, too," Mary cries. "We'll ask Sarah and Sam to help with the money for Hirschel and his wife. He's Sarah's brother, too. She should care what happens to him." At least Hirschel must be saved! But she needs Ray's help; she can't go begging to Sarah and Sam, who despise her because of her craziness twenty years ago.

"You think it's so easy to get someone into America? It's not like it used to be anymore," Ray says reasonably.

"Oh, please, *tayere shvester,*" Mary sobs. She tries to control herself, but she can't. She throws her arms around Ray and wails like a mourner. "*Tayere shvester,* please!"

Ray, her feet wide apart like a flat-footed policeman, extricates herself and holds Mary's hands firm. "Listen, Mary. Just listen to me a minute," she says, like to a hysterical child. "They're not living under the nose of that Hitler. Germany is not like next door to Latvia . . . We'll wait a little while and see what happens."

Together with all her other worries, my mother has to move out of the apartment. The busy season has just started and she's working again, but without Moishe's help she can't afford to keep paying the rent. In the muggy heat of a Saturday afternoon, she walks up and down the East Bronx streets, looking for a ROOM TO LET sign. She's drowning in loneliness and worried sick about Hirschel. What's my purpose in this world? she asks herself as she walks, and she doesn't know. On Longwood Avenue, she sees a sign hanging in a second-story window that's over a little grocery store: NICE AIRY ROOM TO LET. When she opens the heavy door to the building, she sees that the hallway is dark, but there's a bare bulb that lights up the stairs. Somebody has swept the thin carpet clean and polished the banister.

The name above the bell at the door of 2C is Feinberg. The woman who answers has red-rimmed eyes that are small and blue. She's wearing bright lipstick, but only on her bottom lip, as though she'd gotten distracted before she could finish the application. Its garish red accentuates the whiteness of the rest of her face, like the terrible masks that children wear for Halloween.

"Do you inqvire vor di room? Only for vun person. Are you by yourzelf?" the woman asks.

"Yes, it's only for me," Mary answers in Yiddish, because the woman's accent is very heavy.

"I do not speak dat. Ve ver Churmenz," Mrs. Feinberg says abruptly, but she ushers Mary in. The window shades are down in the somber-looking front room. The sofa is covered with a sheet, as though no one ever sits in that room, so Mary is startled when a man in a black suit and bow tie rises from a chair in the corner. "My husband, Herr Doktor Feinberg," Mrs. Feinberg says quickly. He doesn't come forward, but he nods and says a very formal, "How do you do?" Even in the bad light Mary can see that his face has the flaccid skin of a person who was once much heavier. Eyebrows, mouth, dewlaps, everything droops in a visual sob—like a mask of tragedy.

Mrs. Feinberg hurries her on before Mary can even utter an amenity to the Herr Doktor. "You alzo haf kitchen privilege," Mrs. Feinberg says, waving toward the tiny kitchen, and then leading Mary to a little hallway. Mary can see an old-fashioned four-poster bed through a door left ajar, and a big dresser, heavy and dark. They dwarf the room, and Mary knows right away she could not live there because it would depress her; but Mrs. Feinberg opens a door across the hall. "Here vill be your room," she says. The window shade is up and light pours in on a double bed that's covered by an orange and white duvet. The duvet's cheerful print shows a woman in a dirndl carrying a milk bucket, a country swain stealing a kiss on her cheek, geese running about their legs, and cows grazing in the distance. Mary feels the bed's firm mattress and admires the white wicker dresser. She's never had such a nice-looking room. "I'll take it," she declares, though it's three dollars a month more than what she paid at the Poteshes.

Ricki helps her pack her clothes and the few items she wants to keep. She gives Ricki all the dishes and pots and pans, because there's no place for them in Mrs. Feinberg's tiny kitchen. She also gives Ricki the amber-colored ashtray and a lot of the silly knickknacks she's accumulated over the years, like the Venus de Milo statue she won at Bingo Night at the movies. The gilt-framed picture of Hirschel as a boy she wraps carefully in an old silk half-slip, so it won't get banged up. "Oh, Ricki, I'll miss you so much," she says when they finish tying up all her bundles.

"Me too you," Ricki sniffs. They throw their arms tightly around one another and rock back and forth in a sad little dance. Then Ricky loosens her grip on Mary and puts on a cheerful face. "Say, you're not moving to the other side of New York. We can still go to a movie or have a glass of wine sometime. No?"

"Sure we can," Mary says. But they both have trembly lips because they know it can't be the same as when they lived down the hall from one another and saw each other practically every day and talked out their sadness or their anger about the men in their lives.

The smoking jacket and slippers, Mary leaves in the closet.

8

Fall, 1935

TIME ON THE MARCH

Congressman Fontaine Maury Maverick: It seems perfectly apparent that we cannot stop the war; so the best thing is to stay out of it ourselves.

NEW YORK. Three hundred thousand Americans are facing a dark future because the federal government has announced it will close its transient relief centers. It will be back to the road again, back to sleeping in parks or under bridges. Back to the handout, the breadline, the hobo jungle . . . Brother, can you spare a dime? A nickel? A penny? Brother, can I pore through the contents of your garbage pail?

My mother sees little of the Feinbergs. Mrs. Feinberg stays in her bedroom most of the time, and the door is closed when Mary leaves for work in the morning and returns in the evening. Herr Doktor Feinberg seems always to be sitting in the corner of the front room, sometimes holding a book, his mouth moving; sometimes immobile, his head buried in his hands. Mary is always startled, discomfited, when she catches a glimpse of him. He exudes a mute misery. On weekends when she goes into the kitchen, she sometimes runs across her missus, who is always dressed, no matter the hour, in the same faded-blue housecoat that looks as though it once cost a lot of money. Mary musters a cheery voice to say, "Hello, how are you?" and Mrs. Feinberg answers, "Goot day" and nods. She never seems the least bit friendly. The silence between them feels uncomfortable, so Mary usually returns to her room until Mrs. Feinberg has left the kitchen.

Most evenings when Mary comes from work, she stops at the little grocery downstairs and buys herself something to take up for her supper. The owner, Mrs. Rifkin, waits on the customers all by herself, energetically hobbling about the store in her orthopedic shoes. If kids come in to buy candy and then wander around, Mrs. Rifkin is sure they're looking for something to steal, and she yells, "Get out, you little *mamsers*"—bastards. She lifts her food-stained apron to shoo them away like they're flies. If Mary is the only customer, Mrs. Rifkin is very friendly and chatty with her. "Ah, a Litvak"; she can tell by Mary's accent. She herself is a Galitzianer, from Poland, she says. "How long you been here?" she wants to know. She wants to know where Mary works too, and how she likes it, and how she likes living by the Feinbergs. "You never been married, a pretty lady like you?" Mrs. Rifkin asks. Mary thinks Mrs. Rifkin is a busybody, a yenta; but once Mary goes upstairs she'll have no one to talk to the whole evening, and she knows Mrs. Rifkin is lonely, too, so she answers her questions and always asks after Mr. Rifkin, a shut-in with terrible rheumatoid arthritis, who can hardly walk.

One evening, Mrs. Rifkin is wrapping up Mary's farmer cheese and the rolls she bought for her supper and next day's breakfast, and that's when she tells Mary about the Feinbergs. Mrs. Rifkin knows about the Feinbergs because she has a lady friend who's a neighbor of Mr. Feinberg's brother, who lives five blocks away. Mary stands with her back pressed against the tall sour-pickle barrel, feeling funny about listening to gossip, but really wanting to know more about her dour missus and the man who seems never to leave his dark corner or change out of his black suit and bow tie. "Refugees from Stuttgart, in Germany, both of them. A little stuck up, you know, because he was a engineer, a very educated man with a high job in a government office . . ."

The door opens and a customer comes in. Mrs. Rifkin stops her story and nods pleasantly.

"Gimme 'bout a pound of dried plums and a half pound of butter," the man tells Mrs. Rifkin, who hobbles to the dried-fruit bins and scoops plums into a paper bag, then hobbles to the icebox, from which she takes out a tub of butter. With a wooden spatula, she scoops some of it into a little carton. At the counter she weighs first the bag and then the carton on the scale she keeps near the cash register. Mary waits, staring at a Coca-Cola poster with its smiling young blond girl who's brandishing a tennis racket in one hand and a bottle of soda pop in another. Are there really people like that blond girl in the world, who are so carefree and gay and have nothing at all to worry about? she wonders.

The door closes behind the customer, and Mrs. Rifkin resumes her gossip. When the Nazis threw all the Jews out of high jobs, and low jobs too, Herr Doktor Feinberg had no way to make a living in Germany; but the brother was able to get the affidavits and all papers that were needed to bring the Feinbergs to America. Of course they couldn't take any of their possessions or money out of Germany, only ten marks—not more than four dollars. So the brother got them clothes and furniture and found Herr Docktor Feinberg a job in the same private boys' school where he, the brother, teaches German. In a few weeks, the Herr Doktor will be teaching algebra and geometry and calculus, which should be very easy for him. The only complication is that he has to be able to make himself understood by fourteen- and fifteen-year-old American kids, and though he speaks four languages, English is not among them.

"How are they living now?" Mary asks, because she hasn't stopped thinking about Hirschel's letters, and what she's been reading in the Yiddish papers and seeing in the *March of Time* movie newsreels. Hirschel isn't educated like an engineer, but if there's a way for a new immigrant to make a living, she's sure he'd try it.

"I hear the brother slips them a few dollars, and they get a little bit to live on from the Hebrew Immigrant Aid Society, and the rest is from you, for the room she rents out to you. You got the big room up there, no? They gave you the big room so they can get a little more money in rent."

Now that Mary knows the Herr Doktor's story, whenever she passes the front room, she tries to hear what he mumbles. She can make out some words. "I yam, you arrr, he iz, dey arrr . . . Ven in de courz of whoman eventz . . ." She would like to go into the room and ask him things, like whether he thinks people in Eastern Europe are in danger, too, and whether she should try to bring her brother and the rest of the family to America. But she's shy about interrupting him when he's so intent on his study. She wonders how he'll be able to teach kids in a few weeks. When he tries to speak English, it sounds like he's clearing a chicken bone from his throat.

One Saturday morning she's awakened by shouting and pounding on the walls. The Feinbergs are fighting. He's crying like a woman. *Ich kann's nicht mehr!* "I can't do it anymore!" he says. "Impossible at my age. And impossible to be in front of children who will laugh because they can't understand me"—words my mother is able to decifer because their German is so close to her Yiddish.

"What are we supposed to do then, starve to death? Take charity the rest of our lives?" Mrs. Feinberg yells. "You should have left me, even to die! Better there with my mother and sister in my own house than here with nothing."

Mary pulls the blanket over her head. She's embarrassed to be hearing their spat. But the blanket blocks out nothing. One of them pounds with both fists now. "I wish I died there before I ever set foot on the cursed ship. I can't do it anymore!" the Herr Doktor yells.

The next Saturday morning she's awakened again. Sirens. A fire, she thinks. Where? She leaps out of bed and runs to the window. It's an ambulance, stopped right in front of the apartment house. Neighbors come out to the street to watch. Mary sees Mrs. Rifkin running out of her store. "Who is it?" Mrs. Rifkin cries.

Two men jump out of the ambulance with a stretcher. Mary hears them running up the stairs, and then a loud knocking on the door of the apartment in which she lives. Mrs. Feinberg opens the door. The sounds that come out of Mrs. Feinberg's mouth are between a sob and a scream. Mary throws on her bathrobe and runs out of her room. By then the door to the Feinbergs' bedroom is open and the ambulance men are inside. Mary can see the Herr Doktor lying stretched out on the bed, his mouth wide open like he's snoring, and on his face the sun is pouring in through an open window, just like it's a nice day. But he's greenish like lettuce, and nothing on him moves.

"Rat poison," she hears one of the ambulance men say. Mary must hold on to the wall because her head reels and her knees feel like they'll buckle.

Within the hour, two policemen come and a doctor and Herr Doktor Feinberg's brother, a well-fed-looking redheaded man with a pointy russet beard and none of the Feinbergs' moroseness. Mary hears the brother quietly telling her missus not to worry, that he'll go downtown and sign whatever papers need to be signed, and he'll take care of the burial arrangements too. "Gitl, you come live with me and my wife for a while, until you figure out what you'll do," he says kindly.

"No, leave me here!" Mrs. Feinberg keens in German, in a voice so horrible that Mary, listening from her room, is afraid. "I've had enough moving. I should never have moved in the first place." When Mary hears that the policemen and doctor and brother have left, she comes out from her room. How awful to know that just a little while ago someone was living right here, breathing the same air that she breathed, sharing space with her, and now he's a cold corpse in a morgue drawer. She's nauseated by the bitter bile that gurgles up from her stomach; but Mrs. Feinberg is standing at the stove now, waiting for the kettle to boil, and Mary would like to offer some comfort. She doesn't know what to do for this woman who's like a living ghost. "Mrs.

Feinberg?" she says softly. "I'm so sorry for what happened to your husband, for all the terrible things you've gone through. Is there anything I can do for you?" She feels awkward because they've spoken so little.

Mrs. Feinberg looks up at her, stony-faced. "Nothink to do," she says abruptly.

"Well . . . I'm so sorry," Mary repeats. "Please let me know if I can fix you some soup or . . . anything . . . anything at all." She goes back to her room. How will she ever be able to sleep in this apartment? She wants to move out right away. But how can she move when she knows that now more than ever Mrs. Feinberg will need the money she gets from Mary for rent? She'll wait a few months, at least until Mrs. Feinberg gets back on her feet.

Her pity for Mrs. Feinberg is mixed with awful fear. Whenever she passes the front room she sees the Herr Doktor out of the corner of her eye, sitting on his chair in his black suit and bow tie, a tragic ghost, his lips mumbling, "I yam, you arrr . . ." Her stomach flip-flops. When she sleeps, she has nightmares, not just about the greenish corpse that had lain in a bed only yards away from her room, but also about Hirschel; about club-wielding Perkonkrusts; about the crazy-eyed beast in Germany with his spider armband, screaming, *Juden raus!* like she saw in the newsreels.

And yet, she thinks when she wakes up in the dark room, look what happened when the Feinbergs left Europe and tried to make a new life for themselves in America. It's not so easy—to learn a new language, find a job, adjust yourself to a new country. Maybe the Feinbergs would have been better off to stay where they were.

A letter from Hinda. This one says di mameh is back to her normal self, doesn't complain at all about stomach pains anymore. A sweet little calf was born to Shoshana—the cow they'd bought with the money Mary and Ray had sent so di mameh could have milk whenever she needed it for her bad stomach. *I had to feed the calf by hand for two weeks because Shoshana's udder was infected, but it was a good thing for me because it made me forget for a little while my own miseries . . .*

Mary fears what's coming next in the letter—the roughneck bullies again. But that's not it. *Though I had such big hopes, dear sister, things didn't work out with Yossel, the butcher who I was keeping company with. I have to say I'm lonely after I got used to having him so much in my life.* (Just like me,

Mary thinks. What irony—two sisters, a whole ocean apart, haven't seen each other for more than twenty years, and we're suffering from exactly the same trouble.) *But I have my health, thank God, and di mameh, who's so darling and sweet in her old age, needs me very much. So I really can't complain.* And not a word of antisemiten in the whole letter. Maybe Ray was right, Mary tells herself. Jews just have to accept that anti-Semites have always been around; they come, but they always go away again.

My mother still hasn't told Ray where she's living. Every Wednesday night they meet at the Automat on East 170th Street. That way Ray doesn't say, "Where can I get hold of you?" My mother would like to unburden herself about the ghastly greenish corpse and the appalling story of the Feinbergs' suffering, but she doesn't want to get into a discussion with Ray about how long she's lived at the Feinbergs and why she had to leave her last place.

Now she rushes to the Automat with the letter from Hinda in her pocketbook. Ray has gotten there early and hasn't waited for Mary before choosing her dishes from the steaming buffet table and the dozens of little glass doors that slide open when nickels are deposited into the slots. She carries her tray to a table for two. She doesn't take off her brown pillbox hat, but she puts her blue coat on one of the chairs and sits down on the other. When Mary arrives, Ray is already forking bites from a steaming plate of liver and onions into her mouth. "I had to go ahead and start so my food don't get cold," Ray says with a full mouth. "You go get what you want, too."

"It's all right. I don't mind." Mary hands her Hinda's letter before she drapes Ray's coat on the back of the chair and sits down. "It sounds like things aren't so bad over there right now. Maybe we don't have to be so worried," Mary says, though her brow is as wrinkled as a washboard because she's not really certain they don't have to be worried. If she and Ray were more educated, smarter, they'd know for sure if there was something they needed to do right now; but she feels like they're both stupid as stones.

There's a flicker of anxiety in Ray's eyes when she sees the letter is from Preil. She stops chewing and puts down her knife and fork to read it. Then she chuckles at Hinda's lines about feeding the calf by hand. She's so relieved that the only disaster is Yossel the butcher, because that's not the end of the world. You can live without a man in your life. Ray has no man in her life either. "See, like I said to you already, Latvia isn't Germany. We just have to watch and wait. A lot of people say this whole crazy thing will come to an end soon, even in Germany."

"Yes, you're right. A lot of people are saying that," Mary agrees. Even some of the newspapers are saying that. One of the pressers in her shop said that last week. Mary doesn't tell Ray that when the presser said that, a cutter called him a damn fool who had his head up his ass. "This idiot didn't hear from the Nuremberg Laws that just gave Jews the same rights as dead fish. Simpleton, you didn't hear they're making bonfires in Berlin and throwing in Jewish babies together with Jewish books? You should burn in hell your-self!" the cutter screamed. Mary didn't see whether it was he or the man he cursed who started it, but when she heard the crash of a dummy and looked around, the two were already scrambling in a death grip, their fingers clamp-ing one another's necks, blood already gushing from the presser's nose. Four other men finally managed to pinion their arms and stop them. The cutter was a German Jew who had two brothers in Germany. They'd been taken off by the Gestapo a month ago for questioning and never came home. But like Ray, Mary wants so much to believe that what's happening in Europe will blow over.

Maybe it's because they've tried to agree about something for a change, or maybe Mary feels weak because of the Feinbergs' calamity and is so tired of hiding her pain about that and about Moishe from the only person in her family she can be with. She isn't sure what makes her do it, but suddenly she blurts out, "Moishe's gone. He left me." Her lip quivers after she says it, but she won't cry because she won't give Ray that satisfaction.

Ray says none of the nasty things Mary thought she'd say. Instead she pushes back her plate of liver and onions and goes over to Mary, and right there in the crowded Automat she bends and hugs Mary to her big bosom. "Oy, *shvester*," she murmurs and puts her lips on Mary's head. That show of sweetness makes Mary have to suppress a sob that's gurgling in her throat. When Ray sits down again, still she doesn't mention Moishe, never says, "See, I told you so." She only reaches across the table and takes Mary's hand and asks, "Are you all right?"

Mary wants to kiss her for being so kind. She's about to blurt out the terrible story of the Feinbergs too, but suddenly she's afraid that Ray will say something crazy, like, "It's bad luck to live where someone has killed himself." She'll try to make Mary move in with her, which for Mary would be worse than death . . . (Yet it feels so good, that little sign she was given that her sister loves her.) "Yeah, thanks . . . thanks for asking. I'm doing okay," is all Mary says.

When they finish at the Automat, they walk arm-in-arm together down 170th. Mary has not walked arm-in-arm with Ray since they were little girls strolling around the Preil marketplace more than a quarter-century ago. Mary barely notices now the things she's snickered at for years, like Ray's funny hat and her tan shoes that lace up like an old woman's. "Mereleh, what can I do to help you?" Ray asks.

"I'm okay, just a little like Hinda though . . . I get lonely," Mary confides.

Ray pats the hand that's tucked under her arm. They don't talk much, just stroll like two sisters till they reach the building on 174th where Ray lives. Ray's missus is home, fixing her supper, so Ray invites Mary to sit with her for a while on the fire escape. They step over the windowsill in Ray's room and settle themselves on the old towels she's dragged out to put over the rusty iron slats.

"Listen, Mary," Ray begins, "nobody has to be lonely in a city like New York where there are so many Litvaks." She means Jews from the same part of Eastern Europe from which she and Mary have come. She smoothes Mary's hair and pats her cheek like a *mameleh*. "You'll come with me next Saturday to the Litvishe Verein dance. You'll see what nice people you'll meet there." Ray speaks decisively in her foghorn voice, because she knows the simple answer for everything.

Saturday evening: my mother wants to please Ray, wants to keep up this new peace between them, but she doesn't have good feelings about going to the dance. She should be doing more serious things now, like figuring out whether Hirschel and di mameh are in danger. And anyway, she's seen Ray's friends who go to the Litvishe Verein—that Molly and Dolly and Betsy. They're like Ray . . . But she's promised.

She looks in her hand mirror as she puts on her lipstick and Maybelline. She can't help thinking as she does it of the times she used to get ready for her dates with Moishe, and how for so long she was sure he was the one. Oh, then she was happy, then she was beautiful. She scrutinizes the dark shadows under her eyes. Yes, the face is a clock. She'd had that thought last year, when she was afraid Moishe would think she looked too old for him. But she was so young-looking then compared to now.

Mary takes the subway across town to the address Ray gave her, on the Lower East Side, a settlement house on a street that's mostly Italian these days but used to be mostly Jewish when the Litvishe Verein began meeting there thirty years earlier. She stands outside the building, disgusted with herself for caving in to Ray's cajoling. She can't bring herself to go in. What would be the point? She turns and hurries back toward the subway station.

A man is walking toward her, graceless and paunchy. She figures he's heading to the dance; but when he gets closer she knows she's wrong because he has a swarthy look, unlike a Litvak. They pass. She looks straight ahead, but she feels him staring at her. Then he turns around and is following her. She walks faster; she doesn't want to deal with some masher who thinks he can pick up any woman on the street just because she's alone. Down the street is a sign that says BORELLI'S GOOD EATS! She hurries toward it, sure he won't follow her into a restaurant.

"Mary? Is that really you?" he calls out as she's about to open the restaurant door. She stops and looks at this man who knows her name.

He's put on twenty pounds, and an enormous forehead has replaced his coarse dark hair, but his soft brown eyes and full lips are the same. "Dominick?" The man she dated years ago, in the 1920s. They yelp and laugh and throw themselves into each other's arms.

"Mary! Mary! Oh, lemme look at you," he cries and holds her at arm's length. "As beautiful as ever," he says in a hoarse voice. "What are you doing here on the Lower East Side? I heard you moved to the Bronx. I just got through eating at The Sicilian, down the block . . . Remember, that restaurant I used to take you to? Oh, oh, my God, I can't believe I ran into you," he says and laughs again and stumbles over his words because he's so amazed that the gods, or Saint Christopher, or whatever, should set him on just this street, at just this moment, to run smack into the woman he's never put out of his mind. "So, are you married . . . or what?" he dares to ask.

"No," she says. She won't tell him about Moishe. "How about you?"

"Yeah, I was. A nice Italian girl . . . really wonderful. She died in childbirth. The baby, too. It's been four years already."

Mary hugs him and says, "I'm so sorry, Dominick."

"Yeah, me, too." He shrugs. "Life goes on, I guess. Say, are you busy . . . or do you have time for a cup of coffee now?"

She feels a momentary panic. What should she do? She has serious things to think about and doesn't need distractions. Anyway, she certainly doesn't want to start again with this man. He actually asked her to marry him once, and then he said, "It would break my parents' heart if my wife wasn't Catholic." Not that she would have married him in any case, but she was flabbergasted: Yes, it was true she worked hard to act American, but how could he know her so little as to believe she could stop being Jewish? It wasn't religious, it was who she was. She sent him packing that same night.

"I have to get up pretty early tomorrow," she tells him now.

"Hey, just for old time's sake. Come on," he says softly, opening the door to Borelli's.

When Dominick comes to pick my mother up on Saturday evenings, he brings her a dozen red roses and chocolates in a fancy tin box—every Saturday—and he only laughs when she says, "Dominick, you have to stop this. You'll bankrupt yourself."

They go to movies a lot. Dominick always slips his arm over her chair, his fingers grazing her shoulder. She barely notices because she's so deeply troubled by the *March of Time* newsreels—dark and white flags, millions of them, their vicious black spiders dancing in the wind; the German führer, shooting his arm up over and over like a mechanical toy, his screaming eyes sinister like a murderer's; men with carved concrete faces moving in menacing columns, a juggernaut powerful enough to crush the whole world. She studies the newsreels with all her might, as though they will tell her what she must do.

After the movies, Dominick takes her to a restaurant for a bite to eat. It's better than eating alone in Mrs. Feinberg's dreary apartment. She tells him of the Feinbergs' terrible story and of her constant worries over what's going on in Europe. She tells him about her confusion over Hirschel and the rest of the family. "Maybe I need to be figuring out a way to bring them to America, but the Feinbergs were so unhappy here. I just don't know what I'm supposed to be doing."

"I'd help you, Mary," Dominick interrupts. His gaze is solemn. "I don't know a lot about it, but if you want to bring them here, I'll find out how. I'd like to help you any way I can," he says fervently.

When they say goodnight, he gives her a hug and a peck on the cheek. For weeks he asks for nothing more. "I don't know how I ever let you get out of my life," he tells her, as though he's forgotten how annoyed she'd once been with him.

One evening, after they've been going out for almost two months, he orders a whole bottle of red wine at The Sicilian and drinks most of it himself, then orders one more glass. Mary knows he's trying to gather courage to make a move, and she feels a little sorry for him. In the empty train back to the Bronx, he puts his arm around her and turns her face to his. "I'd like to really kiss you, okay?" he asks, and she nods.

She's been kissed by no one but Moishe for three years. It feels strange when Dominick places his lips on hers, his mouth so unfamiliar. She can't remember whether she liked his kisses ten years ago. She doesn't really like them now . . . yet he's so kind and gentle with her. He walks her from the subway station to the house where she lives. "You didn't mind, did you?" he asks at the door. In answer, she gives him her lips again.

(But he's not the one! It's the other one, the selfish one, the one who won't grow up, the phony movie-gangster one. He's the only one! I know what I know, and I can't be distracted.)

My mother tells herself she doesn't want Dominick to get too attached to her because she can't return his feelings, but soon she's going out with him two or three times a week. He asks about her sister Ray. He remembers she didn't like him, called him a *shaygetz*. He says he always wondered if she was the reason Mary wouldn't marry him. He tells her that his father died eight years ago and his mother has been dead for five years. "But you're still Catholic, no?" Mary asks. Now why in the world did I say that? she thinks the minute the words are in the air. What difference does it make unless I'm gonna marry him? And I'm not.

"Naw, not practicing. Not really. I did it for my mom," he says simply. Mary doesn't remind him what he said before she broke up with him ten years ago.

One Saturday evening, just as she begins dressing for their date, the doorbell rings and when Mrs. Feinberg doesn't answer it, Mary goes to the door. It's Ricki, looking glum. "Aw, Mary, I'm through with that bastard," she announces. "He stood me up one time too many." She means the young lifeguard from Steiger's, whom she's been seeing since the summer season was over and he came to the city to work as a waiter. "Say, you wanna go out for a glass of wine or something?"

Mary tells her she's got a date with an old flame and was just getting ready.

"Mazel tov!" Ricki shouts and throws her arms around Mary in a bear hug. "Now, didn't I say you'd find a nice guy to replace that heel?"

Ricki is still there when Dominick arrives because she wants to take a look at him. Mary introduces them, surprised at how nervous she feels. "Ricki, Dominick; Dominick, Ricki . . . Ricki's my old friend from when I lived on Charlotte Street," she explains, glancing at Dominick to see what Ricki sees. Ricki likes handsome young men so much, and Mary can imagine what she must be thinking. Dominick probably bought the blue-serge suit he's wearing at least ten years ago: it's too tight around the middle, and it's shiny with age. His beard is so heavy under his dark skin that he looks unshaven, like the cavemen in the *Alley Oop* comic strips; and he's wearing a polka-dot blue and yellow bow tie, which makes his face look fat and round. Mary is embarrassed that Ricki is seeing this man she's going out with, who's nothing at all like the handsome, elegant Moishe. She tells herself it's foolish to care what Ricki thinks about Dominick's looks, or to let a man's appearance matter so much to her. But she can't help it. She loved Moishe's looks. She doesn't like Dominick that way at all.

"Say, you better treat this lady right. You got a real gem here," Ricki says to Dominick with a big wink.

"Ah, madam, I'd like to spend the rest of my life treating her right," he answers, slipping his arm around Mary's waist, nuzzling her cheek.

When Mary goes to her room to get her hat and coat, Ricki follows her. "Well, he's nobody's dreamboat, but what a nice guy!" Ricki whispers. "You got lucky. A real gentleman."

Part II

9

TIME ON THE MARCH

First Lady Eleanor Roosevelt: I am sure that everyone has been going around with a lighter heart recently after reading that Hitler has agreed to join the League of Nations in the discussions about the present European situation. I have always felt that in a tense situation, if time could be given for everyone to discuss what was going on before they actually went to war, we might come to our senses.

Berlin is being beautified for the Olympics. The city is being scrubbed and scoured, illuminated with new rows of electric lights and dotted with swarms of courteous attendants. *Elderly American tourist, interviewed near his hotel on Berlin's main boulevard, Unter den Linden:* This is the kindest country. I never had so much attention. Why, coming in on the train the conductor visited me every few minutes. Was I comfortable? Would I like something to drink? Would I like my window up or down?

For a while in 1936 it was almost like the antisemiten, as my mother always called the Jew haters of Europe, were too busy to hate the Jews: Europe was distracted by the leadup to the colossal spectacle of the Berlin Olympics, where Hitler outdid himself in order to show off his Aryan Supermen and to convince the world, most of it, anyway, that he wasn't really a bad guy. Since the Jew haters took a little vacation, my mother also took a little vacation, or tried to, from her worries about them. She also tried to banish from her thoughts that failed *besherter,* that heartless deceiver—he who was her most sorrowful disappointment. She "kept company" with Dominick.

"Darling, I want a picture of us, so I can keep it in my wallet and look at you all the time," Dominick tells my mother on a Saturday afternoon, and implores her to go with him to Giovanni's Professional Photography Studio. Giovanni poses them in front of a huge cardboard crescent moon, then stands behind the big camera, a black cloth over his head, and waves a hand in the air. "Look this way," he says.

"Hey, I'd much rather be looking at her." Dominick beams at my mother and ignores the waving hand. In every photo Giovanni takes, Dominick is either gazing at a smiling, forward-looking Mary, or he's hugging her with both arms, his lips pressed to her temple.

Any girl in her right mind would think he's a jackpot prize. He makes her feel like she's the most beautiful woman in America. "I utterly adore you," he tells her every time they're together. He's educated too—came to America a baby in his mother's arms and went to school till the eighth grade. His older brother, the one who introduced Mary to him ten years ago, was only a presser in the same shop where Mary worked; but Dominick was already a senior clerk in the New York Hall of Records. Now he's a supervisor, making better wages in a week than she makes in a month; and he's a good, kind man too.

But he isn't beautiful to her. She doesn't understand why life has to be like that, why somebody can be so good to you, but still he doesn't set your head spinning; and somebody (that damn lousy somebody Moishe) can be a rotten swine, yet he can make you feel like you'd give up half your life just to be with him.

The next Wednesday, Dominick takes my mother to The Sicilian again. On the way, walking down a Lower East Side street, Dominick's arm around her waist, my mother sees in the distance a slim man with a dark fedora, and she's sure it's Moishe. It's his tough-guy walk, and the hat on the man's head is raked at just the angle Moishe likes. She stops like a pulley halts her and pretends she suddenly needs to get a Kleenex from her purse, just so she can extricate herself from Dominick's grip because she doesn't want Moishe to think that Dominick owns her.

But when the man gets closer, she sees it's not Moishe. It's just some guy with a skinny face wearing a hat that almost covers his right eye. A sadness washes over her because again she knows she'll never love a man the way she loved that lousy heel.

After Dominick gives the waitress their order, he spreads the photographer's proofs out on the table in the pool of light thrown by the flickering candle. "Choose the ones you like the best, and I'll have Giovanni make some for you too," he says.

She picks up each page of proofs and holds it close to the candle so she can better scrutinize the rows of images. "They're wonderful," she says. In truth, she's disappointed, though she keeps a smile pasted on her lips. Dominick is in profile in all the photos, but you can see he's jowly and there's a little pillow of puffy flesh under his eye. He looks even more southern Italian than he did when she first knew him, darker, with a substantial nose and a sort of squatness, like all those elderly Italian men she used to see playing bocce ball in the little square on the Lower East Side. He looks every bit of his forty-nine years . . . But she looks old, too. She pulls the candle even closer to better see herself in the proofs. Not many wrinkles yet, she thinks, but that freshness, that look of eagerness I always had in pictures. All gone now. "Ah, the bloom is off the rose," she says aloud about herself.

"What, you? Don't be silly! You still don't look a day over twenty-five." She knows he's flattering her, but how can she not be touched by his sweetness?

Yet—oh, the terrible perversity of the human being—his sweetness is often too much for her. She begins to remember that it was like that ten years ago too. "Do you love me?" he would ask her all the time, laying his head on her shoulder and looking up at her with big soft animal eyes. "Do you love me? Do you love me?" She remembers feeling cloyed, and like she wanted to smack him away. Surely she never believed herself in love with him. Anyway, now that she knows what love feels like, she certainly can't trick herself again. But it's so hard to go home every night to her lonely, depressing furnished room, where she gets the creeps because she keeps imagining that Herr Doktor Feinberg still sits in his corner wearing his black suit. So she lets Dominick take her out and distract her every Wednesday and Saturday evening.

When he brings her home she says goodnight at the door. If he tries to kiss her, she gives him an exuberant, loud-smacking, closed-lip kiss, as though she's saying, I like you a lot but this isn't really a romance. Ten years ago she'd gone to bed with him a few times, but it's different now. They're more like good friends, she thinks.

Sometimes after they go out to a movie and supper, he asks, "How about coming over to my place for a little nightcap?" She knows what that would lead to, and she's pretty sure she doesn't want that with him again. "Oh, I had a long day," she says, or, "I've got to get up early in the morning," or, "My sister is coming over first thing tomorrow."

For months, he accepts her refusals; he insists on nothing. She senses that the wounds life has inflicted on him have robbed him of the confidence to make demands. She feels guilty accepting so much and giving nothing in return, like a thief. She thinks about their situation as she stands pinning fabrics on her dummy or rides back and forth to work on the subway train or even as she's trying to fall asleep in her bed. It's not fair to him; she needs to let him go so he can find a woman who can love him. He's a wonderful person but it's just not there for her . . . And yet if she let him go, she'd be so lonely. And even if she met someone else, it still wouldn't be there for her, because he wouldn't be Moishe.

Late spring. All the newspapers and newsreels are saying Europe is calm. Practically everyone in my mother's shop (the German-Jewish cutter has gone elsewhere) agrees that Hitler has already spewed out all his venom, and now the Jews aren't even in his mind anymore. An ox has been lifted off of her back and she's not feeling too bad these days. "Let's do something different this Saturday," she tells Dominick, because they've gotten into such a rut—movie, supper almost always at The Sicilican, and a kiss at the door when he takes her home.

"Great idea! Coney Island!"

Coney Island. That first year with Moishe, they used to go all the time to Coney Island. Once he caught the brass ring on the B&B Carousell at the entrance to Luna Park, and instead of throwing it back into a barrel like you were supposed to, he pocketed it. Later he put it on the index finger of her right hand, like Orthodox Jews do with their brides. They both knew it was a joke; she'd been going out with him only a few months then. But still . . .

Oh, she's not sure she can bear to go back to Coney Island.

But Dominick is already excited about taking her on Luna Park's huge Wonder Wheel, which is all lit up by neon tubes at night; and the Fire and Flames exhibit, which is not for scaredy cats but is so breathtaking, so magical. His animation is infectious. Mary's mood becomes lighter as they catch the subway train that takes them all the way to Coney Island's Stillwell Avenue stop.

The last ride they go on in Luna Park is called the Slums of Paris. Dominick puts his arm around her shoulder as they float in their gondola-for-two through an artificial underground canal. They drift slowly past illuminated windows that reveal wax figures of underworld characters looking so alive it's hard to believe they're not real: A murderer holding a knife that's dripping blood, his hair standing straight up in horror at what he's done. A prostitute in a negligee that's cut low to the top of her nipples and outlines her shapely thighs; she leers and crooks a finger at a fresh-faced youth. For long moments as Mary and Dominick drift, everything is completely dark, and then there's light again and another window that reveals another lawless scene: A man (who looks a little bit like Moishe), sneering, his muscles bulging beneath his form-fitting shirt; he holds a whip above a crouching figure of a woman; her head is buried in her hands, her black dress clinging to her rounded buttocks that are high in the air, their cleave evident, as though she wears no panties. It all affects Mary so strangely. Dark, and then another scene—a shirtless man standing over a woman who's recumbent on a bed, her eyebrows high in surprise or shock; her bright red lips are the same color as the garters that are exposed under her hiked-up dress. At the next dark spot, Dominick's hand drops to Mary's breast and he places his mouth hard on hers. A quick wave of revulsion sweeps over her, and then it dissipates. He's been so good to her. She lets herself relax to his touch. She gives herself up to the moment.

"Let's go over to my place, okay?" Dominick says huskily when the gondola exits the Slums of Paris and they're back into the bright lights of Luna Park. This time she doesn't tell him that she's tired or that her sister is coming by early in the morning. She only nods.

The trolley they take is almost empty because it's so late. He holds her tight about the waist, and sometimes he nuzzles her ear. She lets him. But when she realizes they're in Brooklyn, she's worried. "Dominick, where's Ocean Parkway?" she asks. How humiliating it would be if Sarah and Sam saw her walking into or out of a building with this man.

"Oh, we already passed it. It's way on the other side of Brooklyn," he says, and she feels freer. He plants soft kisses, one after the other, on the side of her neck; and she lifts her head slightly so that his lips may reach where he likes.

He lives in an old apartment house, dilapidated but with curlicue ironwork on the windows and little gargoyle mouths around the rainspouts, as though the building once had pretensions. "Not the kind of place I'd chose, a lot of really old-country Italians around here," Dominick tells her as he fumbles nervously for his key, "but Angela wanted to take care of my mother when she got sick, so we moved in with her." It's the first time he's mentioned the name of his dead wife. She's truly sorry for him; she knows what agony it is to love someone and then lose them.

He closes the door behind them and pulls Mary close. She lets him, though she feels confused, like she wandered onto a strange street and can't figure out how to get off of it. "You don't know how much I wanted this," he says.

10

TIME ON THE MARCH

RUMANIA. Alexander Cuza, whose Cuzists parallel the Nazis in Germany and the Endeks in Poland, is openly urging the extermination of the Jews. Jewish passengers are attacked in Rumanian railway trains, some are thrown from the railway cars while they are in motion. Jews are brutally assaulted in broad daylight in the parks of Bucharest, Chisinau, and other cities. A state of tension makes the safety and the lives of Jews as precarious in many parts of Rumania as they are in Galicia and other parts of Poland.

After the summer of 1936, the Jew haters of Europe resumed their business; and by the late fall, that business was flourishing, spreading east, just as my mother—ignorant in book learning but prophetic as Cassandra—feared in her bones that it would. Her old worries about the family's peril were renewed.

And in the interstices of those worries, she worries about the crazy foible inside her—perversity, what else could it be?—that ties her still, though she keeps company with Dominick, to that dirty rotten heel who toyed with her, just like a cat toys with a bird before tossing it aside. She can't get him out of her mind, not even if her very life depended upon it.

What a puzzle she is to herself. First to fall madly in love with a scoundrel who's ten years younger and too educated and too fancy for her, and to keep loving him even though she hasn't seen him (thank God) for more than a year—and then to go to bed with an Italian, a *shaygetz,* whom she doesn't even love and refused to marry ten years ago and certainly wouldn't marry now. Maybe it is true, what Ray once said, that a devil dances inside her—though it was very mean of Ray to say it.

But mean or not, who else but Ray does my mother have in this country of her own flesh and blood? During the warm months of 1936, she'd arranged to meet Ray in River Park every Tuesday night. Mary would sit on a particular bench under the dark lush leaves of an elm and watch the Bronx River roll by just a few yards from her feet; and if Ray found something to nag about, she'd tune her out and study the way the river's color went from blue to green to slate in the changing evening light. But now it's winter and too cold to sit in the park. They meet at the Automat again, where it's not so easy for her to escape from Ray's nagging.

This evening, though, Ray is too perplexed to nag. She's gotten a long, disturbing letter from Hirschel. When first she read it, standing up in her missus's kitchen, she grabbed her chest and had to sit down. What should she believe? —She remembers Hirschel as a very emotional boy when he was young. Maybe he's exaggerating. Just a few months ago she saw in the Yiddish papers that Eleanor Roosevelt, who's such a smart woman, was going around everywhere saying things will be okay in Europe. Would the president's wife say that if it weren't true?

Ray has brought the letter to Mary. As Mary reads, Ray fishes at the bottom of her purse until she finds three nickels. Then she goes to buy herself an apple strudel from one of the dessert windows. She takes it back to their table, but she's so upset about the letter that she doesn't have the appetite to eat strudel.

Hirschel writes that the president of Latvia, Karlis Ulmanis, is sounding more and more like Adolf Hitler every day. He makes hysterical speeches saying Latvians (by which he does not mean Jews, of course) are underprivileged in their own country. He wants to be called *vadonis,* which means the same as führer. He's nationalized all the Jewish-owned banks. Hirschel fears for his job because Jewish-owned textile factories—he works for one of the biggest in Riga, Solomon Grynberg—have also been nationalized. Jewish owners of all kinds of large businesses are being forced to sell out to non-Jews at bargain prices. *Our dear Vadonis doesn't threaten to kick the Jews out of Latvia or kill us, yet. He wants to dispossess us and make us poor first. You'd have to be a mole not to see where this is going . . .*

Mary finishes Hirschel's letter, then reads it over again. Her palm is pressed hard to her cheek.

Ray picks at a hangnail. "Listen," she says after Mary lets the letter drop to the table, "we need to send him some money right away, in case he loses his job."

"Good, that's what we'll do!" What else can they do right now? She wishes the post office were still open and they'd run and buy a postal order this minute. She's been saving up money to buy herself a new winter hat, but the old one will have to do. She'll send Hirschel everything she's saved. "Let's meet tomorrow during lunchtime and go send the money right away," she cries.

"I just don't understand," Ray says. "Even the wife of the president of America says it's okay in Europe."

That night Mary can't sleep because she worries so much about what Hirschel wrote in his letter. "Oh, my God in heaven," she moans. She knew in the core of her, even last summer—when almost everyone was saying there was nothing to worry about anymore—that things would get worse over there.

The next morning at the shop she can think of nothing else. She keeps looking at the clock, wanting to push its hands ahead to twelve noon. And then she runs first to the bank and then to the post office, where she and Ray send Hirschel a postal order.

That evening, my mother has a date with Dominick to go see *Camille* at the Loew's State. She always freshens up and changes clothes for a date, but tonight she's not in the mood to do more than rinse her work from her hands and face before she goes downstairs to wait for him in front of Mrs. Rifkin's grocery store. She can't stop thinking about what Hirschel said, that you had to be a mole not to see what's going on, that they don't threaten to kill the Jews in Latvia *yet*. Mrs. Rifkin has two sisters in Eastern Europe—somewhere in Poland. Mary wants to ask if they write her about how things are going there for the Jews. She peers through the store window and can see that Mrs. Rifkin is busy tending to the knot of customers who are shopping for their supper after work.

Mary is still staring through the window, hoping she can have just a minute with Mrs. Rifkin, when Dominick steals up and plants a big kiss on her neck. "Oh, boy, I missed you," he cries.

"Can we just walk around or something, Dominick?" she asks. "I'm not in the mood for Greta Garbo. You don't mind?"

"No, of course not." He leads her down the street, his arm hugging her waist the way he always likes to walk with her. "Tell me what's the matter, darling," he says. She just shakes her head; she's too upset to talk.

They turn the corner onto a street where the buildings have stoops and he sits her down on one of them. She covers her mouth with a hand because her lip is trembling and she feels like she's going to cry.

"Let me help, Mary. I'm here to do anything you want."

Finally she tells him about Hirschel's letter—that the president of Latvia wants to be called führer, just like in Germany, that Jewish business owners are being forced out . . . But now, talking about the letter, she's unsure whether things are as drastic as she's been thinking they are. Hirschel doesn't own a business; he's a little man. And nobody in Latvia is burning synagogues or killing Jews.

A gaggle of scrawny-legged little girls run out of the house and push past Mary and Dominick. They're giggling, yelling, "'Scuse us! Pardon us!" They dance around on the sidewalk, their dark heads bobbing like blackbirds. *Ringa rounda rosy . . . ashes, ashes, we all fall down.* They sink to the ground as though they've been machine-gunned, then leap up, resurrected, and skip down the street, shrieking with laughter like there's nothing to fear in the whole world.

"That's what it is to be young." Dominick smiles.

Mary watches them impassively until they turn the corner. "So I don't know what to do," she resumes. "I feel like my sister and me ought to do something, but she says for now we should just send money. Maybe she's right. I feel so ignorant. I dunno, sometimes I think I need to help him get out of there and come to America. Maybe I feel that way just because I promised to bring him here years ago and I didn't keep my promise."

"Is that what you want? To bring your brother here?"

"Maybe . . . Maybe that would be a good thing, considering what I hear is going on all over Europe. I'd have to bring his wife, too, of course. And maybe later the rest of my family . . ."

"I'll help you, Mary. I told you before I'd help," Dominick says fervently. "Let's start with your brother and his wife. I'll find out everything we can do. You know I love you, darling." His dark eyes are as solemn and sincere as a sepulcher.

"Me too you, Dominick," she answers, but her thoughts are elsewhere.

They circle the block back to her building. She can see through the store window that Mrs. Rifkin is almost alone except for one customer whose bread and eggs she's ringing up on the cash register. "Dominick, I've got to go in and talk to her. She has family in Europe, too. I have to find out what she's been hearing from them," Mary says, pecking a goodnight kiss on his cheek.

He knows this isn't an evening to ask for more. "Okay, go. I'm gonna check things out for you," he tells her. "Just gimme a couple days."

Mary has already slipped through the door. She waits at the pickle barrel while the customer hands Mrs. Rifkin a dollar bill and Mrs. Rifkin puts the change in the woman's upturned palm. "You got a minute, Mrs. Rifkin?" Mary asks after the customer closes the door behind her.

Mary tells the grocery lady about Hirschel's letter. Mrs. Rifkin, large-faced, arms folded across her big breasts, inclines her head in a posture of attentiveness. Today she looks to Mary—who's feeling so confused again—like somebody who really knows what's what. "What do your sisters in Poland say?" Mary asks anxiously.

"Well," Mrs. Rifkin says deliberatively, "it's true from time to time there's bad things going on over there. I heard, for instance, that not long ago they boycotted all the Jewish stores in Przytyk, and they even looted some of them. But that's been happening over there for maybe a thousand years. When hasn't there been bad things going on for the Jews over there? If that's where you have to live, you learn to live through it."

Mary nods. That's what Ray always says, too. Maybe it's right.

"Now, where my two sisters live, in a little city called Bendin, the Jews are in the majority, twenty thousand of them, and nothing bad at all has happened recently. They live like always. Sometimes good and sometimes not so good," Mrs. Rifkin says philosophically.

"My brother worries they have a president in Latvia who's like a Nazi," Mary ventures.

"Sure, and here we have Nazis, too—that Father Charles Coughlin, Gerald L. K. Smith, the German American Bund, the Silver Shirts, the American Liberty League . . ." She enumerates till she runs out of fingers. "Where isn't there antisemiten? Anti-Semites is ancient history."

When Mary gets out of work on Friday, she finds Dominick waiting for her downstairs, at the door of the building. "I got a lot of information for you," he says. His dark face is splotched red and he's out of breath, like he's been running a race. He's excited by what he's found out for her. He steers her by the arm to a cafeteria nearby on Seventh Avenue and leaves her sitting in a booth while he gets them bowls of minestrone and thick slices of bread.

"Listen, Mary," he says, depositing the tray on the table. "You have to tell your brother and his wife if they really want to come to America, here's what they gotta do: First of all they have to go together to the consulate in Riga and apply for exit visas and passports. They'll need both." He slurps his soup energetically and tears off big chunks of bread with his teeth. "And they'll need photographs too. Both profile and full face. And fingerprints—not just the thumb but all ten fingers. They can probably get those at the consulate." He leans forward, way over the table; Mary leans back, as though he's blocking off her air.

"Listen, they'll also need doctor's certificates saying they're healthy. They'll need everything in triplicate. They'll need a bunch of vaccinations too. The doctor will know which ones." No man has ever shown her he cared the way Dominick does. But he talks so quickly, so very earnestly, that she feels dizzy, as though she's on an out-of-control merry-go-round. "They've got to do all this right away, Mary, immediately, because it can take quite a while to get everything. When they've got all that stuff in order, they'll turn it in to the consulate, and then they'll get a number and they'll have to wait their turn, because there aren't a lot of people from that part of Europe who are let into America each year. It can take maybe two, three years, maybe even more. They're also gonna need relatives' addresses here in America. But the most important thing they gotta have is an affidavit from a male relative promising he'll vouch for them morally and he'll take financial responsibility so they won't be a public charge."

"But the only male relative we have here is my half sister's husband . . . and I haven't talked to him in I don't know how long."

"Mary, I could be their relative." Dominick's Adam's apple bobs like he's swallowing hard. He reaches for her hand, imprisons it in both of his. "You know I make enough to support a wife and a couple of her relations. I'd give that affidavit."

His words knock the breath out of her. She could bring Hirschel and Dweira here, take them out of harm's way. Maybe eventually Hinda and di mameh, too; Chana and her family, if they wanted to come . . . And not just that—it would be so good for once in her life to be taken care of, not to have to worry about when she'll be laid off and whether she'll be able to find another job, so good not to have to keep moving from one lonely furnished room to the next. She doesn't love him—but she'll never love anyone else anyway; and she really likes him.

But she'd be Mrs. Torelli. Mary Torelli. How strange it sounds, like the name of somebody else. Impossible to will herself to be someone other than who she is—she can't! She wants to jump up from the table and run as fast and far as her legs will carry her. "I don't know, Dominick . . . The fact is, Hirschel didn't exactly tell me he wants to come to America now," she says, gently extricating her hand from his, ignoring, as though she never heard it, his proposal of marriage.

He sighs like a man who's winded. "Well, maybe you should tell your brother and his wife to just start the procedure anyway, in case they ever decide they do want to come over," he says quietly.

The first Saturday in November. November 7. When my mother was young she sometimes tried to think what her life would be like when she was, say, forty—but she couldn't imagine herself that old. And now here it is. Today she is forty.

She lies in bed for a long while. How did all those years of my life go by already and nothing to show for them? she wonders. *Drek mit bulbes,* shit with potatoes, as Goldie used to say. She mocks herself with a derisive little laugh. In a minute, she heaves herself out of bed, but she feels like she's become decrepit overnight. The first thing she does when she's on her feet is open her dresser drawer and take out her hand mirror. She stands by the window where there's the most light and turns her head right, left, forward again. "Oh, why do you make me look so old?" she wails to the innocent glass.

She's not thought about it consciously, but suddenly, as though a long internal debate has been resolved, she knows what she must do today. She makes up her face—powder to cover the dark shadows under her eyes, lipstick to give her some brightness. Now Maybelline to make her lashes thick like they used to be . . . She can just imagine what Ricki would say if she knew what Mary was about to do. And Ray. She won't even think about Ray.

She puts on her coat and hat because she can hear the wind roaring outside. She turns the coat collar up and hurries down the stairs and to the trolley stop.

She gets off the trolley at the Grand Concourse and walks toward the street where Moishe lives. She doesn't want anything of him. She doesn't know what she wants. Only to see him, one more time, today on her fortieth birthday when youth has fled for good and old age begins. He has been terrible to her, but he is the love of her life, and even if she should decide to marry Dominick, it will always be that way.

It's started to rain. She pulls at the brim of her hat to cover her forehead. She tries to think of what she'll say if he opens the door, if his mother opens the door, or his sister or father, whom she's never met, opens the door, or if they close the door in her face. Her heart is rat-a-tat-tatting like a drill break-ing concrete. What if he doesn't live there anymore? What if he's already got-ten married to the mayor's grandniece that his mother picked out for him?

In the distance she sees a slim figure in a camel hair coat, a long brown scarf, an angled brown homburg. It's him, of course. She'd recognize that walk among a thousand million billion walks. My God, it's him. She dodges up the stoop of an apartment building and into its dark hallway.

Rat-a-tat-tat, rat-a-tat-tat. Through the glass door she can see him as he passes by. He walks with his hands in the pockets of his coat, shoulders slightly hunched, a tough-guy walk, though he's carrying a thick book under an arm that's pressed close to his body. She waits until she knows he's far enough down the street, then she follows. What if he tells her to go to hell?

He stops at a building and opens a door. Mary ducks her chin deeper into her upturned collar and keeps walking. When she passes the door she sees a stenciled sign, Shroeders Coffee Shop breakfast all day. She walks all the way down the block, then back up, past Shroeders again. She can see through the window that he's sitting at a table by the wall, ordering some-thing from the waitress.

She walks down the block again, then up again. Rat-a-tat-tat. Her head is so light it could drift off her shoulders and fly away like a balloon. Though she's never in her life fainted, she thinks this must be the way people feel just before they faint. She stops in front of the door to Shroeders and pulls it open. There's a smell of warm cinnamon buns. He's sitting at the table, reading his book, bringing a cup of coffee up to his lips without taking his eyes off the page. He doesn't look up until Mary is standing right in front of him. "Morris?" she says.

His beautiful eyes blink and for a moment he's perfectly still, then he chuckles. "Hey, there's my doll," he says like they haven't been separated a whole year. He rises slowly to his feet. He pulls her so close and so hard that she thinks she may suffocate on his starched white shirt and silk tie. She doesn't care if she suffocates, she doesn't give a damn what happens to her, as long as she's near him.

11

TIME ON THE MARCH

The curb on Jews is official in Poland: anti-Semitism is now part and parcel of the program of the new government party. *Colonel Jan Kowalewski, Party Chief of Staff:* The Jewish question in this country is one of the most important national problems. The Jews are too numerous. We cannot wait until the problem solves itself by the disappearance of the Jews, for we must without delay find employment for the Polish population in trade, industry, and handicrafts. We must spare no effort to Polonize.
BERLIN. Third Reich schoolteacher Elvira Bauer has just published a book of Hitler's favorite nursery rhymes.

Little girl, reading with a German accent:

One steak is lying on the floor,
the next a cat is pouring o'er.
The butcher Jew finds that okay:
the dirtier, the more they'll weigh.
Such filthy things, Phew! Pee-oo!
A Jew, and Jew alone can do!

Breadlines get longer and longer all around America: The latest estimates say that there are nearly ten million unemployed. Local relief throughout the country is pitifully inadequate. *Anonymous relief worker:* Even in the eighth year of the Depression, we don't seem to know what we're doing . . .

I think that during the first months of 1937 my mother again let herself be enchanted. If she woke from her slumber to remember those she loved on the other side of the ocean, she must have rehearsed everything she'd told herself earlier that had calmed her: If Mrs. Roosevelt, who is such a smart and good woman, is going around saying that things would be okay in Europe, then surely they'd be okay. Otherwise, why would she say it? And in any case, Hirschel and the rest of the family weren't the rich Jews who were making the gentiles feel underprivileged. They didn't own banks or factories; they were only little people, barely getting by themselves. So why should she drive herself crazy with worry when they weren't in any danger?

Until the truth shook her by both shoulders and made her teeth rattle, my mother gave herself up to enchantment.

She isn't a complete idiot, of course. Her memory isn't so short that she's forgotten the abortion, that the baby she so wanted would have been almost two years old now. She hasn't forgotten that Moishe walked out on her, dropped her cold. But she tells herself stories. Sometimes the story is that she's not deluding herself anymore by dreaming he'll marry her, that she understands the limits of his love, that she knows she can only be sure of *now* with him—yet how can she not want that now? She'll be forty-one years old on her next birthday, and a woman can't continue to feel what he makes her feel indefinitely.

Sometimes the story is different: it's that nothing on earth can loosen her tie to him and his to her, because somewhere—who knows where or why?—it's been destined. That is her favorite story.

My mother's one-room apartment, where she's lived since last November, and for which Moishe is helping her pay the rent, is kitty-corner to the El. If she stands out on her fire escape she's able to see his legs in his neatly creased trousers the instant he begins descending the station steps. And soon she can watch him walk down Tremont, his coat collar turned up against the late winter winds and his homburg low over his forehead. He crosses the street and is coming to her. When she was a little child, she used to sit on the floor by the door waiting for der tateh to come home from shul. Di mameh would scold, "Get away from that drafty door," but she wouldn't budge. "I'm waiting here because he promised to bring me a treat for the Shabbos," she'd explain—but mostly she was waiting to jump into his arms and have her faced covered by his kisses. Now she can't help it, she waits for Moishe with the same eagerness. Her yearlong separation from him has made everything as fresh as a newborn, just like it was at the beginning. She can't help that she loves him like she's learned to love through the Hollywood movies she's seen for so long, the love songs she's heard on the radio, even the Yiddish *bubba meisas* with which she was raised—he's her one and only; she loves him to distraction; she loves him body and soul.

Over her V-necked blouse she wears a woolen jacket, its faux-fox collar clasped around her throat. It's cold on the fire escape, but her cheeks are growing hot with a tactile memory—their rush into that first embrace. Their whole selves slamming into one another. Her breath squeezed out of her. Whommp! She keeps replaying it in her mind. Whommp! . . . and lying close to Moishe on her bed, their skin touching everywhere. Oh, he's rescued her, pulled her from the airless cave in which she'd dwelt for a whole year, as numb and dumb as death. He's distracted her from terrible anxieties too. He's given life back to her.

She idly watches the passing parade on Tremont Avenue as she waits for the whistle of the train—a pregnant woman pushing a baby carriage; housewives lugging bags full of produce from the outdoor market a few blocks away; three girls, arms linked like in a chorus line, roller-skating down the sidewalk. "*Meshugeneh!*"—crazy one. "You'll kill somebody and yourself, too, if you don't watch out!" an old man yells, jumping off the sidewalk to avoid being knocked down by one of the skaters.

"Wheee!" the girl is screaming along with her companions, too exhilarated to notice the near-disaster.

And then the chug and the whistle. Mary can hear it before she sees it. Finally, its giant's eye lightens up the gray day. Its brakes squeal like a chorus of cats. How many times has she watched and waited, right here on the fire escape, even when her clothes were getting soaked with rain or white with snow? At least three times a week . . . equals twelve times a month, multiplied by four months . . . Since they've been together again, she's watched and waited about fifty times, her heart pounding, as Moishe gets off the elevated train and hurries down the steps and up Tremont Avenue, thinking, she's certain (because that's what she's thinking), that soon they'll be making love.

She can hear the loud hiss as the train doors open to disgorge its passengers. He's the first one down the stairs. He's all she sees. She waves to him from the fire escape, as though he's finally returned from a long journey. He always looks for her and waves back as he walks his gentleman-outlaw saunter. Just before he reaches her building, she slips over the windowsill and runs to throw the door open for him.

"I missed you, doll," Moishe says every time, even if he'd been with her just the day before. He kicks the door shut with his foot and pulls her tight against him, whommp, till they're as close as the black-and-white magnet dogs that Dominick once won for her playing pop-the-balloon on Coney Island. And still it's not close enough. They separate just long enough to tear off pants, shirt, skirt, blouse, underwear; and in a jiffy Moishe yanks the

Murphy bed down from the wall, where she'd put it up that morning to make the small room look neater. They sink onto the mattress, he whispering into her ear, so smoothly, musically, "I had a hole in my heart as big as a fist all the time I was away from you, sweetheart."

"Me, too, *boychikel*. I had a hole in my heart as big as this whole room." This blazing, soaring moment—for nothing in the world would she give up this moment.

When they lie in bed after making love she sometimes remembers her miserable year without him. The wretched Feinbergs; the room in which she slept, no more than a few yards away from where the pale green corpse of Herr Doktor Feinberg had lain; how lonely she was before she started going out with Dominick again . . . (Dominick. He loved her. He would have brought Hirschel to America—but Hirschel never wrote that he wanted to come to America! She won't let herself be sorry about that; and anyway, things are quiet over there now.) She's ashamed that she was never very nice to Dominick. The day after her reunion with Moishe, she took the subway train to Brooklyn, to tell him it was over between them. Dominick pleaded with her. "Don't do this, Mary . . . I've had so many losses." It made her feel terrible. "I hope you find someone better than me," she told him. She really meant it. (Oh, God, she prays, may the time never come when I regret it.) She wasn't the right woman for him. But she is right for Moishe and he for her. Who can tell why two people click together like a key in a lock? That's just the way it is.

Of course, my mother and Moishe can't stay in bed forever. When the spring weather comes, they go strolling in Crotona Park. My mother has powerful memories about Crotona Park. That was where, five years ago, she first laid eyes on him, a speck in the distance who turned out to be the love of her life. Now they walk together in the park like Siamese twins, with no daylight between them, their arms clutching one another round their waists. Right there on the path they pause in midstep to smooch, to announce to the whole world that Mary and Moishe are crazy about each other. Oh, take it all in, she tells herself, take it all in!

Yet there's a cluster of worms in the bud of this beautiful spring. The news from Europe is starting to get a little bad again. And Moishe is not always happy. He hates his job, says if he had money he'd open his own business. (Mary hasn't forgotten that Moishe's mother wanted to make a shiddach for him with the grandniece of the old mayor of Nowy Korczyn, whose family was probably rich and would be happy to give Moishe the money to open all the businesses he wants. The grandniece hovers over Mary like the evil angel Malach Ha-Mavis who snatches away loved ones.) He's really trying to better himself, he tells her, but he's got such a hard road to trudge. Every Tuesday and Thursday evening, after a whole day on his feet at Cohn's Fine Suits, he's been squeezing into a kid's desk at Samuel Gompers High and spending three hours there, listening to a night-school teacher talk about how to make money in business.

Today Moishe has brought to the park a schoolbook he says he's got to finish by Tuesday for a test. Mary opens the *Forverts* she's brought with her, so he won't think she requires him to entertain her, and Moishe bends his head and reads his book. But soon he's glancing up and around, fidgety, bored. He flips the book down on the bench and he's yawning, stretching his long legs out before him, kissing the top of Mary's head, watching the ducks paddle in a small circle around the lake. "I don't know what good this going to school is," he says languidly. "I think what you've gotta do to get ahead in this country is take the plunge . . . Say, I hear Katz is out of jail," he tosses off a minute later.

It takes Mary a minute to remember that Katz was the one Moishe almost had a business deal with a couple of years ago. Something crooked, though she never knew what. "Morris! No!" she cries.

"Naw, don't worry. I don't think stripes suit me." He laughs. But she does worry. She knows he still hangs out at that Southern Boulevard gym. Every time the bus takes her past its front door, she sees a knot of the unsavory characters who patronize the place—shifty-eyed toughs, men like that Katz who got himself thrown in jail.

And still another worm has wriggled into their beautiful bud. Moishe is totally uninterested in the world events that trouble Mary, but these days he's furious about communists and fellow travelers in America. Whenever he talks about them, which is often, his eyes look fiery and he waves his arms about like the preachers Mary has seen in movies. She doesn't remember his having been like that when they were together before; it bothers her that he's so angry and nasty about people who, it seems to her, are only trying to help the workers.

One evening they go to a Charles Boyer picture, and holding Moishe's arm as they walk home, Mary is remembering that when she first met him she thought he looked just like Charles Boyer. She's feeling sentimental and romantic, and she wants to savor the mood. But Moishe isn't thinking about the movie they just saw. He wants to talk about the students he's met in night school, whom he can't stand, a bunch of noodles in love with the sound of their own voices, smart alecks, with their Marxism and Leninism and Trotskyism and sour grapes-ism, always ranting about the death throes of capitalism and the poor exploited worker. "It's like a new religion to these idiots. It's that kind of fucking stupid babble that makes the goyim think all the Jews are a bunch of lousy Reds."

This time she can't keep her lip buttoned. "But a lot of fat-cat bosses would gladly pay people starvation wages and work them to death if they could get away with it, Morris," she dares argue, because one thing she does know very well from her long experience in shops and her union work is that there really are poor exploited workers. "The garment workers have to fight those bosses all the time, and it's for that that they're called a bunch of Reds."

"Yeah? How much did they earn in Russia? America is the greatest country in the world," he proclaims.

She'd kept secret from him her part in the strike at Alexander and Schwarz and her marching on picket lines all over New York, but she can't be silent now. "But Morris, all the workers want is—"

"And it didn't get that way through Karl Marx," he shouts. "It's not enough for these nudniks that we have a lefty president for two terms." His nostrils flare like a bull about to charge. "A fat lot of good he's done all these years with his New Deal. Any damn idiot can see things are worse now in 1937 than when he started in 1933!"

"FDR? He saved me from starving to death with his unemployment insurance," she shouts back, exhilarated. But he glares at her resentfully, and then they walk along in strained silence; when they get to her apartment he says, "I'm pooped. I'm going to sleep," and he does. She of course can't sleep at all. She can't believe she's had a bitter fight with him over politics.

Another day, they're going to the delicatessen for Sunday breakfast, and on the corner is a small gathering of people. They're listening to a skinny, long-necked boy with Eddie Cantor eyes under his horn-rimmed glasses.

He's standing on a box labeled PEARS TRANSPARENT SOAP, waving spindly arms as he shouts. These days Mary sees a lot of street-corner orators in the Bronx. More people than ever are out of work or getting evicted from their homes, and most of these speakers blame the capitalist system for what's going on. Mary fears that this young man on the soapbox will do the same, and then Moishe will make a scene. After the wonderful night she's just spent with him, she doesn't want their breakfast spoiled by tirades, and she doesn't want to get into any kind of fight with him again. She quickens her step, hoping to hurry him past the speaker and into the delicatessen.

But Moishe grabs her elbow, like stepping on a brake, and halts her. They stand at the edge of the crowd near a rapt listener, a boy of fifteen or sixteen who's balancing his bicycle between his knees and nodding in vigorous agreement with what he hears. Moishe glares murderously at him, then stares coldly at the speaker. The young man on the soapbox has a nervous squint that can be seen even through his big round glasses, but he shouts his message loud, the cords in his neck visible with the strain. "The rich have the right to pass on their millions to their do-nothing children who live in the lap of luxury while your kids, the workers' kids—"

"Hey, Mr. Communist," Moishe shouts, "why don't you get the hell out of here and go to the Soviet Union?" Everyone's eyes turn to Moishe, who looks as though he's ready to sock someone. One old woman cries, "Bully!" and another shakes her head in disgust. Mary wishes she could dissolve into the sidewalk. She doesn't like Moishe at this moment. *Besherter* or not, she doesn't like him at all.

Fifteen minutes later, when the waitress deposits Moishe's lox and eggs in front of him, he's still scowling. Mary bites into her bagel, wondering how it's possible to love a man so much you'd give up practically your life for him, and yet not like him at all.

The horror that's going on overseas impinges again on her awareness: the newsreels show awful things happening now in Poland; in the *Forverts* she reads that the local newspaper in the Polish town of Czestochowa gave lists of the streets on which Jews hadn't yet been robbed, so the rioters could go directly to where they'd find the most booty. There have been pogroms in a dozen Polish cities and villages—Jewish businesses boycotted, little Jewish market stalls overturned, Jews murdered in their homes or on the streets. If

Poland is so unsafe for Jews, how long will it be before Latvia is just as un-safe? She worries night and day for Hirschel and di mameh and all of them.

In the late spring, she receives another troubling letter from Hirschel. He writes that since Solomon Grynberg's was taken over and most of the Jew-ish workers replaced, he's been patching up rips in men's pants and sewing hems on ladies' dresses in a little tailor shop. The shop, a two-man operation, a dark cubbyhole, is so tight that he and the other tailor can smell on each other's breath what they had for breakfast. The other tailor is the owner of the shop, a Polish Jew who used to have a clothing factory in Warsaw. Every day, Hirschel and his boss sit side by side and sew, and the ex-Warsawite tells Hirschel about the terrors he saw before he fled to Riga with his wife and three children, all his ready cash stuffed into the lining of his four-year-old daughter's winter coat: bands of wild-eyed, bloodthirsty Polish boys roam-ing the streets and public parks, wielding wooden bats and iron rods, hood-lums with no instinct of human decency or pity, looking for any Jew they can find, jumping on old men, women, even little children, beating them and leaving them for dead, and the Polish police watching and smirking. *He says he won't tell me of even worse horrors*, Hirschel writes Mary. *He doesn't want to think about them.*

When Mary mentions to Moishe that she's worried about her family in Lativa, he says, "Yeah, so what can you do about it? Nothing." He doesn't want to hear about any of it.

The next day after work, my mother goes to Ray's house with Hirschel's letter. Ray takes her to sit at the kitchen table because the missus has gone out for the evening. Though it's already seven o'clock, it's still sweltering hot. There's only one window in the kitchen, and it's stuck so that it can't be raised more than a couple of inches. Ray picks off chunks of ice from the icebox. She and Mary rub them across their foreheads to cool off. Ray reads Hirschel's letter, and then starts all over, from the beginning, to read it a second time.

The ice melts and runs down Mary's and Ray's cheeks like tears. Ray wipes them away, but Mary lets the drops run all the way to her neck and chest. They make big dark splotches on her blouse. As she waits for Ray to finish reading, she rubs her diminishing little ice chunk on the back of her neck because it's so hot she feels like she could faint. Finally, Ray puts the letter down on the table. Mary is sure that now Ray is as worried sick as she herself has been—but to her surprise, Ray gives a satisfied grunt. "What?" Mary asks.

"Look," Ray says, picking the thin beige paper up again and waving it, like she's a lawyer in front of a jury and the letter is evidence. "Just look at what he says in the letter. If people are running away from other countries and going to Riga, what does that mean? It means Riga is the safest place to be."

Mary is stunned for a moment; but what Ray says makes sense. If Latvia was so dangerous for Jews, obviously refugees wouldn't be running there. "I guess you're right," she admits.

Ray beams. She, too, has been reading horror stories about Poland in the *Forverts,* and she's so relieved to learn now that it's to Riga that Polish Jews are going for a safe haven. "Of course, I'm right," she says. "Now I'm making us some supper."

She brings out of the refrigerator a jar of borscht and a small carton of sour cream, then pours the borscht into two bowls and spoons out the sour cream. She deposits one of the bowls in front of Mary and sits down beside her to slurp from her own bowl. "You gotta eat. You're skinny like a rail," Ray tells her sister with a nudge to her ribs.

Mary takes delicate sips of the cold borscht. It is refreshing in the heat. And she's grateful for Ray's good sense about what's going on in Europe. It's true Hirschel lost his job, but he found another one. Jews can still make a living in Latvia. She's so comforted by the thought that he's all right that she almost laughs. She finishes her borscht and says yes when Ray asks if she'd like another bowl. She's barely eaten since she read Hirschel's letter. Oh why do I always have to get so upset about everything? she asks herself. Her old nightmares—Hirschel, ten years old, short pants, skinny legs and knobby knees like a little horse, the Perkonkrusts in gray uniforms with black boots, kicking him bloody—those dreams have come back because of what she'd read about Poland. She has nightmares even when Moishe is sleeping next to her . . . But Hirschel lives in a place to which Jews from other parts of Europe are flocking to be safe!

Yet what about the Perkonkrusts that Hirschel has complained of, and the president of Latvia who wants to be called führer? She doesn't know what to believe.

Whenever my mother turns on the radio or sees Hollywood movies, she thinks she must be the only person in America who ever worries. On the radio she hears more silly songs than ever before—"The Dipsy Doodle," "The Donkey Serenade," "Whistle While You Work," "Sweet Leilani." There are more ridiculous comedies at the movies in 1937 than ever before—*Lady*

Behave!, The Awful Truth, Topper, Something to Sing About. Antisemiten like Father Coughlin and Gerald L. K. Smith say that Jews run the whole entertainment industry. But if that's really true, and if there really was something to worry about, then surely there'd be dirges on the radio and not frivolous ditties. Surely there wouldn't be movies that get audiences to laugh their heads off over silliness; there'd be tragic movies that show how bad things are for the Jews in Europe. Mary has never yet seen such a movie.

But despite the dumb songs and movies, despite Ray's lawyer-like logic about the safety of Riga, Mary's nightmares don't stop. She remembers her poor tateh, what the vicious Kristaps brothers did to him—and now such cruelty has become official policy all over Europe. She sees things in the newsreels or reads things in the *Forverts* that drive her nuts with worry. The slogan of the Rumanian Iron Guard is "Rumania has too many Jews," and its leader, Octavian Goga, is expected to be the next prime minister. Jewish businesses are boycotted in Rumania. Rumanian Jews have already been barred from all the professions and most of the trades.

At work now everyone worries like she does. Nobody talks about anything anymore but how the world hates the Jews, not just in Germany and Poland, but in Czechoslovakia, Bulgaria, Yugoslavia, Hungary, Lithuania. Bertha, a finisher in Mary's shop who has family in Vilna, says that after her brother ate lunch in a Jewish-owned restaurant he was beaten senseless by a crowd of crazies who were standing outside, just waiting for customers to emerge.

"It's like Hitler took the lid off a box and all the venom that was tamped down has come flying out," Sam the cutter says in a gravelly voice.

"The Jew haters are waiting for him with open arms everywhere. Mark my words, he plans to move east and swallow up everything," Irv the presser declares.

The horror stories and dire predictions go on and on. Mary wants to hold her hands over her ears, but what good would it do? She knows in her bones what the truth is.

12

Summer and fall, 1937

TIME ON THE MARCH

BUDAPEST. Hitler's men are speaking of Hungary as a Nazi *colony*. Hungary now has thirty-nine Nazi newspapers and other publications. Nazi agents have visited every Teutonic village in Hungary, leaving National Socialist Party cells and military units in each community. Anti-Semitism is on the rise all over Hungary.

Panic on Wall Street, again. Stocks crumbled this week in one of the most general waves of liquidation since 1929. On the New York Stock Exchange, 537 stocks made new lows for the year, a record since tracking was started in 1932.

NEW YORK CITY. City employees who were discharged because of budget cuts made three assaults yesterday on WPA offices. They swung fists, kicked, screamed, bit, and scratched as defending security officers flung them around. The demonstrators continued to sit down in the corridor all day long, threatening a hunger strike, shouting, *Reinstate all 11,000 dismissed workers!*

There are twenty-one Nazi training camps in America now . . . the twenty-first opened last Sunday at Andover, New Jersey. Nazi-American storm troopers march in military formation, in natty new uniforms with Sam Browne belts. Everything is here that could be imported from the source in Germany—the swastika, the goose step, the Nazi salute, and Fritz Kuhn as führer.

Germany, Austria, Rumania, Poland, Hungary—the spread of the cancer inexorable. And on this side of the ocean, a blind eye and a deaf ear: because those who were already here had their own worries, such as how to get food or how to keep from losing house and home. So why would they open the doors to the wretched refuse of that other teeming shore?

How did my mother keep from going off her head? How did she keep going? Moishe was a poor anchor to life—unsteady and precarious—yet all she had and necessary.

She places the scrambled eggs and toast she's made for their breakfast on the nightstand. Moishe sits up in bed, grins at her sleepily, and runs his fingers through his stormcloud of hair. She slips into bed next to him. She's about to hand him a plate when he seizes her wrist and holds her palm to his lips, his dark eyes smiling up at her. He's still a good lover—as long as they don't talk about things on which they disagree. She knows the various subjects to avoid—marriage, workers and bosses, President Roosevelt . . . and now the subject that troubles her day and night.

"So what can you do about it? You can't bring them here. There's a quota system for Jews who want to come to America," he's told her whenever she lets him know how worried she is about her family. "And even if you could get them over here, who's gonna support them?" he's said almost belligerently. He's not like Dominick. He doesn't want to help her find answers. It's unfair, she thinks, that she can't open her heart to him, though he's always complaining about his own life to her. More and more she resents it. But what can she do? What was that expression Goldie used to say? Take it or leave it. Well, she's already found out she can't leave it.

Mary and Moishe sit close together on the bed, their legs and hips touching, and they eat. "Doll, you look so pale these days," he says solicitously between bites of scrambled egg. "You know what you need? A little vacation. That'd put some color in your cheeks."

She's noticed herself she's not looking so good. Of course she's not spending as much time fixing herself up as she used to. She just can't get herself to stand for a long time in front of the mirror fussing and primping like she's done since Goldie first taught her to put on makeup. She has bigger things to worry about now.

Moishe butters his toast, and she catches a glimpse of his beautifully manicured fingernails—neatly trimmed, the cuticles pushed back, a clear gloss covering each nail. The red polish she'd put on last week has chipped and her nails are rough and uneven. She tucks her own fingers into loose fists so he won't see them.

"I got it, sweetheart! I'm gonna take you to Atlantic City, next weekend. I bet you've never been there."

"No, never," she admits. She used to think Atlantic City would be such a romantic place to go with Moishe—to stroll with him on the famous boardwalk and dance cheek-to-cheek with him at the Marine Ballroom that she's heard so much about. Now it feels like Atlantic City is the last place in the world she wants to go, yet she can't help being touched that at least he's concerned about how she's looking. She makes herself muster up a show of enthusiasm, like she would have had a few months ago; she throws her arms around his neck.

Next Saturday, he takes her to the Boardwalk and buys a big bag of saltwater taffy that they eat, mostly he eats, while they jostle together through the throngs. She squeezes his arm; she tries to look happy. What's wrong with her now that she has to pretend pleasure? He's wearing an ice-cream-colored suit that shows off his broad shoulders and slim hips, and every girl they pass seems to eye him. How can she not be proud?

They stand in a line on Steel Pier, where Moishe buys tickets for some attraction called the Diving Horse. Then they cram into the dirty-white bleachers where a thousand other spectators already sit. Boys in red caps are hawking hot dogs and Cracker Jacks, and recorded marching music is blaring over the clamor of the crowd. Mary is dizzy with the noise and movement. She looks away from the bleachers, out at the emerald-green ocean. Oh, take it all in, she orders herself, remembering wistfully how she used to love being at the ocean.

"You okay?" Moishe asks her. She sits taller and smiles brightly, assuring him she's fine. She looks around, feigning interest. In front of them, sticking up in the water, there's a big tank, like an immense swimming pool, and across from the bleachers is a platform about fifty feet high. The marching music gets louder. A girl in a black bathing suit and pink bathing cap leads a sleek white mare up a ramp and onto the platform. The crowd grows quiet. One quick acrobatic leap, and the girl is atop the gleaming animal. The crowd cheers and claps, ready to be made delirious. Mary claps, too, and Moishe looks over at her and smiles and puts his arm around her and pulls her closer.

The girl and the horse stare out at the water where the gigantic tank sits. The canned marching music is replaced by canned rolling drums, and the crowd grows absolutely still, as though everyone has stopped breathing. Then canned cymbals crash as the girl and horse leap gracefully into the air, like a single ballet dancer, and let gravity bring them down, down into the tank. The water splashes high up to the heavens and the crowd sighs a collective "oooh."

I'm in an insane world, Mary thinks, where thousands of human beings sit at the edge of the ocean watching a girl and horse risk their lives to entertain them for a few minutes, while across the same ocean thousands of other human beings are being maimed and murdered or are running for their lives. Oh, God help us all.

"Isn't that great?" Moishe yells above the wildly cheering crowd when the girl and the horse emerge dripping and safe from the water. Mary nods but she can't fake a smile.

The mornings my mother wakes up to Moishe, she fights not to think about her obsession—the events going on across the ocean. She shifts closer to him, tries to comfort herself with the faint traces of the musky men's cologne that he wears these days; she nuzzles his cheek or neck or any part of his skin that's exposed. She tries to block out of her thoughts everything but Moishe, because there'll be time enough to agonize once he's gone.

The mornings she wakes up alone, she's seized immediately by awful visions—the horrors that her family might be going through this very minute . . . her sick mameh, poor Hinda, who's had such little happiness in her life, Chana and her three young sons. Her sweet baby brother, Hirschel, to whom she made a promise in 1914, which she never kept—and now he may be in danger.

She must do something! But she's a woman alone, uneducated, ignorant about how to maneuver in the world. She doesn't know what to do. Maybe Hirschel would be safe in America by now if she'd married Dominick, who seemed to know how to do things. But she couldn't marry Dominick because she couldn't get it out of her head that Moishe was the only man in the world for her. And yet, Dominick had been willing to help her bring her family to America; and now there is nobody who will help her. She is so afraid that someday she will pay dearly for what she did and didn't do.

"Stop already!" Ray yells if Mary tells her of the terrible things she reads about Europe in the papers or sees in the newsreels. "Poland is far away from Riga! Far away from Preil! Far away from Dvinsk!" With the mention of each city in which members of their family live, Ray bangs her fist on the table.

"And Rumania and Hungary are as far away as the moon!" she bellows in her foghorn voice.

If Mary is foolish enough to mention her worries to Moishe again, he makes her feel hopeless. "Okay, so what can you do about it? I told you already," he says with exaggerated patience, like he's talking to an imbecile, "America doesn't want more Jews. There's a strict quota, especially for Jews from Eastern Europe. The politicians and the voters are saying they're undesirables. And even if there wasn't anti-Semitism, there's a depression going on, so why the hell would they want to bring in more people to fight with them for jobs? You know how much chance you've got of bringing your family here? As much chance as you've got of marrying Mayer Rothschild."

One day on the street, coming home from the unemployment office, she runs into Irv the presser from her last shop, a tall man, thin as a needle, with an angular head and a pale, bony face. "Mary! How you doin'?" he says, as though greeting an old friend.

"Fine, thank you," she answers politely and keeps walking because Bertha once told her that going up to the shop in the crowded elevator Irv grabbed a handful of her behind. "And then the door opened and that bastard puts a look on his ugly mug like butter wouldn't melt in his snake's mouth, and he slithers out before I can even tell him, 'Go to hell and fry.'" But now Mary remembers that Irv was the one who made the terrible prediction that Hitler would keep moving east, "swallow up everything," he'd said. That's exactly what she fears—what she feels in the freezing, aching core of her.

"Irv!" she turns and calls out, because she's so ignorant and lost, and maybe he can help her figure out what she needs to do. "Irv, stop!"

Though he's already at the end of the block, he hears her, and he turns around and waits, watching with a surprised look as she runs to him, breathless.

She tells him that she has family in Latvia and worries about them. She asks if he thinks it's dangerous for Jews there now.

"All over Europe, everywhere you look, things are getting worse by the day," he declares. His face looks like a death's head to her, and she feels her skin shriveling with disgust. But who else can help her? Maybe he knows how she can bring her family to America, she asks him.

Irv nods thoughtfully. "How 'bout we go for a cup of coffee. I'll tell you what I know." He takes her arm, and she lets herself be led to a corner coffee shop where they sit at the counter and he orders two cups of coffee.

"It's nice to run into you, Mary. I been thinking about you since we were laid off. So, are you working now, or what?" He puts a hand on her back.

"No. Just getting unemployment insurance." She's annoyed because he's acting as though she'd stopped him to flirt. She frowns and stiffens her back hard, like she's shaking him off. He removes his hand and gets an offended scowl on his face. But she's offended too, that he tries to take advantage of her when such awful things are going on in the world. And how ugly I must be looking these days, she tells herself, if this lecher who's as appetizing as a stick thinks he can make time with me. "So do you have any idea what I need to do?" she repeats determinedly.

Irv's expression has changed. He's completely businesslike, as though he never intended anything personal. "America's just about impossible to get into now unless you're a big muckety-muck like Albert Einstein," he says. "But you ought to look into getting your relatives in somewhere else for the time being. Somewhere they can wait until things loosen up here."

"Okay, how can I do that, Irv?" She swings her stool to face him, to listen closely.

"Well, let's see. Cuba's letting foreigners come in on a temporary basis. My cousin who's a CPA just brought his father and sister over there from Bialystok, so I'm pretty familiar with the details of what you need to get somebody into Cuba." Mary nods eagerly. "First of all, you gotta get visas. A Cuban visa cost two hundred and fifty American dollars for each person. And then everyone who wants to come into Cuba has to have a letter of credit saying they're backed by at least two thousand dollars, so they'll have enough money to live there until another country accepts them. It's no small thing, huh?" he says when he sees Mary swallowing hard, fighting tears. "You also have to have a round-trip ticket from your point of departure, so that if no other country accepts you, Cuba can send you back to where you came from," he goes on. "And the companies are really jacking the ticket prices up for the boats these days because they know people are desperate and will pay as much as they got. Even for steerage class, a round-trip ticket can be four hundred dollars a person."

She feels the shame of the powerless. "I don't have that kind of money," she says quietly. She won't let him see her cry.

"Then that makes it impossible, doesn't it?" His smile is ironic.

A gum-cracking waitress pours more coffee into both their cups. "Want anything else?" she asks.

"Just the two checks," Irv says.

Mary fishes a nickel out of her purse and puts it on the counter. She just wants to get out of there. Her helplessness pains her like a thorn in her heart. Maybe because I insulted him he's exaggerating the difficulties, she thinks. "Thanks for your time," she tells him, swinging off her stool.

"See you around," he says, waving her off with an abrupt toss of his hand.

After the dark cool of the coffee shop the sun seems even brighter and hotter, but she walks, the rays beating down on her head. She doesn't know what else to do. She turns down a side street where there are a few trees and a bit of shade. She passes a young woman sitting on a stoop, nursing an infant, the big bonnet she wears sheltering them both from the sun. She passes a man carrying a big sack of groceries, laughing happily at something the pregnant, waddling wife at his side just said; then a boy of about twelve taking a wrinkled handkerchief from his trouser's pocket and patiently wiping chocolate ice cream from his little sister's face and dress. Everything she sees makes her feel so alone.

She wanders aimlessly, up one street and down another. Maybe she shouldn't have been so cold to Irv. How much could it have cost her if she'd let him keep his hand on her back in a coffee shop with a dozen people around? Maybe he would have been more helpful if she'd been nicer . . . maybe even offered to lend her enough money so Hirschel and his wife might get into Cuba. Irv could probably borrow the money from his cousin who's a CPA . . . *No!* She won't ever sacrifice herself that way. She didn't do it with Dominick and she won't do it with any man. But if she'd sacrificed herself to Dominick, Hirschel might be in America already. Dominick was her main chance. She feels sick with the thought.

Even before my mother unlocks her mailbox, she sees a thin beige envelope through the slots. A letter from Latvia. She takes it out of the mailbox and just holds it. These days she dreads letters, fears the bad news she's sure she'll find in them. She can see by the handwriting that this letter is from her brother. She sits down on the stoop to read it.

My dear darling sister, he writes. *I have wonderful news for a change. My beloved Dweira and I are expecting a baby—next March, if we are counting right!*

A baby. Her baby brother will have a baby! She shoots to her feet. She wants to run and tell someone. She sees him still as a baby himself, and now he's going to have his own baby. She must do something to help them be safe. With enough money she can get Hirschel and Dweira into Cuba. The baby can be born there, and they'll have a safe place to wait until they can come to America . . . But that's a pipe dream.

Suddenly a plan jumps into her head: she's seen all sorts of odd ads in the *Forverts,* people asking the readers for help to find a lost husband or a lost samovar or to buy a dry goods store in Schenectady. That's what she'll do—she'll place an ad asking for help! She needs Ray's assistance because Ray writes Yiddish better than she does. The ad should be carefully worded, brief and to the point, but forceful too. Mary runs to the bus stop a block away, where she paces anxiously, waiting for bus number 40, which will take her right to Ray's house. But it doesn't come. She steps off the curb every few minutes, to peer into the far distance, but only cars are coming down the street. She waits ten minutes more, and still the bus doesn't appear. She gives it up. She walks, she runs, toward her sister's house. But when she's almost halfway there, she decides she really doesn't need Ray's help to write an ad in Yiddish. Ray probably wouldn't even do it, anyway. She'd say it's a silly idea and try to discourage Mary from doing it, too. Mary turns around and marches home with giant strides, her heels stabbing the pavement, echoing her resolve.

She pulls a pencil and pad of paper from the nightstand drawer, and sitting on the bed, using the nightstand as a writing desk, with much chewing on the pencil and erasing and rewriting and pulling on her hair and a dozen wadded-up pages with false starts, she finally composes the ad to her satisfaction, though she's sure she's misspelled many of the Yiddish words. *URGENT. Please help me get my brother and his pregnant wife out of Riga, Latvia. He has a good trade as a tailor and will pay back all money plus interest very quickly.* She reads it over a half-dozen times. Perhaps "will pay back all money very quickly" isn't quite true, but anyone generous enough to help will surely be patient. In an old *Forverts* she finds the newspaper's address on East Broadway. She'll bring them her ad as soon as they unlock their doors in the morning.

The next day, the minute she wakes up, the first thing she does, even before she gets out of bed, is to pull open the drawer of the nightstand where she placed her composition. She sits up in bed and rereads it. She reads it over and over. She realizes it won't work. It's foolish. In these desperate times, who would give her the money she needs just because they saw an ad like that?

She wads the paper into a ball and with a frustrated whimper throws it violently across the room. She's got to think of a smarter way.

Every day my mother sees the same skeleton-thin girl of about thirteen, and her little brother, his nose already running with a bad cold though summer is barely over, sitting on the ground near the steps of the El. The girl holds a cracked plate in her lap. Once in a while a passerby, disturbed by the pathos of the two children, rummages in a pocket or purse for a coin. It clinks when it's tossed on the plate, but both the girl and her brother keep their eyes down in shame or misery. Downtown, too, Mary sees scruffy children extending filthy little palms, crying, "Please, sir!" "Please, lady!" She sees gaunt and tattered men and women holding up dirty pieces of paper or ragged bits of cardboard with crude lettering: HAVE NOT EATEN FOR THREE DAYS; NEED MONEY TO GET TO SYRACUSE FOR A JOB; WILL WORK FOR FOOD. Whenever Mary gets change in a store, she separates out the pennies and carries them in her coat pocket to dole out, because at least she's not starving.

It's much worse in this fall of 1937 than it's been for years. Practically every week in Mary's neighborhood there are city marshals carrying piles of possessions out of the apartments of the evicted—bedding, shoes, framed photographs, pots and pans, toys. The marshal and his men wear officer's badges so everyone will recognize who they are and will be afraid. They stack everything indiscriminately on the sidewalk for all to see, people's private little lives made public. They usually come early, when folks are still half-asleep and don't have the vigor to put up much of a fight. They know if they wait until later in the day, they risk more resistance.

The one evening eviction Mary witnessed on Tremont Avenue resulted in a pitched battle between the marshal's men and a bunch of neighborhood kids whose own families, too, were only a step away from being thrown out on the sidewalk because they couldn't pay the rent. As soon as the marshal and his helpers started carrying furniture out of some family's apartment, the angry youngsters knocked over all the trash cans that the super had already brought out to the street for the next morning's pickup. The officers were diverted by the heaps of trash, and the kids started carrying the evicted family's possessions back into the same apartment from which they'd been taken out. The officers swung billy clubs and bloodied a couple of heads, while a few of the bolder kids shouted "Fuckers!" and "Assholes!" at the uniformed men, who kicked them in the *kishkas* for their troubles. The kids finally ran off, but soon the older neighbors (a bit more cautious than the youngsters) began congregating on the rooftop.

One man, his beard stark white by the light of the moon, stood on the ledge and, looking like an Old Testament prophet, blew a shofar to alert the whole neighborhood to come up to the roof and protest what the marshal and his men were doing. Before long the roof was swarming with angry people. "Cossacks!" "Nazis!" they yelled down at the marshal's men. They cupped their hands into makeshift megaphones and hooted boo with every object that was carried from the apartment. Of course it didn't make much difference. In less than half an hour, all the evicted family's possessions were again littering the sidewalk. About midnight, somebody showed up with a horse-drawn wagon, and several men of the neighborhood lent a hand in loading the couch and two beds and everything else the family owned on to it. Mary never saw that family again.

This morning it's a little after seven o'clock when Mary leaves her apartment to walk over to the El, but already there's a dazed and tired-looking woman in a housedress standing in the street beside a rusty stove, a mattress, and a little pile of children's clothes. A dirty Raggedy Ann doll and an open box of Kotex, half-empty, sit atop the stove. Mary feels embarrassed for the woman, who looks too miserable to be embarrassed herself. Her little girl, thumb in mouth, a faded knitted blanket around her shoulders, sits on an old rocking chair in the middle of the sidewalk and rocks.

The fall season has started, and my mother is working again at Seidman and Sons. She knows she should feel very lucky to have a job, but she hates going to work, because it takes time away from her real work now—figuring out how to bring her brother and his pregnant wife to safety. It's the constant motif of her thoughts.

She's been reading many different Yiddish papers, hoping for information about how she can do it. She discovers in *Der Tog* that there are indeed organizations to help Jews who are fleeing Europe. There's the Emergency Committee in Aid of Displaced Foreign Physicians, there are the Emergency Committees in Aid of Displaced Scholars and Engineers and Writers. —But there's no emergency committee in aid of poor tailors and their pregnant wives. The world doesn't give a damn whether a simple man lives or dies, no matter that he's dearer to her than all the physicians and scholars and engineers and writers put together.

"But he won't die!" she cries aloud to no one. She'll figure out what to do, or die herself trying. Her obsession with Hirschel's rescue kicks out of her head even her ancient obsession with Moishe. She castigates herself yet again that since she came to America she hasn't been a serious person. She remembers with burning shame how she was thrown out of Sarah and Sam's house twenty-three years ago, just as she was about to ask them to bring Hirschel over. He would be safe now if she hadn't been such a fool then. Now she must be, she will be, serious, because if she doesn't help the brother she loves so much no one will.

But nothing she tries works. She feels like Bugs Bunny in the cartoon where the fox catches him and lifts him by the ears, and his legs keep pedaling, pedaling, though he's going nowhere.

The one good thing about being in the shop is that there, at least, she can hear of places to which the European relatives of other Jewish workers are fleeing. Gone are the days when the workers gossiped or sang or read Tolstoy or Sholem Aleichem to one another in the shop. Above the hiss and whirr of the sewing machines and cutting machines and pressing machines, the main topics of conversation now are the events in Europe and where Jews are seeking refuge. Even when the workers smell the cigar smoke that always heralds Mr. Seidman's appearance, they don't shut up. They know he's worried, too, because his very elderly mother lives in Hungary, which is now as Nazi-infested as Germany, Poland, and Rumania. Even when the workers go up on the roof to eat their lunches in balmy weather, that's all they talk about.

Yetta the finisher says she has a young brother in Warsaw who's going to Argentina, where there's a large community of Jews. But a couple weeks later Yetta reports, "They're not giving my brother a visa."

"Why?" those around her ask.

"Because Jewish refugees can't come into Argentina anymore unless they have relatives already there who own their own house and make a promise to support them."

"Yep, Brazil, too," a cutter says. "My uncle just wrote me."

"My cousin who's trying to help his wife's family get out from Lodz found out the same is true for South Africa," another finisher says.

They sit in little knots, sometimes forgetting even to unwrap the sandwiches or open the lunch pails or thermoses they've brought with them.

Sonya the buttonhole maker says, "Last year my nephew in Stuttgart heard that the president of United Fruit Company was going to give refugees jobs in Guatemala. But it didn't work out."

Yankel the presser says the year before, a French Jewish organization was negotiating to buy half a million acres in Ecuador that refugees could farm. "My sister's whole family packed up and were ready to go, but they're still in Krakow."

On the shop floor, if anyone has learned anything new, the workers put down their work and gather in clusters around him to listen. Jack the cutter, a gruff man with black moles all over his face, is everybody's main source of information about what the American press is saying, because his English is good enough to read the *New York Times*. "The Polish government wouldn't mind dumping all the Jews in Madagascar. They're negotiating with the French about it," Jack reports.

"Sure, where there's yellow fever and all the other tropical diseases to kill the Yiden off quick," another cutter says grimly.

"You can get into Shanghai without any restrictions," Rosie the baster says, and everyone laughs without mirth at the idea of a European Jew speaking Chinese with a Yiddish accent.

"What about Palestine? That's where I'm going if things get bad for us in America," Paula, Mary's old draper friend with the leg brace and limp, says. A few titter halfheartedly at the idea of shtetl dwellers in the desert or Paula on a camel; but nobody thinks anything is really funny these days.

"Palestine's hell to get into," Jack warns Paula. "Last year the British cut the Jewish immigration quota for Palestine by more than two-thirds."

"Yeah, but I hear that Jews who are already there are managing to sneak in boatloads of people that can't get regular immigration certificates," Rosie says.

"From the frying pan into the fire. The Arabs hate them just like the Nazis. They're shooting at them the minute they get off the boat," Jack says.

Everyone is silent, struggling with their own worried thoughts. For Jews, every single place in the world has a DO NOT ENTER sign. There is nowhere that their mothers, fathers, sisters, brothers—everyone they love and left behind in the shtetlach and cities of Europe—can run.

On Friday after work, Mary and Bertha the finisher, whose brother in Vilna was almost killed last spring by the crazy mob outside the Jewish-owned restaurant, take the same elevator down to the street. Mary has worked with Bertha in a half-dozen different shops; she remembers her from years ago, a jolly girl with huge bosoms, and skirts that were always too tight around the hips. Now, though Bertha says her brother recovered from the attack, she habitually wears an expression of someone who's sitting shiva, and her clothes look like they were made for a woman thirty pounds fatter. While they walk to their trains, Bertha tells Mary about something called the Hebrew Immigrant Aid Society. "I hear they're helping refugees, God knows how. I'm going over there to register for my brother. It's on Lafayette Street near Broadway. You should go over and talk to them, too," Bertha urges Mary, because she and everybody in the shop have heard about what Hirschel writes from Riga. "I hear they're so busy with all the people who are coming that they even keep open on Sunday. You should go over this Sunday; that's what I'm doing."

When Mary and Bertha say goodbye at the subway station, they look at each other and tears of commiseration puddle in their eyes. They both know what it is to be worried sick about a brother.

Sunday morning: it's a warm day. On the Third Avenue El, my mother cracks the window open. Whenever the train comes to a halt, only yards away from the sooty tenements where the Irish live—156th Street, 149th, 138th—no matter the stop, she can hear the boom of the same portentous voice. "A Christian Front will not fear to be called anti-Semitic! . . . Let this be a Christian America, not guided by the principles of atheists and Jews!" She already knows those rolled *r*s, that pseudo-Irish brogue: Father Charles Coughlin, the anti-Semite radio priest.

When she glances into the tenement windows, she sees men in undershirts or still decked out in Sunday church clothes; women with hair rolled in curlers or glossy and coifed, dressed to go to a fancy Sunday dinner; the aged sitting in rocking chairs or lying in their beds; youngsters, toddlers held firm on their mother's knees—all glued to that hypnotic voice coming out of their radios. "You have been victimized by a Jewish economic system!" the voice bellows at the 138th Street stop.

She's heard Jack the cutter complain that this Father Coughlin gets more fan letters than President Roosevelt. "Twenty to forty million listeners every

Sunday—not just Catholics, but Protestants, too. You know what that means? Some weeks a third of our dear fellow citizens are gathered around the radio just to hear a priest's Jew-hating babble." Like in the shtetlach at Easter time, but a lot worse, Mary thinks now. Who can withstand such hatred? —Tens of millions of people who don't know a thing about me or Hirschel or Hinda or di mameh, who don't care if we're rich as a czar or poor as a rat, if we're guilty of whatever sins they've imagined in their goyish heads or as innocent as a cabbage—all hating us viciously just because we're Jews. Mary's heart quakes in impotent outrage.

She gets out near Lafayette Street and finds the old Astor Building, where the Hebrew Immigrant Aid Society is housed, a big brown structure with round, arched windows and doors, like a synagogue. At the side there's a playground, children flying through the air on swings, turning upside down on monkey bars, whirling round and round on a little carousel. They call to each other in Yiddish, German, Polish. Refugee children. So, here's proof that Jews can be brought to America. She stops to watch them before she goes into the building. She sees that a few of the older ones look scared or sad, but the younger kids are as carefree as the little children who play on her own block in the Bronx. She imagines Hirschel's child, looking just like Hirschel, running about among them on chubby little legs . . . Oh, she loves that unborn baby as though it were her own.

A redheaded boy of eleven or twelve, dressed in a new-looking shirt and short pants, gazes at her curiously, and she asks him in Yiddish where she can find the Hebrew Immigrant Aid Society. "Lady, it's the whole building," he announces in his new English, pointing proprietor-like to the various windows. "We got offices there on the first and second floor, we got rooms where we live there on the third and fourth floor, we got there the little synagogue, we got there classroom for us kids." Mary tells him she's come to find out about bringing relatives to America. "Say, you definitely come to the right place, lady," he tells her, taking her by the hand, leading her to the office of refugee inquiry where he says she must go. She let's herself be led by this small Moses. Oh, she could weep with relief, she thinks, because she's found such an amazing haven, and soon she'll be coming to this building to visit Hirschel and his wife and new baby.

The office is mobbed with people—standing in line, leaning up against the walls, sitting on benches or the floor. Mary stands in line next to a mournful-looking little man in a black three-piece suit. He clutches a black derby hat to his chest, his fingers nervously drumming the brim. He turns around to her and tells her about a telegram he's just received from his nephew in the Free State of Danzig, which Mary had never even heard of. They're burning Jewish buildings there, seizing Jewish property, arresting Jews for no reason at all. Three weeks ago, they came in the middle of the night to arrest his brother, the nephew's father, and now someone who'd been in the prison with him says they've already killed him. The nephew begged his uncle to find a way to bring the rest of the family out. "But I don't have that kind of money," the little man wails with a helpless shrug. "My brother had a furniture store; but a lot of good it does them. The new law in Danzig says Jews can't sell their property, and if they're leaving they can't take out anything of value."

He's called up to the counter by a Hebrew Immigrant Aid Society worker, and a minute later Mary is called up by another worker, a harried-looking young man with frizzy hair and rolled-up shirtsleeves. "Can I help you?" he asks in a weary drone, because he's already asked the same thing at least twenty times today, and most of the time he really can't help—too many people in danger, too small an immigration quota to bring a significant number of them to America, not enough other countries that will take them in, not enough money to send them to the few places that might accept them if they had financial backing.

She steels herself. She must find the right words to explain to the young man. "I came here because my brother and his wife who's pregnant live in Riga, and it's becoming very bad for the Jews there." She's dizzy with nervousness, but she must go on. "Please, sir, can you help me bring them over to America before the baby is born?"

"Riga's safe. Probably the safest place in Europe right now," the young man snaps. He looks over Mary's head, as though dismissing her, ready to call up the next desperate person in line, whom he most likely can't help.

"But my brother says . . ." She sees he's not listening. Her high hopes have already come to nothing. She puts a hand on the counter to steady herself against the cannon of cold water he's fired on her. Her legs are trembling so bad she's afraid she'll fall down in a heap.

"And anyway, there's no chance you could bring them here right now," he glances back to her for a moment to say. "You know what the quota is from Latvia now? Two percent of the Latvians who were in America in 1890. That makes close to nothing."

Mary flushes with anger at his brutal bluntness. "I thought the Hebrew Immigrant Aid Society was here to help Jews."

"We are, madam. This year alone we've helped over eleven thousand refugees, mostly from Germany."

The gray-haired woman who works at the counter not far from him sees how distressed Mary is. She excuses herself from the little man in the three-piece suit, who hasn't finished telling her about his family's tragedy in Danzig, and comes over to Mary. "Miss, if it looks like Latvia is in trouble, we have a Hebrew Immigrant Aid Society office right there in Riga. Your brother will go there, and you'll come here, and we'll help you fill out the right documents and transfer the money for the tickets, and we'll find a place for him to go. Everything will be fine," she says sweetly. "For now, though, he's okay. Trust us. Our people in Riga say everything is still okay in Latvia."

13

TIME ON THE MARCH

Hitler enters his native Austria for the Anschluss. In Vienna, a two-mile procession of German Army and Storm Troops. Six tanks lead the way. German bombers black out the sky. Austrians scream, *We see our leader! One führer, one Reich!* Many drop to their knees as Hitler's Mercedes passes. After it has gone by, some grovel in Hitler's wheel tracks, scooping up handfuls of the Austrian earth into which the tread of his German tires has bitten. The Jewish quarter of Leopoldstadt in Vienna is invaded by triumphant Aryan crowds celebrating the Anschluss. Jewish families are called out from their homes and forced to kneel and scrub the pavements while the crowds shout *Perish Jewry!* and *Out with the Jews!*

The Gallup pollsters ask the man on the street, Do you think the persecution of Jews in Europe has been their own fault?

23% say not at all
49% say partly
12% say entirely
16% have no opinion

The picture is not bright for American workers this spring. *Secretary of Labor Frances Perkins:* U.S. factory employment is down again. It's at 81 percent of the pre-depression norm. Since last year, there's been an increase in non-agrarian unemployment of 2,245,000.

By then, as she would tell me all through my childhood, she felt in every cell of her body that those she loved were mired in a quicksand over hell. Month after month of 1938 went by, and people who should have been throwing lifelines turned their backs. They pretended that Hirschel, his unborn baby, di mameh, Hinda, Chana—all those who meant everything in the world to her—were not being sucked down, were not choking, the sand at their necks already, their feet already scorched by infernal fire.

But what do you do if no one around you feels what you feel, sees what you see? Isn't that a definition of insanity—when you cling to a separate reality no one shares? My mother feared she was going crazy.

It's March, 1938. Through the slots in her mailbox, she can see a thin beige envelope with three red stamps. She fishes in her purse for the little key, her blood racing as it always does these days when there's a letter from Latvia.

Congratulate us, my dearest sister! Hirschel writes. *On 26 February, a little bit premature, my Dweira gave birth to a beautiful boy.* "Oh!" Mary exclaims, clasping her heart. *Five pounds, three ounces. Dweira is still a little weak because she had more than twenty-four hours labor, but the doctor says with rest she'll be good as new. We named him Avrom Itzhak Luft, after blessed Tateh.*

Mary sinks down to the cold stoop, so relieved, she could cry. But her relief doesn't last a minute: these are such terrible times in which to bring a Jewish baby into the world. She jumps up as if shot from a gun. She'll take the letter to Ray. They must do something. Now. Because there's not just Hirschel and their sisters and di mameh to worry about, there's the baby. Avrom Itzhak Luft. She and Ray must go to Sarah for help. After all, he's Sarah's nephew, too, named after Sarah's father, too.

Mary doesn't wait for the bus to Ray's house. She runs the twenty blocks, thinking all the way how mortifying it will be to go begging to Sarah and Sam. She'll make Ray do the begging. They always liked her. She's a carbon copy of them. For herself, Mary wouldn't ask Sarah and Sam for a piece of bread, even if she were starving in the streets. But it's not for herself.

My mother and Ray go to see their half sister the next Saturday, when they know Sam will be home, because as Sarah's husband he's the one who'll have to sign the affadavits. As my mother walks up the stairs to their apartment, her face flames remembering her humiliation in this same place. She's not that silly girl they kicked out into the streets anymore, but she knows that that's the way they'll always see her.

Sarah opens the door wearing the same floral-print housedress Mary thinks she remembers from 1914. She feels tears sting her eyes and a lump the size of an egg in her throat, because Sarah is her flesh and blood and was once kind to her, and Mary relinquished her half sister's love to run after foolishness, *Americana mishegas,* as Sam called it.

Ray, a regular guest at Sarah and Sam's, steps inside. Mary lingers at the threshold, feeling awkward; but Sarah grasps her to her big bosom, like she did when they first met at Ellis Island. "Mereleh, Mereleh," she coos, as though their history weren't a thing of disgrace that will mortify Mary till the day she goes to her grave.

Sam is sitting in the living room where Mary slept all those months. He rises to greet Ray with an embrace, calling her *shvester*. He extends a gentlemanly hand to Mary and she takes it, but she senses his old disapproval. She's accomplished nothing in the almost quarter-century since he last saw her that would make him think better of her.

"You got the letter I sent?" Ray asks him without preliminaries.

"Sit, sit first," Sarah says. Mary obediently sits on the chair that's now in front of the door that hides the Murphy bed in which she used to sleep. If she could run, she would.

"Listen, Buna Rivka." Sam addresses Ray by her shtetl name. He hasn't looked at Mary since they shook hands. "To send money, I'm happy to do. To try to get the affadavits, I'm happy to do." Mary watches him, hypnotized by the wagging beard that used to terrify her when he scolded her. "But I think it's really no use. I read the newspapers, and I know what's going on in America. They're letting very few people in these days. It's not like it was when we brought you over in 1923. No matter what I would be happy to do for them, I don't think it'll do any good. It's wasted time."

Mary jumps from her chair. "Brother, please, it's not wasted time!" She throws herself on her knees at his feet, her hands clasped like she's praying to him. "Please! We have to try. I'm so scared for all of them, Brother. Hirschel has a little baby now. Avrom, after our tateh, Sarah's tateh, too. I'll pay you back every penny, Brother."

Sam pushes back deep into the sofa cushion, discomfited by her frenzied plea. "It's not the money," he says curtly. "That has nothing to do with it. I don't have enough for all of them, but for two I have—Hirschel and his wife—and the baby goes for free. But that's not the point. If they're not letting people in, we can stand on our heads, and it won't do any good."

"Try, at least, Brother. On my knees, I'm begging you to try." She waves her clasped hands like she's praying to an obdurate idol. She doesn't give a damn for the mortification she feels. "Please, Brother, for the memory of your wife's father. Please!" She doesn't stop until he resignedly says, "Okay, I'll go get the affidavits and I'll try."

———

Moishe has quit night school. He's in a bad mood. He and Mary have gone to the park, but she may as well not be there for all he notices her. He sits and stares at the lake. She moves closer to him and cups his cheek with her hand. "What is it, *boychikel?*" she says. She needs him still, because what else does she have in her life?

He cracks his knuckles loudly. "I dunno . . . I've got to make some changes," he says with finality.

"Like what?" she cries.

"Nothing to do with us," he says and won't say more.

All that night while he sleeps soundly, little puffing snores escaping from his lips, she's scared. She's sacrificed so much for this relationship, and if he's tired of her, what will she do? She drapes her arm around him, hugging him tight. He won't help her with the most important thing of all, but she needs the comfort at least of his warm body, at least to be able to reach out and feel him in the bed, next to her, to hear his breaths as he sleeps.

A few days later he tells her he's quit his job. He's going into business with a guy from the gym.

"Oh, Morris, no, not that Katz who got arrested!"

"No, no, it's not Katz," he says gruffly.

"Who then? How did you get the money to start a business?"

"Hey, you mind your business and I'll mind mine." He won't tell her anything about what he'll be doing.

She persists. "Morris, it's not something that'll get you in trouble, is it?"

"Do you think I'm a goddam idiot!" he yells, so loud that she recoils like from a dog's bark in her ear. "Look, it's perfectly legit," he says more quietly.

Whatever the business is, it requires that he travel. He goes up to Rochester, Buffalo, Albany, to Philadelphia, even to Boston. Mary hates it when he's out of town. When he's with her she has a little bit of respite from thinking about what's going on across the ocean and worrying herself sick about whether Sam will really try to get the affadavits and if he does whether they'll do any good. When Moishe's around she has to make herself stop imagining she's standing on a high cliff watching shipwreck victims, those she loves, floundering in a sea far below. When she's alone she feels like she's going insane. She fears the women Moishe must meet in his travels too—younger than she is, probably smarter, better educated. New faces. She frets all the time, especially when she learns he's going to Philadelphia, because she's never gotten the mayor's grandniece out of her head. If she loses him now it would be a calamity. It's not so much their lovemaking anymore. She just feels so alone when he's not with her.

"What do you do evenings in a strange city when you're not working?" she dares to ask him one evening, making sure to keep her voice matter-of-fact so he won't think she doesn't trust him. She's sitting on the bed, unhooking her stockings from her girdle. She doesn't even let herself look up at him.

"Nothing much." He stands above her, still wearing his socks but nothing else; he's already almost hard. "Listen, I get lonely as hell for you all the time, doll," he says huskily. He wraps a strand of her hair around his hand, and he draws her head to his groin. It gives her less pleasure than it used to to take him into her mouth; sometimes it even makes her choke a little, as though she's forgotten how to do it; but she musters up the old show of lust. She wants to please him. If she can't make him happy what good is she?

When he's out of town, the time rolls out in front of her like a vast and scary desert. She has to stop herself every day from running over to Sarah and Sam's and demanding what's taking so long. "It's been weeks already!" she wants to yell at them, but she tells herself she has to be patient and mustn't pester, because Sam has no warm feelings for her as it is. But she doesn't know what to do with herself, how to keep her mind from going wild with worry. A few times she's invited to go eat Chinese or go to a movie with a bunch of the new girls at the shop, but she says no. She likes them well enough—but it feels funny, because most of them are nineteen or twenty years old; she'll be forty-two next birthday, old enough to be their mother.

One evening after work my mother takes the elevator down to the street and finds Ray standing there, waiting for her. Ray looks even more unkempt than usual. She's forgotten to put on the hat she always wears, and her coat is lopsided, the left side hanging two inches longer than the right because she was too upset to pay attention when she buttoned it.

"What?" Mary cries, images of death and destruction already rolling in her mind like there's a movie camera.

"Bad news. Two letters with bad news. I brought them for you," she says grimly.

"Give me!"

"Wait. Let's go sit down in that restaurant across the street," Ray says, taking Mary's arm, leading her to the stoplight on the corner and then across the street to the cafeteria.

"Give me the letters," Mary keeps saying. She knows there must be something terrible in them for Ray to be looking as she does.

"They won't jump out of my pocketbook and run away," Ray says. She's already standing in the cafeteria line. When the server asks what she'd like she points to the liver with onions and the mashed potatoes. She says that to drink she'll have hot tea. "You gotta eat, too," she tells Mary, and orders the same dishes for her, because Mary keeps repeating to Ray, "I want to see those letters" and won't tell the server what she'd like to eat. Mary is furious with Ray, but she makes no protest when the server places liver and onions and mashed potatoes on her tray, because she just wants to get to the table and have Ray give her the letters.

The minute Ray sits down, she digs into the liver and onions, despite her worry. "Eat first," she orders Mary.

"I can eat and read," Mary says. She takes a bite of liver, pushes the potatoes around on her plate, and holds out her hand for the letters. "Okay, give them to me."

"I wanted us to have some supper first before we talk about them," Ray says. But she does reach into her purse and pulls out one letter that she puts in Mary's open palm. It's from Sam. He thought about it for a long time, he writes, and then he went to his rabbi, who told him it would be foolish even to go to the trouble of getting the affadavits. *Twelve people in the congregation who have relatives in Europe already tried to bring them here, and only one—a man from Dresden—succeeded, and just in bringing his old mother, nobody else. The rabbi says there's no chance for your family. They're letting hardly any Jews in from Eastern Europe, no matter how much money or what kind of promise to support them you give. Hirschel would have to sign up now and wait maybe ten years, so what's the good?*

"That lousy rotten bastard! He didn't even try!" Mary cries. "And where was Sarah in all this? She doesn't give a damn."

"Listen, we gotta think of someplace else they can go if they can't get in here," Ray says, handing her the second envelope.

This one from their sister Chana. Surely some new disaster. Di mameh, who's past seventy-five already? Mary's hands tremble and her mouth is dry as a stone as she slides the pages with Chana's careful Yiddish script out of its thin envelope. But the letter doesn't mention di mameh at all. It's about Chana's husband, Mendel, who owned a bakery in Dvinsk, right in the center of town; he employed a dozen workers, Jews and gentiles. But in the last year there's been almost no business because the antisemiten started a boycott of Jewish shops. And now all businesses with over ten workers are being nationalized. *They made Mendel liquidate and gave just a little bit of money, maybe 20 percent of what the store used to be worth. Tayere Shvester, we'll be starving before long.* And that's not even the worst problem, Chana goes on. In school, Dovid and her middle son, Lev, and all the other Jewish boys are forced to sit on the floor in the back. In Dovid's class, if he raises his hand to say something, the teacher usually pretends he doesn't see him. If he bothers to call on Dovid at all he says, "What does the Jew Boy want?" and the gentile kids laugh. They gang up on the Jewish boys after school too. Lev lost a front tooth in a fight. He and Dovid refuse to go to school anymore. The youngest, Shlomo, was supposed to be in his second year, but Chana and Mendel are afraid to send him.

Please, please, dear sister, Chana ends, *for the sake of your poor nephews if nothing else, find a way to help us get out from this hell. We know it's hard to get into America now, but maybe Palestine, Argentina, anywhere . . .*

"We'll go back and ask Sam for the money so they can get to Palestine," Ray says.

Mary pushes her food aside, but its smell still nauseates her. She feels like she's losing her mind with so much worry. "Sam doesn't give a damn. They don't want to help," she says angrily.

"What are you talking? He went to the rabbi who said America is impossible, that's all."

But Mary doesn't trust him. He kicked her out in the cold when she was seventeen years old, and Sarah did nothing to stop him. Everything might have been different now if they hadn't done that . . .

"Okay, okay, listen," Mary says. "Sam only has enough money for two people, and Chana has a husband and three kids. If we have to help her right away, we gotta find more money, and we gotta find out how we can get them into other countries . . . Listen, maybe we oughta go to the B'nai B'rith." It's the only big Jewish organization she's heard of that she hasn't yet tried. She closes her eyes and breathes deeper because she knows it will be a long struggle, and she's so tired already.

"I went to B'nai B'rith, yesterday afternoon, the minute I got the letter from Chana. They already told me they're not the one to go to. They sent me to the Hebrew Immigrant Aid Society."

Mary opens her eyes. Bile rushes into her mouth because she sees that Ray is still forking down liver and onions. "Can you stop eating for a minute?" she cries, and Ray puts down her fork. She looks like she's about to weep, though with the back of her hand she wipes at her lips and not her eyes.

"Listen, I went to the Hebrew Immigrant Aid Society already, last year," Mary tells her. "They said they can't do anything for Jews from Latvia because things were still all right there compared to Germany."

"Yeah, I took off from work and went over there this morning. They told me the same thing," Ray says. She searches in her purse until she comes out with a wrinkled handkerchief. She blows her nose, and now she wipes her eyes. "They said the real danger in the East isn't Latvia but Poland, Rumania, and Hungary, where they're killing people on the streets. But this afternoon a lady from my shop gave me another place we could go. Wait, I'll find it." She fishes in her purse again and pulls out a folded piece of paper. "The American Jewish Joint Distribution Committee, it's called. That's where she got help for her sister whose husband was killed in Linz on the day of the Anschluss. Let's go try there."

Mary can't get enough air into her lungs—like she's been running for miles, though she hasn't moved an inch.

The next morning, my mother wakes up and her head is spinning. She thinks she's been feeling nauseated ever since the liver and onions. She rushes to the bathroom so she can throw up in the toilet. She barely makes it, and she heaves and heaves. She feels like she's emptying her whole stomach. But on the train to work she has to get off at a Bronx stop and find a bathroom in which to throw up again. By the time she arrives at Seidman and Sons her stomach feels more settled. Thank goodness I got all that cafeteria junk out of my system, she thinks. But that afternoon, as she's pinning a bodice on a dummy, a burning tingle radiates from both her nipples, like a hot wire is threaded in them. She remembers that feeling from four years ago.

But how can she be pregnant again? She's hardly seen Moishe for the past month, and whenever they've been together he's worn a rubber like he always does. And she's almost forty-two years old. She tries to remember when she last had a period. She's stopped paying much attention because in the last couple of years they've gotten less regular and she can't predict them anymore. She doesn't remember having menstruated in the last month . . . She's not certain about the month before.

Again a burning tingle radiates from her right nipple. And then another from her left nipple. Now she's sure it can be nothing else.

14

Summer, 1938

TIME ON THE MARCH

President Roosevelt convenes an international conference at Evian, France, asking thirty nations to open their doors to Jewish refugees fleeing Nazi persecution. *Head of the British Delegation to the Evian Conference, Lord Winterton:* A sudden rush of Jewish refugees might arouse anti-Semitic feelings. *Australia's Chief Delegate, Colonel White:* As we have no real racial problem in Australia, we are not desirous of importing one. *Head of the Swiss Delegation, Dr. H. Rothmund, Chief of Federal Police:* Switzerland, which has as little use for these Jews as has Germany, will take measures to protect itself from being swamped by Jews.

Pleas by refugees swamp the consulates. The summer isn't yet over, but America's yearly quota limit of 27,370 for immigrants from the Reich has already been filled.

Pollsters stopped the man on the street this week to ask, What is your attitude toward allowing refugees into the United States?

4.9% answered, We should encourage them to come even if we have to raise our immigration quotas.

18.2% answered, We should allow them to come in but not raise immigration quotas.

67.4% answered, With economic conditions as they are, we should try to keep them out.

9.5% didn't know.

For most of my adult life, I've tried to understand certain choices my mother made. Sometimes they anger me. Though she's been dead for more than thirty years—she died at the age of eighty-three—in my thoughts I compose lectures to her: *Twice you screwed up. Okay, in 1914 you were only seventeen years old, but what about when Dominick would have helped?*

Cataclysms were happening left and right and you let yourself be swept up in your stupid passion for that phony movie-screen gangster, that transparent deceiver, that stuffed Arrow-shirt man. For a second time you were a fool! (Oh, but if she hadn't been, how could I have come to be?)

Sometimes I only imagine her anguish, and I'm mute. I do not know how she endured it. I have to force myself to remember all the details of her stories, to relive them and tell them. When I do, I marvel at her strength to have survived it all. Oh, Mama, I think you were a better woman than I.

The American Jewish Joint Distribution Committee office is jam-packed with harried-looking people desperate to get their loved ones out of harm's way. My mother and Ray take their place in a huge line. The corpulent man in front of them is holding his hands to his heart; every minute or two he takes a huge breath, like he can't get enough oxygen into his lungs.

"Mama, darling, please don't get your hopes up too much," a well-dressed woman down the line implores an age-shrunken dowager with red-rimmed eyes who stands beside her.

"I don't need to hear that, like you're giving up on them," the old lady answers bitterly. She sucks on her wrinkled lip.

"But, Mama, even if we can get them visas, they've still got to go to the consulate in Prague and be examined by an American doctor there," the younger woman persists in Yiddish. "He'll see that Manny has tuberculosis."

"Shhaahh! Be still!" the old mother hisses.

Ray stands with feet wide apart and arms crossed at her chest. She looks fierce as a bulldog. "We'll try now for Chana and her family because things are so bad in Dvinsk. Let's ask for America first; and if they can't help with that, then Palestine."

"No! Not America!" Mary whispers fiercely, her pulse pounding. There's a baby growing inside her, and if she keeps it and Chana comes here, it would be terrible. She'd report Mary's disgrace to the whole family. It would kill di mameh. Mary struggles to get hold of herself. "Don't you remember, for godsakes, Sam found out already America's impossible." A hideous prayer escapes her before she can stop it: she's praying Sam was right and Chana won't be allowed into America.

But the feeling of guilt for that treachery pricks her like the pitchforks of a hundred devils. She must find a way to help her sister now, and her baby brother, and all of them. That's what must come first. And she knows what she needs to do about what's growing inside her. She'll do it on Monday.

The two young men who have joined the line in back of Mary are talking about places that could accept refugees if they wanted to. She turns around and listens to them. They look like brothers, both tall and skinny as poles, their black hair in high wavy pompadours. "That lousy England owns half the world," the younger one says. "Why can't they take in the Jews somewhere? Australia, New Zealand, Canada, India, Palestine, Rhodesia, Tanganyika, British Guiana . . ." He counts on the fingers of both hands.

"They're making the excuse that if they opened their doors to refugees, Hitler would right away dump a half million on their doorstep . . . Bastards," the older one breathes.

"The French own the other half of the world," the man who's taken a place in line behind them says angrily. "They got colonies on every continent—Asia, Africa, you name it. Why can't they let the refugees in just till somebody manages to assassinate that damn Hitler?"

"Yeah!" Mary jumps in, her voice shrill, "there's a whole world outside of Europe and America. Why can't Jews be let in somewhere, anywhere?" How can it be that on the entire earth there's not one damn place to which those she loves can run for safety?

"President Roosevelt called a big international conference for next month, someplace in France . . . Evian," a young woman down the growing line says hopefully. "He's bringing together more than thirty different countries just to figure out how to help the refugees."

"Yeah, sure, they'll pass the buck, just like they been doing," the man beside her snickers, and the two brothers nod mournfully.

"I heard yesterday the Dominican Republic will accept a hundred thousand refugees if only the Joint will give them a million dollars up front," a gray-haired lady farther down the line says.

Mary and Ray are finally called up to a desk. Their interviewer is a plump, pretty woman with a habitually sympathetic expression. When Ray explains the terrible things that have been happening in Dvinsk, the woman's warm brown eyes become shiny with tears, though she must have heard a thousand such stories.

"What about America? Isn't there any way we could bring them here?" Mary asks right away, though she's sick about it. Even if there was no baby, Chana would find out about Moishe.

"No," the woman says sadly. "There's almost no chance for someone from Latvia. Congress won't expand the quota. I know your sister and her family are suffering," she tells Mary and Ray, "but Latvia's really not in trouble the way Germany and Austria are. Right now the Joint is trying to resettle refugees from Germany and Austria. We're bringing them into the parts of Europe that are safe."

"But nowhere in Europe is safe! And Latvia's in big trouble!" Ray yells in her foghorn voice. The woman looks startled for a moment. "Look, I brought the letter from my sister. Read it!" Ray shoves it under the woman's nose.

The woman shakes her head wearily and says, "You told me already." She won't take the letter.

Mary's heart is pounding in her ears. "If not America, what about Palestine?" she asks.

"Next to impossible legally," the woman says, composed and sad again. She absentmindedly picks up a yellow pencil from her desk and twists it round and round with both hands. "The Arabs protested because the British were allowing too many Jews in. Now they'll let in no more than a couple hundred a year."

"Then not legally!" Mary cries.

"Then not legally!" Ray echoes, banging her fist on the woman's desk, yelling so loudly that the whole room seems to grow quiet for a minute.

"Shhh. Please, there are other people here, too," the woman says, looking annoyed, waving the pencil like it's a wand that will quiet the funny-looking lady in front of her. Ray bites her lip and glares.

Finally the woman says in a low voice, "I can tell you that five boatfuls of Jews from Austria just arrived in Palestine illegally. But you'd have to go to a Zionist group to get more information."

"We'll do that right now. We'll do anything. Where can we find them?" Mary demands.

The woman's eyes look shiny again. "I'm sorry to say that if you're hoping to get your sister and her family into Palestine, it's probably no use. The Zionists are looking for young, single people that they can teach to build kibbutzim and work in agriculture. They don't want families with young children now."

On Sunday afternoon my mother hears his key in the lock. He comes in carrying a paper sack. "Say, doll, I can't stay for more than a couple hours today," he announces, taking out a bottle of the red wine he likes and getting two glasses from the cupboard, just like he hasn't been gone for more than a week. "I've got to take my mother to Philly because one of Tamara's grandkids is in a piano recital tonight." He sighs like one put upon. Then he reaches for Mary, and that's when she tells him she's pregnant again.

He stares at her bug-eyed before he opens his mouth. She doesn't need to hear what he's going to say. "We'll have to go back to that place for another abortion," she says before he can say it.

But he's shaking his head resolutely. "I'll give you the money," he says.

"But you'll come with me, no?"

He juts his jaw stubbornly and keeps shaking his head. "Listen, Mary, I'm sorry it happened again, but I can't go with you. I just read in the *New York Times* that a man was thrown in jail after his girlfriend had complications from an abortion."

Her head spins for a minute, like she's been running in circles. "You bastard!" she screams. "You think it's my responsibility alone?" She howls like a goaded animal. "Is that the kind of love you have for me?" She lunges at him, to scratch his eyes out, to pull his hair out of his head, to tear his flesh off.

He struggles with her, pinions both her wrists in his big hands. "Stop, wildcat, stop!" he hisses between gritted teeth, then slaps her face so hard she sees double for a minute. She wants to kick him, but he pins her flat against the wall with the force of his whole body so she can't move. She lifts her head and keens like somebody has died.

"Shh, shh," he says over and over. "I love you, doll. Shh." He kisses her forehead. She can't stop sobbing. He lets her loose and then pulls her back to him in an embrace, patting her back as though she's a child who's wept herself into hysterical hiccups. She goes limp in his arms, a deflated balloon. "Shh, sweetheart. I'll be there for you. I never meant I wouldn't. I just can't go with you. You wouldn't want me to end up in jail, would you? . . . Look." He takes a pen and a little notebook from his pocket. "I'm writing down the telephone number where I'm going to be the next few days. I've got to go up to Rochester, but I want you to call me the minute you're out, person to person, collect. I'll be worried till I hear from you, sweetheart. You understand about my not coming, don't you?" He looks anxious about her now. Liar, damn lousy liar, she thinks. He tears the page out of the notebook and puts it in her hand. He closes her fingers around the slip of paper. Then he pulls her to him again and holds her close. She can smell his musky aftershave.

The odor almost makes her gag because she can't stand strong smells of any kind now, and she breaks away.

He takes out his wallet from a pocket on the inside of his suit jacket. He counts five ten-dollar bills. "That ought to be enough. I think it was only thirty-five bucks the last time," he says, grasping her resisting hand and stuffing the money into it.

"You call me the minute you're out. Don't forget. Person to person, collect. If somebody else answers, tell them you're my sister—okay, sweetheart?" And he leaves.

I've made a very bad bargain with life, and now I have to resign myself to the consequences, Mary thinks. She swipes at her eyes with the back of her hand. She remembers what Goldie always used to say: You make your bed, and then you gotta lie in it.

My mother can't sleep that night. She'd resigned herself to going alone the next day, but she remembers girls at work talking about all the terrible things that could happen—her womb could tear and she could bleed to death, she could die from an infection. If she died, the doctor (if that's even what he was) would be scared he'd go to jail for doing an illegal operation; he'd probably take her out to some field and pile the dirt on top of her. She'd read about such a thing happening. Nobody would even know she was dead; they'd assume she just ran off. Hirschel would think she deserted him. Wouldn't it be safer to have the baby? . . .

She feels like she's going insane, like a woman she read about in the *Forverts* who was carted off to the crazy house in a straitjacket. But she can't give in to the escape of insanity. She has to think clearly: she'll go over to Ricki's and tell her she's got to go for another abortion. Maybe she can even get Ricki to come with her . . . But she hasn't seen Ricki for so long, and she's too ashamed to have to tell her that she let herself get pregnant with that heel's baby again.

A couple of hours later, Mary, shivering like she's in a snowstorm though the summer heat has set in, takes the bus to Ray's house. She'll tell Ray where she's going . . . in case she dies on the table.

As the bus lumbers toward 174th, Mary looks out the window, trying not to think what Ray will say, though she can hear that foghorn voice in her mind. Didn't I tell you that louse was a no-good? If di mameh knew she'd kill herself! Mary tries to pay attention to the sights—kids everywhere, because it's early summer and school is out. Bunches of kids cavorting in the heavy rush of water that's shooting out into the street from the fire hydrants they've managed to pry open. Bunches of kids playing kick-the-can or broomstick baseball. When the bus approaches, they scatter in a wave from the middle of the street onto the sidewalk, and then drift back again as soon as the bus passes. The mothers all seem to be outdoors, too, lolling on stoops, gossiping, fanning themselves as they watch their broods. Mary thinks that right now she'd give anything to be one of them, to lead a predictable, passionless life. But such peace is not for her in this world.

"What happened?" Ray cries in alarm when she opens the door and sees her sister, who never just drops by.

"Moishe . . . " Mary begins.

"Oy, I thought somebody died," Ray slaps her heart and cries. "Come in, come into my room. The missus is in the kitchen." She leads Mary by the hand into her dark little room and shuts the door behind them. They sit down together on Ray's bed. "You look terrible. I can't believe you're back with that miserable user!" she yells but not loud enough so the missus can hear her. "What's wrong with you that you keep going back?"

"I'm pregnant."

"*Gott in himml!*" Ray cries. "Is that no-good louse gonna marry you?"

Mary doesn't look at Ray. She shouldn't have come. But she had nowhere else to go.

"You're gonna have a baby from that miserable bastard and he doesn't care about your shame even?"

"You go to hell!" Mary yells and rises to her feet. But Ray clutches at her skirt, pulls her back down, and throws her arms around her. Mary sinks back on the bed and they rock together, rock and moan, sisters grieving for losses they've had and losses to come.

Ray finally breaks away, crying, "Listen, Mary, it'll be okay! I just figured out what we gotta do. I'll go with you to the Jewish agency that does adoptions—I read about them in the *Forverts*. It's for Jewish girls that can't keep their baby. They find good homes."

"No, I'm gonna have an abortion! It would hurt me too much to have it and then have to give it up. I couldn't stand that. I'll jump out a window first."

Ray's bullying stare dissolves when she sees that Mary means it. "Well . . . you can't go by yourself. I read in the *Forverts* you can't trust those doctors." Ray is already putting on her hat.

On the train ride home, Mary is sure she's dying. The sharp pains are like hyenas gobbling up her guts, and she's clammy and wants to vomit. Ray says, "Lay down with your head on my lap and you'll feel better." Mary is so weak that she doesn't argue. She curls her legs up on the seat and lets her head loll on Ray's ample thighs, her cheek against Ray's belly. She tries not to think that there'd been a baby growing inside her and again she had to have it killed. She opens her eyes and sees that Ray is white as a kitchen wall, though she's stroking Mary's hair with a firm hand. Neither of them gives a damn that people are staring.

Mary refuses to hold on to Ray's arm as they walk down the El station steps, though she's so weak she can hardly put one foot in front of the other. She totters. Ray stops, her fists on her hips. "Listen, I'm taking you to the hospital right now. I'm calling a taxi."

"No!" They'll know what she's done. She could be sent to jail. And the doctor, too, and maybe Moishe also if they found out he was the one. She grabs on to the iron railing and begins to struggle again down the stairs.

"Take my shoulder at least!"

Leaning on Ray's shoulder, she hobbles up the street toward her apartment. Then suddenly she remembers—she wants to turn around and go to the candy store on the next block, where there's a telephone. "I promised Moishe. He'll be worried if he doesn't hear from me."

"How can you call that *paskudnyak,* that no-goodnik?" Ray cries, but when Mary starts limping toward the candy store, Ray goes after her. "You need to be in bed. Listen, I'll go call him for you."

Mary is too weak to argue. She lets Ray help her up the stairs and into the apartment. She lets Ray help her take her clothes off. "Lift up your arms," Ray says, and pulls Mary's nightgown over her head. Ray eases her onto the bed and tucks her under the covers. "What can I get you now?"

"I'm okay," Mary says. "You promised you'd—"

"Okay, okay, I'll go call him, the *mamser,*" Ray spits.

"Person to person, collect." Mary hands her the slip of paper on which Moishe had written the Rochester telephone number, and Ray goes down to the candy store.

Mary lies there motionless, staring up at the ceiling, waiting for Ray to return and tell her what Moishe said.

Ray comes back looking sour as vinegar. "That miserable louse thanked me for calling," she reports dutifully. "He said now he has to go over to Albany for a few days, so he can't come see you until the weekend. He said for me to tell you he loves you." Ray growls a string of bitter curses in a rasping witch voice. *Kakn zol er mit blit un ayter.* May he shit blood and pus. *Trinkn zol im piavkes.* May leeches drink his blood. *Krichen zol er afyn boych.* May he crawl on his belly. "Are you going to see that lousy son-of-a-bitch again?" she demands.

Mary turns her face to the wall.

Ray fixes crackers with butter, and bullion soup and soft-boiled eggs, and she brings them to Mary in bed. She plumps the pillows. "You'll choke if you eat laying down," she says, and helps Mary sit up. When Mary gets out of bed saying, "I want to see if my legs are strong enough yet to walk," Ray runs to her and says, "Here, lean on me before you fall and break your neck," and she extends her arm. She stays with Mary for four days, until the fever breaks, sleeping on Moishe's side of the bed.

But they hardly talk. Mary doesn't want to hear what her sister has to say about him.

Mary receives a small photograph of the baby Avrom, taken in July, when he was five months old. He's naked on a piece of rug and grinning like the world is dandy. *Here is the joy of my life,* Hirschel has written on the back of the picture.

There's no joy in the letter that accompanies it . . .

Dweira is still weak, but the doctor says that's to be expected because she lost so much blood when the baby was being born. Hinda and di mameh have come from Preil to take care of her and Avromeleh while I work. Hinda looks good, but di mameh is complaining of bad pains in her stomach again, the way she used to a couple years ago. Chana and Mendel came to visit with their children, who are not going to school anymore. Mendel still hopes to emigrate to Palestine because he can't make a living in Dvinsk now; but I had to tell him that I've been reading that people all over are so desperate that they'll take any kind of boat to get to Palestine, and then in the middle of the sea they're robbed of all their possessions, even their gold teeth. A couple weeks ago I read that boats were dropping refugees off on barren little islands around the Mediterranean without food or water even. Chana heard what I told Mendel about these pirates, and she screamed and carried on so much that poor Dweira jumped out of her sick bed to try and comfort her.

It's not just relatives Hirschel worries about.

That conference your president called in France, at Evian, has been the worst thing for the Jews that anyone could imagine. It's shown the whole world that not a single country wants us. And now Herr Hitler is laughing, saying, "See, what hypocrites they are when they pretend to be worried about the precious Jews. Everybody hates them as much as we Germans do." What I'm most afraid, dear sister, is that Evian showed the führer that since the world doesn't care, he can do what he likes. Nobody is going to step in and save us . . .

15

Fall, 1938

TIME ON THE MARCH

BERLIN. Raiding squads of young men invade the Jewish shopping districts, breaking shop windows with metal weapons, looting, tossing merchandise into the streets or into passing vehicles. They leave the unprotected Jewish shops to the mercy of vandals. The vandals hack away at windows, accompanied by the laughing and joking of onlookers. Their targets are easily recognized because all Jewish-owned shops must have the name of their proprietors whitewashed on the windows in large block letters. VIENNA. In the dingy streets of the Second District, reporters film a chase by a mob a thousand strong—roaring execrations at an aged, lame man, a Jew, who tries vainly to run while his twelve-year-old granddaughter aids him. Jews awaiting admittance to the British Consulate-General and the United States Consulate are severely beaten. Many are taken into custody. Apartments are raided and searched and over 15,000 Jews are taken to police stations. *Eye-witness foreign correspondent reporting from police station:* I witnessed a uniformed Elite Guardsman beating and throwing to the floor a very old Jew of patriarchal appearance, who was so terrified he wasn't even able to cry out against his tormentor.

U.S. Senator Robert Rice Reynolds: Hitler and Mussolini have a date with Destiny. It is foolish to oppose them, so why not play ball with them?

November 9, two days after my mother's forty-second birthday. Moishe had told her he had to go to Albany again; but a delivery boy in a red suit rings her bell soon after she gets home from work and hands her a dozen pink carnations tied with a white bow and wrapped in cellophane. *Happy birthday, doll,* —*M,* the card says. She takes the package to the sink, fills an empty borsht jar with water, and arranges the flowers as best she can. She places the bouquet on the nightstand near her bed. But the belated gift makes her bluer, and he's still not here.

She snaps on the radio to keep her company during her lonesome evening. She's expecting to hear the croon of some mind-numbing ballad, some silly thing that might distract her a tiny bit from her troubles. Instead, a booming, solemn voice is announcing the horrors that had gone on across the ocean that day. Almost every synagogue in Germany, Austria, the Sudetenland—up in flames. Jewish cemeteries desecrated. Thirty thousand Jews taken off to concentration camps (Mary had never heard the term *concentration camp* before, nor their names: Buchenwald, Dachau, Sachsenhausen). Thousands of Jews victims of sadistic violence. Seven thousand plate-glass windows of Jewish-owned stores smashed to shards; the undefended stores looted by mobs while policemen watched, jeered, applauded. "The amount of plate glass windows belonging to Jewish businesses that was shattered in German and Austrian cities today is equal to an entire year's production of the European plate-glass industry," the newscaster hoarsely declares.

Mary walks back and forth in the room listening to the horrors. She bumps into the bed or nightstand or dresser, oblivious. She hugs herself hard to still the quaking, but it won't stop. Why isn't Moishe here, to comfort her, to share her terror at least? She snaps the radio off, pulls her coat from the closet, and runs out into the street. She can't face this alone. Where can she go to be with someone? She runs toward her sister's house because she's too nervous to wait for a bus. She needs to be with Ray.

She's panting for breath by the time she arrives at Ray's apartment. Ray's missus answers the door, the look on her face as grim as death. Mary can hear the radio blaring in the kitchen. Another newscaster with the same awful news.

"This is the end of us all," the missus says in a flat voice before she tells Mary, "Your sister's in her room."

Ray opens the door to Mary's knock, her face streaked with dirt, like she's been swiping tears with grimy hands. They throw themselves into one another's arms. Ray wails, "Gott zol uns helfin!"

They sit huddled close together on Ray's bed, listening to the unending radio reports of the disaster. The bare lightbulb on the ceiling casts a harsh light, but they're unaware of anything except the terrible stories they're hearing. The newscasters are calling it the Night of Broken Glass. They say the Nazis claim it's a spontaneous riot. Retaliation after a seventeen-year-old Jewish boy assassinated an official at the German Embassy in Paris. The boy's parents had been deported from Germany along with fifteen thousand other German Jewish citizens who'd been born in Poland—all fifteen thousand dumped without food or water in a small Polish border village of six thousand hostile residents.

One newscaster reads the earnest statement of the young assassin, Henry Grynszpan. He'd been distraught for his parents, who'd lived in Hanover for twenty-five years and had considered themselves good Germans, and for himself, too: "Being a Jew is not a crime. I am not a dog. I have a right to live, and the Jewish people have a right to exist on earth. Wherever I have been I have been chased like an animal." All the newscasters agree that the boy's rash act gave Hitler and his henchmen a pretext, an excuse to unleash on the Jews the mayhem and murder the Nazis had long been contemplating.

November 10: The workers at Seidman and Sons are standing around a little Philco table radio. One of the operators has brought it in and plugged it into the electric outlet that usually powers her sewing machine. No one is sewing now or operating any of the factory's machines. The shop is quiet except for the voices of the radio newscasters, an occasional gasp from one of the women workers, and the nervous cracking of gum by Mr. Jerry, the eldest Seidman son, who stands next to his father and Ezra, the foreman. My mother, who's in front of them, can smell the spearmint on Mr. Jerry's breath, the sour odor on the breath of the other two men, the fetid sweat coming from her own armpits. They listen to a newscaster read an eyewitness report by a U.S. Embassy official in Leipzig—Jewish homes demolished, furniture, clothes, children's toys flung into the streets. "In a poor Jewish district of Leipzig," the newscaster reads, "I saw an eighteen-year-old Jewish boy hurled from a three-story window. He landed with both legs broken on a street littered with burning beds and other furnishings from the apartments of his family and the other Jewish residents of the building."

Sonya, a finisher, lets out a long, low wail and covers her face with both hands.

"Shaa, it's okay, they're not here," Maury the presser tells her.

"I have a sister and three nieces who live in Halle. Only twenty-five kilometers from Leipzig," Sonya says in a groan and covers her face again.

"All of Leipzig has become a hell for Jews," the newscaster intones, his voice funereal. He reads more of the embassy official's report. "I witnessed the insatiably sadistic perpetrators throw many of the trembling Jews they'd rounded up into a small stream that flows through the zoological park. The sadists commanded that the horrified spectators spit at the Jews, defile them with mud, and jeer at their plight." Paula, the lame draper, whimpers softly, bends over, and vomit shoots from her mouth. Mary's stomach tumbles at the terrible smell and the yellow-green bile at her feet. She sees that her left shoe and stocking are speckled with vomit. She breathes through her mouth, afraid she'll throw up, too. She won't let herself. Paula is hanging on to the operators' table as though she might collapse. "I made a mess," she moans, shamefaced. "What should I do?" she asks Mary, who's standing closest to her.

Mary struggles to keep down her own bile. "Come on, let's go clean you up," she says quietly to Paula, taking her by the elbow, leading her as she limps to the ladies' room, while Ezra the foreman runs to find a mop and pail.

Moishe comes by on Saturday morning carrying a gold-colored box prettily tied with a red ribbon. He's in a very good mood. "Another belated birthday present, doll. I picked it up in Philly," he says as he hands it to my mother and kisses her cheek. He doesn't notice right away how grim she looks.

She takes it, baffled, and lays it down on the kitchen table. Hasn't he been following the news? "Do you know what's going on in Europe?" she asks him. "It's terrible."

"You mean the riots. Yeah, it's awful. The whole world agrees they're monsters."

They stare at each other. He's baffled, too—by her tragic expression. "But what can we do about it? I really feel sorry for the Jews over there, but the American government is not going to let them in here. Nobody wants them."

"What to do you mean 'them'?" she says contentiously. "'Them' is 'us'!"

"Yeah, well, we're powerless to do anything, Mary. That's just a fact." He takes off his gray fedora, flicks a speck of soot from it, and places it on the kitchen chair, then unbuttons his coat, slips out of it, folds it inside out, and drapes it carefully over the chair's back.

"So you want to just give up on them?" She's trembling inside. "You have cousins in Poland. Aren't you worried about them? How do you live with this?" A hideous disaster is going on, and he's as aloof as if he just heard that his neighbor lost a pinochle game.

"Yeah, I have a bunch of cousins I used to play with as a kid. I loved them, and my sister loved them. Yeah, I'm worried about them. We all are. I feel awful. But would it do any good to go around with a long face? How will that help them?" He juts his chin out, his expression resentful. "What the hell can anyone here do about it? Just tell me!"

She doesn't know either what anyone can do about it—except tear their hair, bang their head against the wall, go nuts like she's been doing . . . at the least, weep about it. He's not even weeping. "You really don't give a damn, do you, not about anything in the world but you," she says bitterly, thinking about the abortions too, for which she will never forgive him.

"That's bullshit! If I can do something, I do it. If I can't, I just learn to live with it. I'm a pragmatist." He glares at her angrily.

She chews on the inside of her cheek and glares back.

"Hey, look, doll," he says after a while. "I know you're worried about your brother and the rest of your family, but there's nothing you can do right now. And we're here and we're alive," he says earnestly, taking her unyielding form into his arms. "We've got a right to live instead of moaning and mourning all the time . . . Look, you haven't even opened your birthday present yet." He turns and fetches the box from the table where she'd laid it down. He unties the ribbon for her and opens the box because she makes no move to do it. He takes out of the tissue paper in which it's been neatly folded an expensive-looking red silk dress, plunged low at the neckline. He holds it up to her. "You'll look gorgeous in this! See, doll, I think of you all the time. Now gimme a smile."

Jack the cutter brings the *New York Times* to the shop every day. At lunchtime, he and a couple of other cutters carry the multicolored bolts of cloth that are on the cutters' table over to a wall and lean them up against it. They clear the long table of usable snippets and swatches and put them in a big shallow box; they deposit all the scissors in drawers. They make a place for a dozen or so workers whose English isn't good enough to read what the American papers are saying. The workers stand around the table or sit on it. Some have taken their sardine or egg sandwiches or thermoses of borscht with them and, if they have the stomach to, they eat and drink; but all listen attentively while Jack bends his bald head and reads aloud. His wire-rimmed glasses keep sliding down his long nose, but he pushes them up again with one finger and continues reading.

The newspapers are calling the staggering savagery of November 9 and 10 Kristallnacht, "Crystal Night"—which sounds utterly mocking, the workers agree, like a name for prize night at a movie theater. Hitler has decreed that Jews won't be permitted to sell goods or services to non-Jews anymore ... Jewish children will no longer be allowed in German schools. The next week, there's better news. The *New York Times* says that President Roosevelt just declared that public opinion in America is deeply shocked by the terrible acts the Nazis committed the week before. "I myself could scarcely believe that such things could occur in a twentieth-century civilization," the president said. He promised help. The twelve thousand Jewish refugees who are in the United States on temporary visas will not be sent back to Europe. They can stay in the United States indefinitely.

"Thank God!" one of the pressers cries.

"Lange yoren zol er lebn!" Mary shouts. *May he live long years.*

They all bang their hands together or bang on the table with open palms. "A gezunt oyf zayn kup!"—*A blessing on his head*—Sonya, who's been trying to get her family out of Halle, cries.

"Maybe now I can send for my brother in Vilna," Bertha tells Mary, who's grabbed the table, weak-kneed with relief because maybe there's hope that now *she* can send for her brother, too.

"Wait, wait a minute," Jack holds up a hand and says. "Don't get too excited. He's not throwing open the doors yet. Listen what he says next. 'Liberalization of America's immigration quotas is not contemplated.' You know what that means? It means they're not thinking of changing a damn thing except for those twelve thousand German Jews who are already here."

My mother grasps the table harder, this time because she feels like sinking to the floor and staying there forever. So nothing will be different. The Nazis just showed the whole world they're capable of the vilest barbarism, yet no one will come forth to rescue their victims from Hitler's juggernaut. It will spread farther and farther. They'll welcome him with open arms as he marches east. Of that she's certain, because from her earliest years she's known about the antisemiten in Eastern Europe; she's known of their viciousness.

When she catches a glimpse of herself in the mirror these days, it takes a moment before she recognizes who she's seeing. She looks like she's dead already. Her hair is limp, lifeless. The shadows under her eyes are deep, dark hollows. She can't bring herself to put on makeup anymore because she's in mourning for what will come. She's as pale as Malach Ha-Mavis, the Angel of Death himself.

Paula, who's pulled herself together since the day they stood listening to the terrifying news on the radio, wants to help her. "Mary, darling, it scares me to look at you," she says when they're both changing into their work dresses behind the canvas curtain in a corner of the shop. "You got to get hold of yourself. What can I do?"

"Oh, I'll be okay," Mary tells Paula and turns her lips up in a smile, though she knows she looks like a death's-head.

Paula tries hard to make her feel better. The next day at lunchtime she hobbles over to Mary's station carrying a big sandwich wrapped in a torn-apart paper sack. "Say, I made a salmon last night and there was a lot left over, so I saved some for you." Mary puts aside her hardboiled egg and thanks Paula. Paula pulls up a stool beside Mary's and unwraps her own salmon sandwich, and they both eat. "It's very good," Mary says to please Paula, who was so kind to think of her.

"Mereleh, I just want to tell you," Paula says, "that I know things are turning around for the better. You know what I heard Thomas Dewey who's the district attorney for New York say on the radio?" She quotes him in her most careful English: "'The whole civilized world is revolted by Hitler's pogrom. Every human instinct cries out in protest against the outrages.' So, see, we're not alone anymore," Paula says cheerily. "The goyim understand the terrible things that are going on over there, and they're gonna help us." Mary nods, as though she agrees, but nothing will take away her dread.

The next day Paula brings to work an article from one of the Yiddish papers and stands next to Mary's dummy. "Mary, look at this," she says. "Put your pins down and read it," she insists. "Even Sholem Asch the famous writer is saying things will get better. Here, I'm gonna read it to you. He says, just like I told you, 'The spectators are beginning to stand up for us. Through our blood Hitler rose and through our blood he will fall.' See, the whole world knows what those lousy Nazi worms are doing, and now they'll take it seriously like they didn't before."

Sonya, whose workstation is nearby, hears and pipes up, "She's right, Mereleh. We can cheer up a little. Just this morning I passed a goyishe butcher shop on the way to the subway, and they have a new sign in the window, 'People of America: Stop Hitler Now!' right next to a big *chazer* with an apple in its mouth."

"See?" Paula says, hugging Mary maternally. "It's gonna be okay now. The whole world is ready to help."

16

Winter and spring, 1939

TIME ON THE MARCH

The latest Gallup poll asks the man on the street: It has been proposed to bring to America over the next two years twenty thousand refugee children from Germany, mostly of Jewish origin, to be taken care of in American homes. Should the government permit these children to come in?

30% of those polled say yes
61% say no
9% have no opinion

The saddest ship afloat today, the Hamburg-American liner *St. Louis*, with nine hundred Jewish refugees aboard, is steaming back toward Germany after a tragic week of frustration at Havana and off the coast of Florida. No plague ship ever received a sorrier welcome. At Havana the *St. Louis*'s decks became a stage for human misery. Relatives and friends clamored to get aboard but were held back. Weeping refugees clamoring to get ashore were halted at guarded gangways. One man jumped and reached land. He was pulled from the water and slashed his wrists. A second suicide attempt led the captain to warn the authorities that a wave of self-destruction would follow. The refugees could even see the shimmering towers of Miami rising from the sea, but for them they were only the battlements of another forbidden city. Germany, with all the hospitality of its concentration camps, will welcome these unfortunates home.

If any tiny vestige of the old Mary, steeped in the silliness of love songs and movies, survived into her forty-second year, Kristallnacht delivered its deathblow—that's what my mother will tell me years later. Now it's two months later, 1939. After work she stops at the little candy store a block away from her apartment. She always exchanges a hello with Mr. Solomon, the store's ancient owner, who knows to expect her every evening about six thirty and has already taken from their racks the *Forverts*, the *Freiheit*, and

Der Tog, which he hands her neatly folded. She deposits three nickels into Mr. Solomon's gnarled hand and carries the papers home, hugging them under her arm, anxious to get into her apartment and scan them for news even before she makes herself some supper. In the evening and on the weekends, if Moishe isn't there (as he seldom is these days) she's gotten into the habit of snapping on the radio, not to hear what's new on the Hit Parade like she once used to, but to listen to the news broadcasts of H. V. Kaltenborn, Robert Trout, Walter Winchell. Nowadays, if the station to which she's tuned in is playing love songs, she does chores that require attention until one of the newscasters comes on; then she pulls her chair close to the radio and listens intently for any words about Hitler, the Jews, immigration. At work during lunchtime she still goes over to the cutters' table with the others who can't read English well enough to understand the *New York Times,* and they listen to Jack read what the newspaper has to say on those subjects. She can't remember the days she wasn't glued to the news.

At the end of January, my mother reads in her Yiddish papers that Hitler has established the Reich's Central Office for Jewish Emigration. (Does that mean Hitler just wants to get Jews out of his territory, and he won't keep spreading his venom after all?) A few days later, the fascist prime minister of Czechoslovakia, Rudolf Beran, is also demanding a speedy emigration of Jews from his country . . . But to where? In Rumania, the fascists are declaring *Jidanii in Palestina*—Yids to Palestine. Yes, Yids to Palestine would be good! . . . but the Arabs are demanding of the British, who have juridsdiction over the country, "Keep the Yids Out!" As far as the whole world is concerned, there's no place for Jews but out of it.

My mother can't make sense of it all. It's like trying to navigate a labyrinth drawn by some evil spirit—you run here and there through its sly twists and turns that might lead to freedom but end always at menacing walls, black and stoppable as death. When she's alone and the news is very frightening, she can't control her anxieties. She feels impending horror, just as sure as she feels her splitting head and splintering heart. She runs round and round, bumping into furniture, tearing her hair, tearing at her clothes. She bites her lip so the neighbors won't hear her shrieking and call the insane asylum. But she must get hold of herself, for the sake of Hirschel and di mameh and Avromeleh and all of them: she must keep looking for more avenues to try, though her hopes are less substantial than a puff of breath on the January air.

In *Der Tog* she reads that the Quakers are starting a farm they call Scattergood, and they will take in refugees to work there. She runs to Ray's house. Ray has already put on her coat with the huge shoulder pads that make her look like a football-playing dwarf. She holds her little pillbox hat in her hands, about to put it on. "Listen, I'm meeting somebody for lunch. I can't talk to you right now."

"This can't wait." Mary shoves the article from *Der Tog* into her hands. "We gotta write the paper right away and find out what to do."

Ray reads, her hand pressed to her cheek, her heart. "A dank Gott!" *Thank God!* "We always grew vegetables!" she cries as she unbuttons her coat and throws it on her bed. She looks around her room for some writing paper and a pencil. They hurry into the kitchen, where Ray lifts the oilcloth off the table so she'll have a hard surface on which to write. Mary hovers over her while they compose a letter to *Der Tog*, which Ray painstakingly prints in her best Yiddish hand: How can they find out when the Quaker farm will start? How far from New York will it be located? Will the Quakers help Ray and Mary Lifton bring family members from Latvia to the farm?

"Tell him Hinda knows how to take care of a cow, and di mameh sells the vegetables she grows herself," Mary leans over Ray's shoulder and dictates. "Tell him that Hirschel can fix machinery. Remember when he was just a little boy he fixed the broken sewing machine that not even der tateh knew what to do with!

"Tell him they'd be very happy to learn any work they have to for a farm, and they'll all work very hard." Mary keeps nudging Ray, pushing at the small of her back.

"Stop already!" Ray yells, shrugging her off. But she writes down everything Mary says. A few days later Ray receives a formally worded letter from *Der Tog*'s editorial office in Brooklyn. *Der Tog* is sorry to inform the Mesdames Lifton that it is *Der Tog*'s understanding that for the time being, the administrators of the Quaker farm, which will begin operations this coming July and will be located in Iowa, are intending to bring only thirty German and Austrian Jewish refugees there for resettlement.

A few weeks later Mary reads in the *Forverts* that an Orthodox Jewish group called the Agudah is hoping to meet with President Roosevelt and convince him to use his influence to let in more refugees from Eastern Europe. They're going to promise him that they'll take full responsibility for the refugees, so none of them will be a public charge. Mary rushes to Ray's apartment again, clutching the newspaper, her head throbbing with plans for her family. If Agudah will help, they can have three little apartments, Hinda and di mameh, Chana and her husband and kids, Hirschel and his wife and baby. Or maybe two apartments will do. Chana may take in Hinda and di mameh . . . Maybe they can all live in Brooklyn, near Sarah, who's their relative, too . . . Maybe Sarah will even take in Hinda, and Chana can take in di mameh . . . Mary can go see them all after work—she'll go several times a week. She'll be there as much as she can. Hirschel, Avromeleh! How wonderful to hold her little nephew . . . There's no reason anyone needs to find out about Moishe . . . As she's hurrying to Ray's place, she sees a yellow cab passing, and she waves the driver down. She knows the cab will cost more money than she makes in two or three hours of work, but she doesn't want to waste any time.

She rings the bell hard, and the door is opened by Ray's missus, who always has a panicked look since those terrible days last November, like she's expecting the other shoe to drop any minute now in America. "Your sister went out about a hour ago, but she said she won't be long," the missus tells Mary in a feeble voice. "You can come inside if you like and wait in her room."

"That's okay. I'll just wait here on the stoop," Mary says. She's too agitated to sit alone in Ray's dark room. "Thanks anyway, Mrs. Levine." She turns her collar up against the cold. In a few minutes she sees Ray coming down the street, shoulders hunched, her features twisted in a scowl.

"Look, read this!" Mary yells, skipping down the steps, waving the folded-back newspaper, the article showing, at her sister's face. "We gotta go put Chana and di mameh and all of them on the list in case President Roosevelt agrees."

Ray pushes the paper out of her face. "I read it already. I went to find out already from somebody who knows. That's where I been. The rabbi at Tifereth Jacob, the shul I go to for the holidays, he says the Agudah wants to bring over Talmudic scholars and young yeshiva students. Not bakers and old ladies and tailors. It's not for people like us," Ray says with a bitter shrug.

I can barely imagine how my poor mother lived through those desperate days. Moishe must have seemed to her her pearl of great price, since it was for him that she gave up Dominick, who might have known how to help her. Of course she would cling to Moishe: to throw away what she'd paid for so dearly would have made her emptiness terrifyingly complete. She was bitter that he wouldn't lift a finger to help, disgusted that he didn't give a damn that the world was smashing to pieces—yet how could she even keep going without the occasional comfort of his presence?

Late winter, 1939. He'd told her he had to go to Boston for a few days, but that was ten days ago. My mother is simmering with anger like a slow-boiling pot. She needs him, and where the hell is he? There's a hole in her heart, but he doesn't give a damn. And on top of everything else she has to worry that he'll leave her. She's as sure as if she had a crystal ball before her that he's got another woman in Boston—he's probably got them in Albany too, and Rochester, and all those places where he goes, for what reason she still doesn't know.

Finally, late Monday evening, she hears his key in the lock, and in he walks. She'd been sitting up in bed, reading a newspaper. She puts the paper down but stays where she is, waiting for him to give her his excuses about why he stayed away so long this time. He pulls off his snow-dusted hat and coat and drapes them over a chair, not saying a word. She can see from his glowering expression that something is wrong. "What?" she asks.

"That jackass Kowalski blew the whole thing, and now he's run off to Canada."

"Who? What whole thing?"

"The guy I've been working with. The fucking idiot! Don't worry, there's no way anything can be pinned on me." Moishe sits down on the bed, sighs hard, buries his head in his hands.

"Morris, what do you mean 'pinned'?" She sees how shaken he is and she's alarmed. She throws her arms around him, forgetting she's been furious. "Won't you tell me what happened, Morris?"

He lets himself be hugged for a minute, then shrugs her off. "It's too complicated to explain," he mutters. "Anyway, it's over now . . . Look, Mary, I'm bushed. Do you mind if we go to bed?"

She's afraid to think about what it is that he hasn't been telling her all these months. "Yes, of course," she says. She kisses the top of his head maternally. She'll only let herself think that right now he needs her, and she wants to give him whatever he needs. He's what she has, all she really has.

She takes out of a drawer the sheer black nightgown he's always liked on her, and she goes into the bathroom with it. She gets out of the plaid woolen bathrobe with its ripped breast pocket that she wears when she's alone, washes herself everywhere with a soapy cloth, rinses it with warm water, and scrubs at herself again. Then she dabs a little bit of Evening in Paris on her neck, her wrists, behind her ears, like she always does for him. She combs her hair and applies rouge to her cheeks and eyeshadow to her lids. Finally, she puts on the nightgown.

When she comes out of the bathroom, Moishe is still sitting on the bed, his head buried in his hands again. He gets up and goes into the bathroom. After a minute, Mary hears the toilet flush, and then he's back in the room with her. He pulls off his clothes, hangs up his shirt and suit in the closet, and drapes his tie over them. The look on his face is distracted, like he's deep in thought. He turns the light off before he climbs into his side of the bed.

She reaches for him. She slips her hand under the waistband of his shorts and strokes his flat belly lightly, moving her fingers downward. But his muscles contract at her touch and he clutches her wrist. "Not tonight, sweetheart," he tells her. She rolls away quickly, like he's slapped her face, and curls into a tight ball, her back to him. Why did he bother to come to her this evening if he doesn't even want her?

"Hey, don't be mad," he says into the darkness. "Things have been a mess. Nothing bad—it's all legit, but it shook me up." He turns her around and nuzzles his rough cheek against her breast. "I just had to come over here. There wasn't anyplace else I wanted to go. Hey, I love you, sweetheart." He lays his head on her shoulder and clutches at her waist. She puts her arms around him and wills herself to believe him. In a minute she's petting his head like he's a little kid with a skinned knee. Pretty soon he's sleeping. She inhales his musky pomade. At least when he's with her, no matter how disturbed she is about what's happening in Europe, she can't go crazy running the maze. She needs his presence so much.

The window shade isn't pulled down all the way and enough moonlight comes in through the window that she sees Moishe's face. There are hollows under his eyes, and she can see from the occasional tic on his eyelid how tense he's been. It makes her sad for him. She places her lips on his forehead softly, so it won't awaken him.

Eventually Moishe gets a new job. This one he's not mysterious about—assistant business manager at Rosenstein Knitting Mills. He isn't traveling anymore, but he's gotten out of the habit of seeing her every couple of days.

More than ten days can go by before he comes around, and then he's usually in a lousy mood. He loathes his fucking imbecile boss, he says. "This isn't the job for me either. I don't know where I belong," he snarls. Half the time he doesn't even want her.

Oh, Mama, my Mama, what hell you lived through then, terrified you'd lost him, that spurious pearl for which you'd paid so dearly; terrified at the same time you'd soon lose all else that was precious to you. Not one thing would be left to tie you to this earth.

Spring, 1939. Ray is wearing a dark little hat with a veil that makes her look like she's at an interment, but she's sitting next to my mother on a bench in River Park. "There's no more places we can go to ask for help," she says grimly. "Only God can help us."

My mother jumps up, seizing her sweater from the back of the bench. "You're saying you want to give up on them. You bitch, you! I'll never do it!" She shouts so loud that a boy on a scooter stops to see what's going on, and she storms off. Ray calls her back, but Mary keeps walking. She'd rather die than give up on Hirschel.

The next day after work, she and Paula squeeze into the crowded elevator together. Mary worries that Paula, who's not very steady on her braced leg, will be knocked about, and she holds on to her. "Say, did you happen to hear Mrs. Roosevelt speaking on the radio last night?" Paula asks. "Such a nice lady, a friend to the Jews even more than her husband is."

And as Mary is walking to the train station, she has an idea. Why didn't she think of it before? She'll write Mrs. Roosevelt and tell her that the anti-Semites are much stronger in Latvia than people in America know. She'll tell her about Hirschel losing his job, Hinda being assaulted, her brother-in-law losing his bakery, the children afraid to go to school. She'll tell her about all the places she and Ray have been to or written to, and nobody has wanted to help them rescue their family; everyone is saying there's no danger in Latvia, and even if there were, Jews from Eastern Europe can't get into America. She'll beg Mrs. Roosevelt for help. She'll open her heart to this fine person.

Mary hangs on to the overhead strap in the crowded train, and as she's jostled about, she's writing and rewriting the letter in her head. But she can't write English. She'll have to find someone to write the letter for her . . .

Impossible to ask Moishe. He'd say the president's wife is too busy to read the thousands of letters she gets from strangers; he'd make her feel foolish for even thinking of it.

Who does she know who writes English? Selma! Her old friend from Seidman and Sons. Selma went to school in America till she was fourteen, and she stopped only because she had to go out to work when her father died. Mary ran into her last year, pushing a baby carriage and leading her little girl by the hand. "Promise you'll come visit—4444 Webster Avenue. It's easy to remember," Selma said. "The name on the bell is Karsh. Mr. and Mrs. Howie Karsh."

The next Saturday morning, my mother walks over to Webster Avenue, remembering how she and Selma sewed Selma's wedding dress six years earlier. Ah, they'd had such a good time doing it, such laughs and merriment. "You'll be next, Mary!" Selma said. My mother had been sure that was true . . . But she can't let herself grow maudlin now about her old disappointment when she needs to be thinking about the letter.

Mr. and Mrs. Howie Karsh live on the first floor of a six-story brick building. The baby carriage Mary saw the year before has been exchanged for a stroller, which is parked in the dimly lit hallway next to the door of the Karsh's apartment. Mary can hear a little girl laughing and then footsteps when she rings the bell.

Selma, wearing a quilted housecoat and big metal curlers in her hair, opens the door. "Mary!" she squeals, and they throw themselves into one another's arms. "Oh, it's so good to see you! Come on in. Pardon the mess," Selma says, pulling Mary into a front room cluttered with a big tattered couch and chairs and a playpen with a toddler inside it who's chewing on a Zwieback cracker and shouting, "'lo, 'lo" and waving at Mary. A toy train is circling the tracks, humming quietly, around the perimeter of the playpen.

Selma is no longer the young woman she was when she worked with Mary in the shop, and she's even more twisted with scoliosis than when Mary ran into her a year ago. But she's as lively as ever, and her face is still as sweet and round as an apple. "Howie! My friend Mary is here," she calls. "Rosalie, this is Mommy's best friend from the shop," Selma says to the big-eyed child who's now peeking out at Mary from behind her mother's legs. "Mary and Howie, you remember each other, don't you?" she says when a short, barrel-chested man in an undershirt appears in the living room. His coarse hair sticks out like hedgehog bristles.

"Sure, you're the one who helped Selma sew her beautiful wedding dress," Howie says affably. "She told me a lot of times that of all her friends from the shop she misses you the most. Good to see you again!" He shakes Mary's hand vigorously.

"Good to see you, too, Howie!" Mary feels a twinge of guilt, because when she met Howie six years ago she thought, How will Selma be able to sleep with such an ugly man? But now Mary sees his warm brown eyes and sweet manner.

"I'm making some coffee," Selma says and is already on her way to the kitchen. "Come on in and talk to me while I do it, Mary."

Sitting at the little table in the kitchen, my mother tells Selma about the alarming news she's getting from her family, and that she's been turned away at all the places she's gone to beg for assistance to get them out of Europe. "So I came up with this plan of writing to Mrs. Roosevelt for help." She worries when she says it that Selma will think she's dumb to write to the wife of the president.

But Selma cries, "Mary, what a great idea! We'll do it right now." She stops her coffee making and throws open several cluttered drawers to search for a pen, an envelope and stamps, some nice writing paper. "My whole family— my *zaydeh* and *bubbeh*, my mother and father, two aunts and an uncle, two cousins, my sister—all of us came from Poland on the same boat when I was a little kid," Selma says as she takes stacks of things out of drawers and stuffs them back in again. "So I have no one left over there, thank God. But I know how worried you must be about everything that's happening . . . You know, I bet Mrs. Roosevelt will do something to help you. She's such a nice person." Mary is thankful that Selma thinks she's doing the right thing.

Selma finally finds all the writing paraphernalia she needs, and she clears the kitchen table. She sits down, ready to write. She squeezes Mary's hand encouragingly while Mary tells her everything that must go into the letter. Selma says she'll put it all in, just as Mary said, and she bends her head to the task. Mary watches Selma form the English words in her careful, round, schoolgirl hand. As Selma writes, Mary thinks, I'm so happy for her that she's got a nice life; she deserves it. But she was lucky too. Maybe if I hadn't come all alone to a strange country when I was such a young ignorant girl, maybe if I'd had my whole family with me in America from the beginning, I wouldn't have—I couldn't have—done the things that cost me so dearly . . .

Selma wants to copy the letter over because her pen leaked and there's an ugly ink spot on the paper. Mary says she doesn't want to trouble her to redo the whole letter; but Selma insists. "If you write to the First Lady it's got to be perfect," and she bends her head to the task again.

The little girl Rosalie suddenly peeks around the corner and then paddles into the kitchen, looking at Mary shyly. "Mommy, you been in here so long," she tells Selma, tugging on her housecoat. "When can we go for a walk?"

"In a little while, dumpling. I'm helping my friend Mary with something very important."

Rosalie juts out a lip. "But you and Daddy promised we'd go get me a Charlotte Russe today."

Even pouty, she's a darling child, Mary thinks, with her big brown eyes and honey-colored hair. "Do you want to come sit on my lap and I'll sing you some songs?" Mary offers.

"That's a good idea," Selma says, her head still bent over the letter.

Rosalie sidles up to Mary, and Mary lifts her onto her lap, remembering a Yiddish nursery rhyme from when she was a child. She takes Rosalie's little hands in hers and claps them together softly in time to the rhythm: *Patche patche kikhelach, der tateh vet koifn shikhelach, di mameh vet shtriken ze-khelach, far di maydeleh mit roite bekhelach.* Pat, pat, little cookies. Father will buy little shoes, and mother will knit little socks, for the little girl with rosy cheeks . . . Mary used to recite it to Hirschel when he was just a baby. She'd said *yingeleh*, little boy, instead of *maydeleh*, little girl. It was *his* little feet she'd hold and clap together gently, and then she'd tickle him, all the way from his tiny feet to his rosy cheeks. He would laugh and laugh, just as Rosalie is doing now. How hard to believe that was more than thirty-five years ago.

"More, more," Rosalie pleads, and Mary starts all over again. She loves the warm smell of the little girl's hair and her sweet little hands and silky skin. Mary thinks she would have given anything to have had a child like this one.

Selma finishes the letter and addresses the envelope to Mrs. Eleanor Roosevelt, First Lady, The White House, Washington, D.C. She and Mary go out to the front room where Howie and the toddler are sitting together on the floor, running the toy train. "I'm going to get these curlers out of my hair and put some clothes on, and I'll walk over to the post office with Mary so she can mail her letter," Selma tells Howie.

"Say, why don't I take the kids to the park, and you two spend some time visiting, go to a movie or something," Howie offers. Rosalie plops in his lap. "I'll get this pumpkin over here that Charlotte Russe, and we'll go on the merry-go-round and the swings too," he says, stroking his daughter's pretty head as she nods an energetic yes. "My wife needs a little vacation," he tells Mary. "She hardly ever gets out away from the kids."

Mary and Selma mail the letter at the post office and then walk arm-in-arm, the way they used to when they palled around years ago, over to the Fox Theatre. They buy their tickets and then stand in the concession line, because Selma says that hot-buttered popcorn is her big weakness whenever she goes to the movies.

"Mary, do you mind if I ask what happened to that fella you used to go out with who bought you all those nice presents?" Selma says as they're waiting.

Mary feels her face grow hot. She's ashamed to tell Selma that she's still with him after all these years and that she's never gotten him to make an honest woman of her. "Oh, that was so long ago," she answers vaguely.

Inside the theater, Selma munches popcorn as they wait for the movie to start. "Say, I just thought of something, Mary," she says suddenly. "Howie has a cousin—a really sweet man who lost his wife two years ago. No kids and a good job in cloaks. I know he's really lonely. He'd love to meet someone like you. How about it?" She squeezes Mary's arm excitedly. "Meet him at least, okay?"

The theater darkens, which means that everyone must be quiet and Mary doesn't have to answer Selma's proposal. After the *March of Time* newsreel and the cartoons, the music blares and the RKO emblem—a radio tower atop a globe—appears on the screen. The main feature is a movie called *Love Affair*, with Charles Boyer and Irene Dunne. It's the kind of movie that, long ago, Mary loved—about people who are used to lives of pink champagne. Boyer and Dunne, lovers, are sailing to New York on a luxurious ship, crossing the Atlantic from somewhere in Europe. All the women passengers are dressed in ermines or minks and long evening gowns, and the men are in tuxedoes and white bow ties. They all have lavish staterooms in which to sleep. They eat in dining rooms decorated by white tablecloths and tapering candles in silver candlesticks. They sip cocktails with dainty straws and take cigarettes from gold cigarette cases. On their Atlantic Ocean, there is no sign of a ship called the *St. Louis* and the nine hundred souls who have been denied safe harbor everywhere and are being returned to Europe and certain death. There is no sign that the whole world is poised for war and that millions will soon be killed. No sign even that the worldwide depression continues and many are starving. No life-and-death struggles of any kind. This is a world in which the only thing that matters is the two lovers—a man and a woman figuring out how they might spend their opulent and carefree lives together.

17

Summary, 1939

TIME ON THE MARCH

The Senate Committee on Immigration has amended the Wagner-Rogers bill that would open American doors to twenty thousand German-Jewish refugee children over the next two years. Under this proposed change, the children would be counted against the quota for all German immigrants. *Senator Robert F. Wagner:* This is unacceptable to me. It would convert my bill from a humane proposal to help children who are in acute distress to a proposal with needlessly cruel consequences for adults in Germany who are in need of succor and are fortunate to obtain visas under the present drastic quota restrictions.

More than six weeks have passed and no word from Mrs. Roosevelt. Another dead end. My mother feels like a mouse trapped in a wall—darting here, there, up, down, searching in vain for the obscured opening. Where can she go that she hasn't already gone?

In twenty more years, I'll be a cocky young American woman, nothing in my pockets yet, but confident that soon the world will be my oyster, which I with sword will open. I'll explain to myself and anyone who cares to listen that my mother was a poor illiterate immigrant who knew nothing about the workings of the world. I'll boast, "If I'd been alive at that time, I'd have known what needed to be done to extricate our family from hell and find them safe harbor."

Fifty years later, more steeped in the facts and somewhat less brash, I'll understand that there was probably nothing at all she could have done to change their fate.

One evening she comes home from work, and through the mailbox slots she can see a long white envelope. The return address in the upper left corner says THE WHITE HOUSE. Her heart thuds as violently as it used to when she was waiting for Moishe. She fumbles with the little mailbox key, unlocks the box, seizes the envelope and tears it open. In her haste she rips a corner of the heavy stationery on which the letter is written. It's more a note than a letter. The language is simple enough so that she can make it out. She sees with disappointment that the signature is not even Eleanor Roosevelt, First Lady, as it had been in her lovely fantasies. It's signed, *Yours truly, Malvina Thompson, Secretary to Mrs. Roosevelt.*

My dear Miss Lifton:

Mrs. Roosevelt is very sorry to hear about your family and knows how worried you must be over their situation. She has learned through the State Department that the yearly immigration quota from Latvia, which is based on 2% of the number of Latvian immigrants in the United States in 1890, is 286. She advises you to have your relatives register with the American Consulate in Riga.

And that's all. Mary sinks down on the stoop, too livid with disappointment to budge.

Mr. Kronin, the middle-aged widower who lives across the hall, comes out the front door, his lunch pail under his arm, wearing the faded overalls in which she always sees him going off to work. He'd asked her for a date once. It was a time when Moishe hadn't come by for a couple of weeks, and for a moment Mary thought, It would serve that bastard right if I went out with somebody else, anybody else . . . But what would be the point? "Oh, thank you, but I'm engaged," she told Mr. Kronin straight out. It was barely a lie because she's been engaged body and soul to Moishe since she first laid eyes on him, though to what end she still doesn't know.

Mr. Kronin has remained friendly despite her rejection. She slides over to the side now so he'll have room to come down the steps. "You okay, Mary?" he stops to ask.

She realizes she must look bizarre, sitting there so morose with a letter dangling from her fingers. "Oh, yeah, sure. Just getting the fresh air," she says brightly.

"Wish I could. I got night shift at the factory this week. Well, have a good evening," he says.

"Okay. Don't work too hard," she tells him. She waits until he walks off toward the El before she rereads the terse note from Malvina Thompson, secretary to Mrs. Roosevelt. Then she wads it into a tight ball. She'd like to throw the balled-up piece of White House stationery at Malvina Thompson's head. Did Mrs. Roosevelt even see Mary's letter? Damn fool, she castigates herself. How could she believe even for a minute that the First Lady of America would take an interest in the sufferings of poor Jews from a little place she probably never even heard of? And now what the hell can she do? To whom can she go? She's tried everything already. She looks up and down the empty block. She jumps to her feet, peers at the blank cloudless sky. God in Heaven, what else can I do? Tell me! she screams silently to the blue ether. She waits a long time, like a madwoman or an idiot, like she's expecting a booming voice to answer back.

The news from Europe grows steadily worse. The Gestapo is now firmly established in Czech Bohemia and Moravia. And the Polish government is getting as bad as the Reich, enacting laws to obliterate Jews from the country's economic and social life. Terrified Polish Jews, tens of thousands of them, are fleeing the prelude to the unspeakable. But those who manage to get as far as Rumania are expelled, back to Poland again: Rumania will no longer allow emigrants even to pass through that country. The appalling procession of events doesn't stop. Pro-Nazi Lithuanians greet the German Army with frenzied joy when they come to seize Kleipeda, Lithuania's only access to the Baltic Sea.

With all these calamities to worry about, my mother is ashamed she expends anxiety on Moishe, but she can't help herself. The worse things get, the more desperate she is to keep him. She has nothing else to hold on to. It's not the sex that she needs from him anymore; she just needs him to be near. He's her one bit of respite from the apprehension that's settled like a ghoulish lodger in her head.

At the end of June, she gets laid off from work because the season is over, and now she has nothing to do all day except tear her hair about Hirschel, di mameh, Avromeleh—and wait for Moishe. When she first moved into this apartment on Tremont, when their romance had sprung to life again after a year apart, if he couldn't come see her, he'd call. They arranged with Mr.

Solomon at the candy store that whenever she got a phone call, Mr. Solomon would immediately dispatch his granddaughter to her. The girl—a somber little person of nine or ten who lives with Mr. Solomon and his wife in the store's backroom—would arrive breathless from her speedy dash down the block and up three flights of stairs. She'd pant, "Miz Lifton, he's on the line and said he'd wait till you got down to the telephone," or "He doesn't have time to wait for you to come down 'cause he gotta get back to work, but he says he'll see you tomorrow night." Mary had gotten in the habit of saving nickels to tip the child; but now the nickels pile up or she hands them to the beggars on the street.

Sometimes when Mary goes into Mr. Solomon's store to buy her newspapers, if she hasn't heard from Moishe for days she can't help herself: "I didn't get any phone calls, did I, Mr. Solomon?" she asks.

"Mereleh, would I keep your phone calls from you?" the old man says with a sad little smile, his always-red-rimmed eyes looking as though they've cried for her. "Whenever you get a call, I send my Sheila over right away, just like always."

Mary is embarrassed to have asked, and embarrassed that a stranger is witness to her business and feels sorry for her. She promises herself she'll never ask again—until the next time, of course, when she can't help herself.

One Sunday morning, Mary wakes up, alone, and remembers a dream she was having—about Selma's little daughter, Rosalie. In the dream Mary took her to the Bronx Zoo and bought her a strawberry ice-cream cone. Rosalie was licking it with her little pink tongue while they watched the monkeys doing somersaults on the monkey bars. Mary was holding Rosalie's sweet hand, saying, "Look, darling, the way that cute baby is hanging on to its mama's fur," when suddenly Rosalie changed into Hirschel at four years old. And then changed again, into Hirschel's little son Avrom. Though Mary has never seen Avromeleh, she somehow knew in the dream it was his hand she was holding. What bliss. She wanted never to awaken. But she did. And that was when she decided she would go visit Selma and ask to take Rosalie to the zoo. The last time she saw them, Selma made Mary promise she'd come by whenever she felt like it. "Rosalie would love it, too," Selma said.

Mary fixes herself a cup of coffee and sits sipping it at the table, remembering her dream, floating in the strange contentment of it. She'll get dressed right away and go over to Selma's before it gets too hot. She'll buy Rosalie a red balloon at the zoo . . . Mary is at the sink, rinsing her cup, when she hears

Moishe's key in the lock. Anger wrestles with relief inside her. He hasn't been around since Saturday a week ago.

"Hey, doll," he calls when she doesn't run to greet him. His white shirt is half-open and Mary can see he's wearing a black bathing suit, the crinkly hairs of his chest peeking out over its scooped top. "Say, let's go to Orchard Beach!" He takes the cup from her hand, pulls her to him, and plants a rough kiss on her nose.

She rears back against the sink. She's not going to cheapen herself by jumping into his arms when she hasn't heard boo from him for eight days. "I thought you went off to the Hawaiian Islands for a vacation," she says with all the sarcasm she can muster.

"I've been working my tail off, Mary. That Rosenstein is the original Simon Legree."

"But you don't work all night long. Why couldn't you come by at night when you finished working?" She hears her nagging voice but won't change it.

"Look," he says evenly. "I can't function under the pressure I get all day long unless I'm getting eight hours at night, and I don't sleep well these days unless I'm in my own bed."

She's dumbfounded. "But you always said you never slept so well in your life like you do when we're holding each other."

A gamut plays on his face—mad, sad, cold, kind . . . He chooses unruffled. "This has absolutely nothing to do with you, sweetheart. Just be patient, okay? My nerves have been a mess. Let's have a nice time today, okay? We'll go eat Chinese after the beach too. Come on, doll. Go get your bathing suit." He says it like an order. She hesitates. She'd like to tell him, Go to hell. But she needs him. She does.

He's light and jovial as they walk to the bus stop, like nothing at all is wrong between them. He puts his arm around her shoulders while they wait for the bus. She lets him, but she can't get his declaration out of her head: "I don't sleep well these days unless I'm in my own bed." The only hold I've had on him was his desire for me, she thinks, and if that goes, what can make him stay? What will she do if he leaves her? Her heart is a boulder in her chest.

At the beach, she goes into the changing cabin to put on her bathing suit. Three girls, around twenty-one or twenty-two years old, are giggling about the fellas who just tried to pick them up outside. The girls take off their brightly colored sundresses and put on daring two-piece bathing suits that bare their midriffs. In Mr. Solomon's store last week Mary saw Paulette Goddard in a two-piece bathing suit on the cover of *Look* magazine, but hardly anyone wears two-piece bathing suits on the beach. She glances at the girls, who pay no attention to her. She can't help seeing how firm and smooth their bodies are. They're young enough to be her daughters, only about ten years younger than Moishe. They look sexy in their new suits. He must lust for girls like that now, Mary thinks.

She gets out of her dress and underwear and pulls on her old black-and-white swimming costume. Then she rolls her clothes up and tucks them under her arm. Before she leaves, she examines herself in the long mirror near the exit. She once looked so good in this swimming costume, but no longer. She thinks the flesh above her knees has begun to dimple, and there are places on her thighs that look like organge peel, like old lady's skin. And her breasts beneath the crisscrossed bodice of her suit don't look high and firm as they did just a few years ago. She hates the way she looks these days.

He's waiting for her by the drinking fountains. To her he still looks like a boy. The lines under the woolen bathing suit that covers his torso are full of grace, like the picture she once saw of a statue of the young King David. She feels self-conscious and dowdy.

"Hey, you're gorgeous in that, sweetheart," Moishe says, as though he doesn't notice how the years are changing her. She wonders if he says that to make up for how he hurt her when he told her he didn't like to spend the night with her anymore.

He has a week's vacation coming in August. It would be such a help if he would be with her that week, like that first summer they had the apartment on Charlotte Street—a sweet week, like playing house: she cooked for him, they sat together while he read his books, they took walks in the park or window-shopped on Southern Boulevard. A few days of his presence would give her blessed respite from the demons in her head—bogeymen under a child's bed, waiting to grab a leg and trip her up and cut her heart out.

The week before his vacation, he stays with her Saturday night, and the next morning she fixes him bagels and lox for breakfast. She carries it to him on the tray she'd bought when they first got this apartment on Tremont. She gets back in the bed beside him and they eat. She plans to wait until he's finished and then ask if they can spend his vacation week together.

But there's still a half bagel left on his plate when he wipes his lips with the paper napkin, clears his throat, and says, "I promised my mother that during my vacation I'd take her to a reunion at her friend Tamara's in Philadelphia. It's with all the *landsleit* from Nowy Korczyn—you know, where we came from in the old country."

Mary is disappointed because that means she'll lose a day of his vacation; but it would be haggling and probably useless to argue over a day. "Which day is it?" she asks.

"The whole week," he says matter-of-factly. "People are coming from Chicago and everywhere. It's a big thing. We'll leave the Saturday I'm off and come back the following Saturday . . ."

She feels like a twig in a maelstrom swirling out of control. "Morris, what about me?" she cries.

"Sweetheart, it's my mother's birthday. They're honoring her at the reunion. What am I going to do, tell her she can't be there for the honor?"

"But why do you have to be gone the whole week that you're off?" She tries to calm herself. She doesn't want to make a scene. She just wants him for a few days.

"Because the damn reunion is a whole week long!"

"And you're gonna be with that girl the whole week?" The young, educated grandniece of the mayor has never left her head.

"What girl? What are you talking about?"

She senses he knows damn well. "The one your mother wanted you to meet."

"Aw, for crissake, Mary, that was six years ago. She's probably married by now."

"Will she be at the reunion?"

"How the hell do I know? If she's still living in Philly, yeah, she'll probably be there. It's at her aunt's house, for crissake."

My mother doesn't believe he doesn't know whether or not the mayor's grandniece is married. She's certain his mother is cooking something up. She probably said to him, You're almost thirty-three years old and it's high time you found a girl and settled down. Six years ago, when his desire for her was hot, he told his mother he'd already chosen his girl. But it's not the same anymore.

The grandniece of the whilom mayor of Nowy Korczyn becomes another constant bogeyman, romping malevolently in her head together with the ghastly old ones.

———————

He's in Philadelphia with his mother, and Mary forces herself not to think of who else may be there. On Saturday she wakes up early in the morning and goes to Crotona Park to feed the ducks, and on Sunday afternoon she goes to the free concert in the park. Monday night she has supper with Ray at the Automat. Tuesday she and Selma and Rosalie take a bus downtown and go to a new movie in color, in which Judy Garland sings and dances—and for a little while, Mary takes such pleasure in Rosalie's glee at a man who looks like he's made of tin cans that she forgets Europe is on fire; she forgets that her lover may, at that very moment, be falling in love with someone else who his mother thinks is much more suitable for him than she's ever been. She waits for the week to be over. She has to keep believing he'll come back to her.

Wednesday, August 23, the middle of that hard week. Mr. Solomon has put Mary's three Yiddish papers aside under the counter. "How are you doing, Mr. Solomon?" she says when she walks into his candy store that evening. She hands him three nickels as usual.

"Seen the headlines?" he asks excitedly.

"Soviets Sign Non-Aggression Pact with Nazis," all the papers announce. She leans on the counter in the dim, stifling little store, reading the front page of the *Freiheit,* which is on top of the stack he's given her.

"Sit down, sit down," Mr. Solomon says and pulls his chair from behind the counter over to where she's standing. An electric table fan that's turned on high has been whirring in his direction, but he now aims it toward her.

"Oh, no, you enjoy it," she says, because sweat pours from his brow in little rivulets.

"No, sit, sit, in the cool," he insists. "*Nu,* so how do you like that?" He points a gnarled finger at the headline. "The Ribbentrop-Molotov Pact, it's called." He's told Mary several times in the past about his brother and sister and their children and grandchildren in Vilna; he's been very worried about them. "We got reason to celebrate now, Mary. Hitler's gonna stop moving east now," he declares happily.

"Do you think that's really what it means?" she asks. She begins reading the article again. So it's really over, all her agonizing? Has she spent all these years worrying for nothing? It's too good to be true.

"Well, Hitler won't want to make Mr. Stalin mad at him, will he?" the old candy-store owner says. His red-rimmed eyes always give him an ancient, tragic look, which makes Mary think of illustrations she's seen of the patriarchs in the Bible—Abraham, Isaac, Jacob. But today Mr. Solomon is all smiles. "A blessing on Stalin's head," he proclaims, waving a shaky fist in victory.

She wants to share his gladness, but still she worries. What if it's Stalin who won't want to make Hitler mad? She wishes she were working in the shop now, so she could talk to people like Jack who really seem to understand politics and what's going on in the world. Can it be true that all it takes is one stroke of the pen, and all the terrors, all the anguish, her worst nightmares and bogeymen will evaporate like a wispy puff of smoke?

"Mark my words, the biggest problems are over," Mr. Solomon reiterates, "because the Soviet Union protects Jews." He wags his head, and his beard, long like a prophet's, wags too.

An elderly man whom Mary has seen in the store before walks in and Mr. Solomon calls out in triumph, "Pelsky, did you hear? The Nazis signed a non-aggression pact with the Soviets!"

Nine days later, Hitler attacks Poland. Mary's Yiddish newspapers say, "Jews Moving East, Hoping Soviets Will Protect Them."

From what happened later and all I know of him—a man who felt cheated of his rightful fortune and looked always for the main chance; a mama's boy, who never could bring himself to leave the old neighborhood; and yet a practiced seducer, a lady's man ("All the women were crazy about him," his nephew would tell me a half century after his death): from all of that, this I surmise:

The porch of the Philadelphia home of the daughter of Nowy Korczyn's old mayor. Moishe, in the shadows. He sits alone on a canopied porch swing meant for two lovers. The darkness that surrounds him is broken only by a square of light coming through the living room window. Once in a while he pushes off with a foot to keep the swing in lazy motion. The creak and groan of rusty springs and old wood; the slow, hypnotic back and forth, back and forth; the darkness that envelopes him; the sounds of a clarinet and accordion playing klezmer music, and laughter and voices that float out from the living room to the quiet and loneliness around him—they all add to his melancholy. Mary was right, of course, that his mother brought him to this party in Philadelphia to meet the mayor's grandniece, who is still unmarried at thirty, and who has a horsy laugh and a nose like a sickle and saggy breasts that sit almost on top of her ample waist.

"She could be Maimonides' great-great-granddaughter, for all I care," he told his mother testily when they were alone again after the afternoon's introduction. He was incensed that she imagined he'd even consider it, no matter what *yicchus* the girl and her family had. How could a man even get it up? Moishe didn't say that—he always tried to spare his mother crudity—but he was adamant in his refusal.

"Okay, okay, Morris. No is no, and I can't force you." His mother threw up her hands as if in surrender. But they both knew she'd already won something. He had agreed to come to Philadelphia to meet a suitable young woman. If he doesn't like this one, she'll find him another. It's only a matter of time, as long as he's open to it.

Of course this isn't the first time Moishe has thought, This thing with Mary has played itself out and I've gotta end it. But he hadn't been able to do it. Why, he didn't know. Maybe it was inertia . . . or he felt sorry for her . . . or he remembered how she used to excite him and that memory excited him all over again. Yeah, he'd had her under his skin all right . . . Anyway, whatever the reason—though he's slept with more girls than he can count, and when he and Kowalski used to travel around doing their racket he'd had at least two or three of them in every single town just dying to see him—still, he couldn't break it off with Mary.

But now he's quickly approaching middle age and he's so unsettled. No decent job, no consolation of a family to make up for the frustrations life has thrown him. He wants the normal things a man his age should have—a home of his own, a wife he can show off to the world and take to his mother's house for Friday-night dinner. That's what he tells himself as he swings back and forth on the creaky swing.

It wouldn't hurt if she came with a bit of money too. He hates working for someone else, the small-time-crook business is too risky, and even if he'd kept going to night school a couple of times a week how long would it be until he even got a degree? —He'd be forty-five at least . . . If he could marry a girl with some money he might open his own business. Start a knitting mill maybe. He's a hell of a lot smarter than that jackass Rosenstein, who bought his mill with his wife's money. Yeah, he'd like to meet a young, attractive, educated woman with a bit of money who could help him along.

But he does not take his defection from Mary lightly. He knows she's given him everything she has. She's not the kind of person who could hold back anything, and he loved her for it. Their relationship had been a big thing for him, too. Seven years, for crissake.

He looks out at the dark sky, the sliver of a moon, the cold and distant stars. How hard life is, probably for everyone, he thinks. He remembers how in the beginning he couldn't get her out of his head—all the wonderful times they had together. When she danced naked for him, wearing only the green stone necklace he gave her . . . When he used to gaze up at the window of the apartment on Charlotte before he went upstairs, and it was always a good thing he was wearing a long coat because otherwise his excitement at the thought that soon they'd be on her bed would be apparent to the world . . . When they hadn't seen each other for a year and suddenly she was standing in front of him at the coffee shop and they locked together, zap, like there were magnets inside them . . . She'd been the woman of his youth, all right. But his youth is over. And so is their love affair. Like fresh snow that's turned to muddy slush. He won't keep pretending anymore.

There's no use putting it off. He gets up from the porch swing and walks down the dark street toward the lights of the boulevard where he'd gone that afternoon to buy a pack of cigarettes. He doesn't think of himself as a cruel person. He'd like to let her down easy because he believes her when she says he's all she has to live for. Yet how the hell can he sacrifice his whole life to her if he doesn't love her anymore? There's a pay phone on the corner. He'll call the candy store down the block from her and ask the old man to get her. He'll just let her know that things have changed.

Mr. Solomon answers the phone in a sleepy voice. "Do you know what time it is? It's after ten o'clock," he tells Moishe. But Moishe says it's really an emergency, so Mr. Solomon agrees to wake his granddaughter and send her to get Mary.

"Thanks very much. I'll hang on," Moishe says. Why the hell should his heart be thudding in his ears? He rehearses what he'll tell her. They need to stop seeing each other for a little while . . . She's a wonderful woman, but things have changed for him . . . It's best for her, because this way she can meet someone who'll give her more what she needs . . . Nothing he thinks of seems quite right to him.

"Hello?" Mary finally says. He can hear her breathing like she'd been running a mile. "Morris, is that you?"

"Hey, doll . . . I've really missed you," is what comes out of his mouth, like he's a ventriloquist's dummy—just the opposite of what he meant to say. "I'm coming back Saturday, sweetheart. I'll take you to Angelo's. Does that sound good?"

Mary closes her eyes. If only she could push her whole being through the phone wires to be with him this instant. "Oh, *boychikel*, I've been so lonesome for you. Hurry back to me," she breathes.

18

Late summer and fall, 1939

TIME ON THE MARCH

Jerzy Potocki, Polish Ambassador to the United States: Poland has been ruthlessly attacked by the armed forces of Germany without provocation. We did not desire this war. We did everything in our power to prevent it ... The Polish government was the first government in Europe to attempt to make permanent peace with the Third Reich. A non-aggression pact was signed in 1934. It has still five years to run.

LONDON. The British government has published a white paper that accuses the Nazis of inventing tortures almost beyond imagination. *British government spokesman:* The testimony of accredited witnesses had not been given to the world before because as long as there was the slightest prospect of reaching any settlement with the German government, it would have been wrong to do anything to embitter the relations between the two countries. On the basis of prewar reports of our diplomats on the conditions in German concentration camps, we know that victims transported to Buchenwald, where ten thousand Jews were being held, had teeth knocked out, heads bruised, and eyes blackened by guards. They were driven in trucks to the camp with their heads between their knees while guards beat them. At the camp they were driven with kicks and blows into a wire enclosure charged with electric current. After the commandant had lectured them on his views on Jews, guards came in, picked out men at random, and took them outside to be flogged. Fixed on the ground were two footplates to which a man's feet were strapped. He was then bent over a pole and his head secured between two horizontal bars. The men were given up to fifty strokes, except in the case of promiscuous flogging inflicted for sport. Each guard was only allowed to inflict ten lashes lest his strength give out.

President Franklin Delano Roosevelt: Let no man or woman thoughtlessly or falsely talk of America sending its armies to European fields. At this moment there is being prepared a proclamation of American neutrality.

———

In New York City, every week, some thirty thousand people attend meetings which Jews do well to avoid. During these meetings, which are held by groups with names like Christian Front and Christian Mobilizers, the streets of Upper Manhattan and the Bronx resound with cries of *Buy Christian! Down with the Jews!* and *Wait till Hitler comes over here!*

"Hirschel!" My mother calls in her sleep, and the shout wakens her to the pitch dark. For an instant she can't make out where she is. In her dream they'd been in a forest, enveloped in thick morning fog. Hirschel was a small child who could barely stand on his own legs, but she clutched his thin fingers and led him through dank weeds. They paused at a blueberry bush, where she plucked a handful of berries, then turned around to deposit them in his hands, which he held together tightly as though cupping water. She picked one handful after another, at great speed, because suddenly she was sure that only the berries could keep them alive. Each time she turned to deposit them, she saw that his palms were still empty and he'd shifted size—now a toddler, now ten years old and in short pants; now Hirschel the man, whom she's never seen—a man no longer young, with worried eyes and a tremor in the long, thin hands he cupped to receive the berries. She turned away, only for a frantic instant, to pluck another handful from the bush. That was when he disappeared like the smoky fog had swallowed him up—evaporated, as though he'd never existed. And my mother knew—as sure as she knew anything at all—that never again on this earth would she see her brother.

She sits up, wide awake, and clutches the pillow that's Moishe's when he's there. "That was only a dream," she says aloud. She won't let herself be afraid.

But she can't help being afraid when she gets a letter from Hirschel a few days later saying he lost his job and can't find another. The tailor for whom he's been working, the refugee from Warsaw, didn't want to lay him off but had to give work to his own brother, who just fled Poland with only his shirt on his back. *Riga is awash in Polish refugees, and every second one is a tailor. It looks like they're going to stay for a long time too. The Hebrew Immigrant Aid Society in Riga says they should try to become Latvian citizens. It was bad*

enough here before, because there are so few jobs open to Jews, but now there
are even more Jews, all of them looking for work. Please, dear sister, if you can
spare a little bit . . .

She tracks Ray down at the Automat where she always goes on Tuesday
nights with Molly and Dolly. Dolly, her fork poised in the air and her mouth
full, is holding forth, but Mary doesn't stop to listen. She waves Hirschel's
letter in Ray's face. "Listen, we gotta send him money right away," she cries.

"You know, your sister hasn't even had a chance to finish her supper yet,"
Dolly of the spinach-covered buckteeth says.

"Please shut up if you don't know about something," Mary snaps because
she has no patience with nonsense now. "They're starving there, Ray—him
and his wife and the baby."

Ray shoves her meat loaf aside and seizes the letter. "*Gottenu,*" she groans
as she reads.

"Some people are so rude," Dolly tells Molly, and they both shake their
head and glare at Mary, whom they've always thought strange, so different
from her darling sister.

The next day, as soon as the lunch bell rings, my mother runs from Seidman and Sons where she's working again to the bank on the corner of Thirty-
Seventh and cleans out her savings account, forty-two dollars, then runs to
the post office on Thirty-First, where she and Ray will buy the postal order.
Ray has gone to her bank, too, and now she's already standing in the post
office line. She's eating half a chopped-herring sandwich that she's brought
with her in a paper sack. She tries to get Mary to take the other half of the
sandwich. "We don't have time for lunch if we have to stand in this long line,"
she says, waving the grease-spotted sack at Mary.

Mary pushes it away, revolted. "You're not supposed to be eating in a
post office," she hisses at her sister. She doesn't know how Ray can eat when
there's so much to be frantic about. She wants to talk about what they'll do
if Hirschel can't find a job for a long time. She wants to talk about Hitler's
invasion of Poland, and the Poles quick surrender, and what it means for the
rest of Europe and the Jews—and Ray is munching away.

"At least we know he's safe," Ray says between mouthfuls.

"What are you talking about?" Ray's ignorance is infuriating to Mary.
"How the hell do we know that?" she demands.

"You just have to read his letter. Jews from Poland are still running to
Latvia because that's where it's still the most safe," Ray says doggedly.

"But what did he say in his other letters, and Hinda and Chana in their letters? They're in danger there," Mary cries, exasperated that Ray has gone back to her old stupid theory. "The reason Jews are running to Latvia is that they have nowhere else to go, but that doesn't make them safe!" Mary wants to shake her sister, pound her, shout in her ear until she wakes up. A wildfire is engulfing Europe bit by bit. Mary can see and smell the burning. And Ray is as dumb to it as a cow. All she can do is eat.

But if there's nothing she can do to change things, how would it help for Ray to see and smell the burning like my mother does? Cassandra, cursed with visions of horror to come and powerless to prevent the tragedy, went mad with seeing and smelling. That will be my mother's fate, maybe already is. Ray is made of coarser stuff. Ray—the funny monkey, as my mother always called her; My Ray, as I will call her—will agonize with the guilt of the survivor, but she'll keep insisting you have to eat and sleep even if the world might be falling apart, because otherwise you won't survive yourself. I'll forever do battle with her tedious "Eat! Eat! Sleep! Sleep!" regardless of what calamity looms. But when my mother will be maddened by her failures, as helpless as a hatchling in the whirlwind, My Ray will be the rock and sanctuary of my childhood.

"Why do you always have to imagine the worst?" Ray says stubbornly, wiping the herring grease from her lips with the back of her hand.

"The worst keeps coming true!" Mary struggles to keep her voice down but she wants to scream. She balls her fists tightly to keep her hands from trembling like they often do.

Ray starts on the other half of the sandwich that Mary has turned down. A gob of chopped herring slides from between the slices of rye and plops on the marble tile of the post office floor. The woman standing behind them in the post office line tsk-tsks in disgust. "Oh, sorry!" Mary exclaims, as though the fault is hers, and quickly pulls a Kleenex from her purse. She stoops to pick up the bits of herring, then rubs at the smudge with another Kleenex.

September 19, the Soviets come marching into Vilna, one of the biggest centers of Jewish culture in the world. As soon as the 8 a.m. bell rings at Seidman and Sons, Jack the cutter, who reads the newspaper in the morning before work, announces the invasion to the others. "Mazel tov! We should celebrate," the burly presser they call Commie Kennie shouts out. "Just you watch, the Soviets are gonna protect the Jews of Vilna from that hyena, Hitler."

"The Soviets will be lions and tigers!" Yakov, a little bantam rooster who's vice president of the Bronx branch of the pro-Soviet John Reed Club, cries. Some workers bang their hands together, or bang on the tables with measuring sticks or on the floor with their feet. Almost everyone cheers.

My mother isn't sure what to think, but she cheers, too; she's desperate to believe things will yet be all right. If Vilna is safe, that means Latvia is safe. It was to Vilna, about a hundred miles from Preil, that the cart driver took her on the first leg of her journey, when she left her family's home to come to America. She remembers passing the Great Synagogue of Vilna, its handsome white stones and elaborate iron gates gleaming in the moonlight. Der tateh had told her to look for it because it was one of the oldest synagogues in all of Europe, and it was the grandest anywhere, big enough to hold five thousand worshippers. As she drapes fabrics on the mannequins and pins with nimble fingers, the boulder that sat on her chest for so long begins to dissolve like salt in warm water: surely Kennie and the others are right. The Soviets will finally put the antisemiten in their place.

But they don't. The next month, there's a pogrom in Vilna that goes on for three days. Why? Any excuse is a good one—the currency has been devalued, and Lithuanian fascists are accusing the Jews of fomenting discontent over it. The Lithuanian police, instead of quashing the riots, join the delirious orgy, desecrating the Great Synagogue, tearing the Jewish quarter apart, beating any Jews they can get their hands on. The Soviets, who have come to Lithuania to take over military bases, react no more to the ransacking and bloodletting than if they'd heard that a flea was biting a mongrel dog.

Moishe comes and goes. "Working," he says curtly when my mother asks where he's been. She knows she's losing him, like he's on a train that's chugging out of the station and she's running with all her might to keep up, but she can't. Almost two weeks pass and she doesn't see him, and then he shows up again. He takes her to a dark and smoky cocktail lounge he's found in the Bronx. He orders a pink lady for her and scotch straight up for himself. "Bottoms up," he says, a movie gangster again, like in their early years, and he quaffs it in one gulp. He orders another scotch and soon another, while Mary is still sipping her pink lady. She's scared he's trying to raise drunken courage to tell her they're through. "What's going on, Morris?" she asks. She catches him glassily eyeing a redheaded girl in a décolleté orange blouse who's flashed him a toothy smile. "Listen, if you're with me, be with me," Mary hisses and elbows him hard.

"Hey, sweetheart, you're my preferred poison," he slurs and laughs and pulls her to him so hard it knocks the breath out of her. She's never seen him drunk like this.

She grasps him at the waist when they leave the Lethe Lounge because his step is unsteady, and they stumble together into the cool autumn air. She hails a cab, helps him in and out of it, takes a dollar out of his wallet to pay the driver, helps him up the stairs to her apartment, undresses him, helps him into her bed. "*Boychikel,* what is it?" she cajoles him softly, holding his head between her breasts, petting his curly hair, which is still dark like a blackbird's wing. God, don't let him leave me, she thinks. Though he's very drunk, he rolls over on top of her, and soon he's making love to her, hot breath whispering careless words into her ear. He's too drunk to remember that object he's always tried never to forget.

Is this the night the arrow finally quivers in the bull's-eye?

And then he disappears again, and she has no word from him for a week or more. That's okay, she thinks. She just needs to be able to lean her poor roiling, moiling head on his chest once in a while. If he were always around he'd see how hair-pulling-breast-beating-head-banging-circle-running batty she gets with anxieties . . .

Anyway, she's too old for a full-time lover. Her periods have even stopped. For weeks, whenever she goes to the bathroom she expects to see the heralding russet streaks on her panties, but they're never there. She can't be pregnant again, she's sure. Next month, November, she'll be forty-three years old.

Sunday morning, a few weeks after her birthday. She's been awake for at least an hour but she lies in bed. She doesn't know what she'll do with herself all day. She gets up to go to the bathroom and check her pajama bottoms for the streaks. Nothing. She tells herself mournfully, This time it really is the change of life. All my worries have brought it on too soon.

But the instant after she thinks that thought, a familiar burning around her right nipple radiates out in concentric circles. She jumps up from the toilet seat, holds her breath and waits a moment, motionless. Surely she imagined it. Then the radiating waves hit her left nipple. Her heart leaps like it will escape her chest. She knows for certain that again there's a baby inside her.

She remembers the nasty blackbird she saw from her window long ago. How she banged on the glass to shoo it away from the robin's nest, and her banging was in vain. She stood and watched, sick, as the blackbird pecked open every egg and gobbled up the insides. Scraped them clean . . . Suddenly, her mind becomes cool, clearer than it's been in months, in years. She'd kill before she'd allow that to be done to her again. Moishe and Ray and everyone and everything be damned. This is her last chance. She knows the baby will not fill the gaping hole she's certain must soon be her heart. It cannot make up for everything that will be lost, impossible to do that. But it will keep her tethered to life at least. And when everything else is gone, at least her own child will remain and witness and go on.

19

TIME ON THE MARCH

News Commentator Elmer Davis: The voice of pity does not exist anymore in Europe.

Field Marshal Herring, in Charlie Chaplin's The Great Dictator: We've just discovered the most wonderful, the most marvelous poisonous gas! It will kill everybody!

My mother doesn't tell Moishe right away. What if she's wrong? She'll wait a few weeks to be certain. She remembers too that Ricki once said that after the third month you can't have an abortion. He won't be able to try to talk her into it; and if he does try, she'll tell him to go roast with the devil. This baby is mine and I will have it, she'll say.

Nothing can stop her now.

January. She's as tired as if she's been working twenty-four hours straight, but every day she gets herself out of bed and goes off to the shop. On the train, she's always nauseated. Sometimes it's so bad she has to get off and go into a station bathroom and throw up her coffee and roll and last night's supper. She leaves for work fifteen minutes earlier than she used to, so she'll have time to vomit and then catch the next train and not be late punching the time clock. Her breasts are tender too, like they used to be just before her period, but now the tenderness doesn't go away and the bleeding doesn't come. She calculates this might be the end of the third month, maybe even into the fourth.

She hears the click of Moishe's key in the lock on a Saturday afternoon. This is the day she'll tell him—not that she expects him to help her, but he ought to know.

He hasn't been around for so long she's lost track of when she last saw him. He comes in carrying three white roses tied with a fancy red ribbon, like from a nice florist. He's wearing a new pearl-gray coat with the collar up, and of course he's raked his black fedora, one side coming low over an eye, that movie-gangster look. She used to think it so romantic, but now it seems only silly, affected.

"Hey, I missed you, doll," he says, pulling her to him roughly with one hand around her waist. With the other he holds the flowers high so they won't be crushed. "Tell you what, sweetheart, let's go over to the Lethe Lounge and have a couple of drinks, and then I'll take you to a steak house for dinner. How's about it?" He hands her the little bouquet with a flourish. She accepts it wordlessly and for an instant holds it in front of her, a befuddled bride, before she tosses it down on the kitchen table like it's poison ivy. She still hasn't said a word. "Say, is something the matter, sweetheart?" he asks.

"I'm pregnant again," she makes herself say without drama.

He stares at her, aghast, and doesn't speak. He looks as he did six years earlier, the first time she told him she was pregnant—a man facing a noose. She sees his Adam's apple rise and fall above his collar, beads of sweat already breaking out above his upper lip. She'd like to hate him, though she can't because she's been so long in the habit of loving him. But she thinks he's disgusting.

Finally, he says, "Listen, Mary, don't worry. I'll give you the money to take care of it." For a split second she's confused. Does he mean he'll support the child? No, of course not. "Take care of it" means have an abortion, get rid of "it." She folds her hands over her belly, shielding her baby from this man who wants to harm it. "This baby I'm gonna have," she says quietly.

It has taken me a lifetime to understand the strength she had to find and did. A conflagration was gobbling up the light from the world while the man she loved was good for nothing at all but fiddling. Yet she did not let herself put an end to anguish in a padded cell; she kept her head out of the oven; she got up out of bed every day and kept going. That alone amazes me. And on top of all that, at the age of forty-three, in 1940, manless and succorless, she proclaimed, "This baby I'm gonna have."

Her courage takes my breath away. Oh, Mama, my hero, I owe you awe.

He lets out a long, exasperated sigh. "Mary, I'm still trying to figure out what to do with my life. I still have responsibility for my family, and this isn't the time for me to become a father." Anger creeps into his voice; but she's not scared, at least not by his anger. "You know goddam well I can't take responsibility for a kid right now," he shouts.

"I'm not asking you for anything, Morris." She looks him in the eye, and he glowers back with hatred, but she won't be shaken. "I don't expect anything from you, and I don't want anything from you."

"I want you to have an abortion," he says flatly.

"I can't. I'm more than four months pregnant."

"Four months isn't too late. We'll find somebody who'll do it. I'll even go with you this time . . . Look, Mary, I'm not bringing a kid into the world right now."

"I'll be bringing it into the world."

"But if it's here that makes me its father." He spits the word out.

She thinks of her own father, her good tateh, how she would jump into his open arms when she was a little girl. *Mayn geliebste,* my most loved, he would call her. Her baby will never have such father love. "It's my choice and my child, Morris," she says much more calmly than she feels.

She knows, as though this scene has already played itself out in a dream, that now he'll turn on his heel, and he'll walk out. And that's exactly what he does.

She hears the tap tap tap of his shoes on the stairs. She won't call him back. This baby will be hers alone. She stares at the white roses with their stupidly jolly big red bow. She won't let herself cry.

My mother doesn't let herself cry until months later, and then it's not about Moishe.

The Union Health Center doctor has told her the baby is due in July. She holds her mind as rigid as a guardhouse soldier, trying not to let herself get upset about anything, trying to think only of the task at hand, bringing her body and soul safely through the next months so the baby will come out healthy and sound. Time enough after that to be furious with Moishe, who hasn't come to see her since the day he stormed out. Not one word from him, though—to her surprise—he's been sending her postal orders for the share of the rent he's always paid, as though to say, Our story isn't over yet. She cashes the postal order, pays the rent, and tries not to think.

She hasn't said anything at the shop, she's told only Ray, but she knows she can't hide what's in her belly much longer. She wants to keep working until slack season, but she's afraid Mr. Seidman will fire her if he knows she's pregnant. That's her biggest worry—after her worry for Hirschel and Avrom and di mameh, which she tries to push to the back of her mind, though it's constant as the ticking of her pulse. She needs to save up as much money as possible to see her through the early months with the baby. She has it all planned out. In September, when the busy season starts again, she'll get a furnished room by a missus who, for a few dollars extra, will take care of the baby while she goes to work. She remembers that's what a girl with whom she once worked at Reisman Brothers, who also didn't have a husband to support her, said she'd do. She always wondered how that poor girl fared after that fat pig Mr. Reisman let her go. "I can't condone immorality among my workers," he told her when he heard she was pregnant.

In the middle of April, in the ladies' bathroom at Seidmans, my mother turns her full profile to the long mirror that's balanced against a wall. She's in her sixth month. She sees that now she's showing—not huge, but enough. Paula, the crippled draper who's known Mary for more than fifteen years, is there in the ladies' room and sees it, too. "Darling, you won't mind if I ask you something?" Paula says.

Mary is sure that once she tells Paula, everyone she works with will know. Women don't have babies without husbands in 1940. She refuses to feel shame or guilt, but will they say she was having a bastard? She hates that ugly word. Whenever she thinks of it, she hugs her belly against the hurts the world might want to inflict on the baby she loves. But what if they urge Mr. Seidman to fire her?

"Yes, I'm pregnant," Mary says. She lifts her chin defiantly.

"Mazel tov, darling, mazel tov!" Paula cries and kisses Mary on both her cheeks. And then of course she blabs—or maybe people knew already just by looking at Mary and were too polite to mention it. Now it's in the open. "Mazel tov!" the workers come up to her to say during lunchtime or in the elevator or when she meets them in the ladies' room. Nobody asks her about her baby's father. "Do you want a girl or a boy?" "What are you gonna name it?" they ask. Bertha the finisher has a younger sister who had a baby boy last year, and he's grown out of his infant things. Bertha brings in yellow pajamas and knitted booties and peaked hats, tiny like dolls' clothes, and soft yellow blankets and little white sheets, all neatly folded and smelling of nice soap. "It's silly for you to buy new stuff when this is good as new," she says and presses the pile on Mary, who accepts it gratefully because she's been worried about how she'll be able to buy all the things she'll need for the baby.

Stevie the runner, who delivers the bolts of cloth to the factory floor and takes away the racks of finished dresses, carries over to Mary's workstation a white bassinet decorated with pink and blue gingham ribbons, and the younger Mr. Seidman follows behind him. "You know, our baby just graduated to a crib," Mr. Seidman says kindly, "and I thought you might be able to use this. If you want, you can just leave it in the office for now, and when the time comes, I'll have somebody bring it over to your place."

All in all, Mary feels pretty good these days. She walks with her head high and her shoulders back, her belly sticking out like a little round bowl.

But then a terrible thing happens. She comes home from work one evening and sees an envelope through the mailbox slots. There's a black border around it, like there was on the envelope she got during her first year in America—the letter that said her father was dead. Mary's heart races and her hand trembles so bad she can't fit the mailbox key into its lock. If it's Hirschel or his son, how will she survive it? She'll want to die herself, and what about her baby?

She sees the letter is from Preil, from her sister Hinda. She leans against the row of mailboxes as she tears the envelope open . . . It's di mameh! She closes her eyes tight and clutches her midriff. This is my punishment, she tells herself. God is mad at me, after all, for everything I did and didn't do. She starts to walk upstairs to her apartment, but she sinks down, right in the middle of the stairway, not caring who may come by and see her; she weeps all the tears she hasn't let herself shed in months. She can't hold it together anymore. Di mameh, who loved her, who used to call her *mayn ershte trayst,* my first comfort. Mary will never see her again on this earth. She cries loud as an infant, until her face is flushed red and she can't breathe. She doesn't think of her baby now, she doesn't think of anything—except the confused notion that God has punished her for her years of sin and her latest sin, to want to bring a child into the world though she has no husband.

She has to be with her sister. Coatless and hatless, hair disheveled like one deranged, she runs out into the street, up to the corner, and waves down a yellow cab. "Hurry, quick," she yells at the driver after she gives him the address.

Ray answers the door, red-eyed and somber. She's already ripped the lapel of her blouse. Before they say a word to each other, Ray reaches out, bunches the material of Mary's dress in her hands, and pulls until the fabric gives way at the lapel. Then they throw themselves into one another's arms and wail.

"It's my fault," Mary howls. "I did wrong things."

Ray breaks away and looks at Mary, uncomprehending. "What are you talking about? What's your fault? Di mameh had stomach cancer for years!"

"God is punishing us for what I did," Mary moans.

"Shut up! This is no time for crazy talk. She was almost seventy-eight years old. Nobody lives forever." Ray goes down the hall to her room, and Mary follows. Ray bustles, throwing the two pillows that lie on her bed onto the floor because she and Mary must sit shiva, opening overstuffed drawers until she finds the right one, pulling out a wrinkled white sheet. "We gotta cover the mirror first." She throws an end of the sheet at Mary. "Stop being crazy and help me . . . Listen, you'll give the baby up for adoption and everything will be okay," My Ray says, going back to her old song.

My Ray, who, once I'm in the world, will hold me to her heart and cover my head with kisses and call me *mayn geliebste,* my most loved, and make up for so much that he, the man who sired me, took away. "When you were born, the nurse put you in my arms and I held you to my heart, and you crawled in and never crawled out again, little *gonif,* little thief," she'll tell me all through my childhood. Though I'll dog my mother's footsteps as she runs the crazy circles—round and round as she pulls her hair and blames herself and her moral failings for the loss of them all—I'll break free of those circles because My Ray, with her flat-footed sanity, will be there for me. But what she says now is, "You'll give the baby up for adoption."

The loss will come just as my mother—Cassandra in her madness—has long felt it coming, though she will never find out exactly how it happened. More than half a century later, I will be working on a book about another slaughtered people, and suddenly I will be driven to find out myself.

I will go to Preili, as my mother's shtetl has come to be called, and there the kindly mayor of what has been transformed into a small, Soviet-era city will take an interest in my mission. He will fish out of the Preili government archives the eyewitness testimonies that the Soviets, after driving out the Nazis and returning to Preil, gathered in 1945 from gentiles who saw the murders—and he will hand me a copy. I will find graphic printed accounts by some of the few Jewish survivors of the slaughters in Dvinsk and Riga. And I will imagine how it happened to those my mother loved:

June 16, 1940. Russian tanks will roll into Latvian cities. Hirschel will stand at the edge of Riga's central market, watching the Red Army cross over the river by the Iron Bridge and enter the Old Town of Riga. The soldiers, in summer tunics and shiny black boots, will march in tight formation, so close that each almost steps on the heels of the man in front of him. The Jewish peddlers, young and old, will run from their market stalls to line the streets. They will forget the ancient history they have heard about since childhood— they will forget even the pogroms of a few decades earlier, in Kishinev, in the Ukraine, in Odessa, in Makariev, in Kiev—and they will greet the Russians with flowers, candies, kisses, certain that their savior has come to snatch them from the fire just in the nick of time. The marching songs that the Red Army soldiers will be singing will sound to Hirschel, whose historical memory is better than most, like wolves howling for their supper.

Less than a year later, June 13 and 14, 1941, hundreds of open trucks, rattling loudly through the cities and towns, will carry in their beds human cargo—twenty thousand Latvians, including five thousand Jews. KGB soldiers will point fixed bayonets at them as they are driven to marshaling yards in Riga. There these "unreliables" will be loaded onto freight cars and deported to the gulag camps of northeastern Siberia. Ironically, the few Jews who will survive the harshness of the gulag will indeed have the Soviets to thank for snatching them from the fire.

June 22, 1941. The Nazis will honor their non-aggression pact with the Soviets like they honored their non-aggression pact with the Poles—the German-Russian war will begin. In a few days, Hirschel, who has been making a little money by peddling secondhand clothes in the central market, will stop to buy a kilo of potatoes and a loaf of bread to bring home to his wife and child. He will look up at the skies of Riga and see a low-flying formation of thirty Nazi bomber planes, the German Cross stamped on their wings. His blood will pound like he's imploding. He'll dash home as quickly as his crippled leg allows him to dash; he'll drop his bundles of potatoes and bread and unsold clothes in the street because they slow him down. He'll pull the sickly Dweira from their bed, scoop Avrom off the floor where he plays with an old shoe, and hurry them down to the basement of their apartment building. A score of other neighbors will already be sitting there, praying that if the bombs hit the building, the basement will shelter them. Someone will have had the foresight to bring a radio with him, in case the Soviets issue lifesaving directions. When he turns it on, the Nazis' "Horst Wessel Song" will blast out.

Red Army soldiers stationed in Latvia will rip their insignias from their uniforms, take off their heavy boots, and skedaddle.

In Dvinsk, on the morning of June 29, Chana and Mendel and their three sons will huddle together in terror as they peek from a window of their fifth-floor walk-up. They'll see Latvian antisemiten, waiting to welcome Nazi tanks into the city and filling the idle time by smashing the windows and looting the stock of the modest Jewish-owned stores up and down the block. A Jewish apartment building across the way will be burning, and Chana, whose thoughts will shift from deranged to coolly rational and back again, will think, Would it be less painful if we held hands—first the three boys and then Mendel and I—and jumped?

By that evening the Nazis will have arrived in Dvinsk, and posters will be plastered everywhere, instructing all Jewish males between sixteen and sixty to report immediately to the big marketplace. Some of the Jews will be forced at gunpoint to go out on the road and bury the bodies of those who had been killed by the approaching Nazis. The Jews who won't be sent off on this immediate work detail will be brought to the large redbrick building which is Dvinsk's prison. In the prison yard, German soldiers will have some sport. "Jump like a frog"; "Get down on all fours and march with your behind in the air"; "Sing 'Deutschland Über Alles.'" They'll screech their orders into the ears of the petrified prisoners. While the Jews perform, the Nazis will shoot guns over their heads to add to the amusement. Mendel, who was always tone-deaf, will sing "Deutschland Über Alles" badly, and a Nazi bullet will aim for his heart and hit its mark. His oldest son, Dovid the scholar, will be among those shoved in groups of fifteen or twenty into prison cells meant to hold three people. The next day they will be put to work as slave laborers, digging ditches or unloading cement and timber from railcars. Dovid will have a scholar's undeveloped muscles and the work will be hard for him. He'll barely be able to lift a heavy sack of cement and will stumble clumsily as he carries it. A Nazi bullet will find his heart, too.

In Preil, on the same day that Mendel and his oldest son will be taken off to the Dvinsk prison, Hinda will be opening up the top of the door of the hole-in-the-wall store from which she sells a few carrots, beets, and onions, as di mameh used to. Hinda will hear a sound she's never heard before—the roar of motorcycle engines. The main street, Sondergass, through which the motorcycles will pass, is a long block away, but the booming noise will carry. Like in a nightmare, Hinda will drift down the street without thought and see that Sondergass is lined with cheering crowds. Blond girls dressed in Sunday finery will be throwing flowers. The motorcycle riders—many more than she can count—will be wearing helmets stamped with an eagle grasping a swastika. Dozens of jeeps and tanks will follow. Hinda will feel with the certainty of nightmare knowledge that unspeakable horror has arrived.

In Riga, on Friday, July 4, at the beginning of the Sabbath, even before the Nazi tanks roll in, hundreds of Jews will be herded and locked inside synagogues. Local Latvian fascists will pass around bottles of vodka to keep the arsonists amused while they soak their torches. In their little apartment on Saulen Street, Hirschel and his wife and child will hide, mute and trembling, in a room that is dark because he has pulled the window shades down. They will listen to the screams of those who have been imprisoned in the Saulen synagogue a few doors away. And then the torches will be set to this house of worship and soon the shrieks will stop . . . The Nazis will love local Jew-hating inventiveness of this nature. Reinhard Heydrich, head of the Nazi Security Police, will issue an order to the invading Nazi soldiers: "No obstacles are to be placed in the way of the self-cleansing desires of anti-communist and anti-Jewish circles in the areas to be newly occupied. Rather, they are to be promoted."

When the Nazis enter Riga, gentile Latvians, who hate the Soviets almost as much as they hate the Jews, will line the streets and cheer. On July 28, the Nazis will publish an order requiring the Jews of Riga to wear a yellow Star of David no smaller than ten by ten centimeters at the spot of their hearts, and a few weeks later they will be ordered to affix another one at the center of their backs. They will be ordered to walk only in the gutter, never enter public baths or parks, never walk on the seashore or attend public events. They will be allowed one-half the food rations of non-Jews. They will be forbidden to have social contact with non-Jews or leave their quarters at any time other than ten to twelve in the morning and three to five in the afternoon. They will be forced to surrender all their radios, typewriters, weapons, all means of transportation, and all valuables. Men between sixteen and sixty will be conscripted for compulsory labor.

And this will be only the beginning.

In Preil, the small shtetl where my mother was born, the annihilation of the Jews, whose families had lived there for centuries, will be carried out in three waves. In each wave, Latvian Nazi collaborators, organized by the Gavar brothers, younger counterparts of the Kristaps brothers who roughed up der tateh almost thirty years earlier, will go from house to house, forcing Jews out and herding them to the Jewish school on Posadan Street or to the big synagogue on Sondergass. Old people and children who will not be able to keep up will be hurried along by beatings with wooden paddles and sticks. Pits, twelve by four meters in size, will have already been prepared by convoys of Jewish prisoners brought to the Jewish cemetery on the outskirts of town or to a meadow about a half kilometer away.

On July 28, three hundred Jews, the first batch, will be marched through the town to the meadow. The men will be shot first, then the women. Bullets will not be wasted on the babies. They will be thrown live into the pits.

The second wave will take place on August 8. Nine hundred Jews will be rounded up and taken to the synagogue, then herded together to the edge of the Jewish cemetery. One of the Gavar brothers will worry that the two pits may not be large enough to hold so many bodies, so he will commandeer shovels from farmhouses not too far away and force some of the Jewish men awaiting their destruction to dig more graves.

Hinda will be ordered to stand with other women and children at the edge of a pit. She will be numb with fear, already dead though a bullet from the submachine gun that has been mowing down others hasn't yet reached her. Before the bullet hits her chest, she will think one last thought—that she thanks God he took di mameh fifteen months before and her body already lies peacefully under a grave marker only meters away.

The next day, in the third wave of killings, almost all the remaining Jews of Preil will be slaughtered. Of the two thousand who will have been living there on June 30, when the Nazis first arrive, only six will survive—hidden in the homes of two righteous Latvian families, at great risk to themselves.

(Three years later, in June 1944, the war will not be going well for the Nazis. The Nazi leadership that is stationed in Preil will decide that before withdrawing, it would be prudent to cover all traces of their handiwork. They will bring forty partisan prisoners in chains to the meadow and the cemetery, and order them to dig open the burial pits and pour gasoline over what remains of the bodies. One pit will be overlooked. When the Soviets retake Preil on August 8, 1944, a few of the seasoned Red Army soldiers will weep, some will be sick, and some will only shudder at the wretched tangle of bones, hair, and rotted flesh that once belonged to human beings.)

In Dvinsk, the Latvian Auxiliary Police will be happy to exterminate the Jewish population for the Nazis. A thousand Jews will be killed almost immediately after the Soviets desert Dvinsk. The twenty-five thousand Jews who are not taken to prison to be used as slave labor will be herded into Griva Fortress. Chana and her two younger sons will be among them. The fortress, once Latvian Army barracks, will be big enough to house only a fraction of the Jews, but their numbers will very soon be thinned. By the end of August about ten thousand of the inmates will have been marched to the Mezciems Forest and slaughtered by the Latvian Auxiliary Police, their corpses thrown into huge pits and covered over with dirt. On November 8, 9, and 10, over eleven thousand more Jews will be taken to the forest. The job will be too big for the Dvinsk division of the Latvian Auxiliary Police alone: with a team of forty to sixty men to guard the marching Jews and then to carry out the killing, it would take too long to murder eleven thousand people. Thus the Latvian Arajs Kommandos, who are stationed in Riga, will commandeer the city's blue municipal buses and come to help the Auxiliary Police do the murdering more quickly.

Chana and her children will be among those marched to the Mezciems Forest. Large pits will already have been dug out by slave labor, waiting for the Jews who are already as weak as infants from months of starvation, beating, terror, and now this long march. Chana's middle son, Lev, will be feverish with the flu and will be tottering along beside his mother and little brother, delaying the procession behind him. An Arajs Kommando will see Lev stumbling. He'll seize him by the hair, and Chana will shriek and grab Shlomo, her bawling youngest child, and hold him close. The commando will slug her on the side of her head with the barrel of his gun, and drag the now-mute Lev away. Chana will reel, and then right herself and hold tight to Shlomo, realizing this will be the last hour on earth she can hold him. She will hear a shot ring out behind her and know that her beloved middle son, Lev, has gone to be with his father and older brother. She will be too exhausted and sick at heart to weep or be afraid now. She will only want it to be over. She will stagger, dazed, holding Shlomo's ice-cold hand, envisioning them both somewhere else, together again with Mendel and her two older sons. The Jews of Dvinsk will be herded to the edge of the pits in groups. The shooting commandos will be waiting twenty feet away, arranged in two rows, their bolt-action rifles at the ready. The front row will shoot kneeling; the back row will shoot standing. Each Jew will be shot twice, one bullet from the front row and one from the back. Chana will grab Shlomo in her arms. Only three bullets will be spent on them because they will fall together into the pit before the back-row commando can discharge his rifle at the child.

In Riga, barbed wire will be put up around a few square blocks of the most dilapidated and desolate area of the city, where the ramshackle houses are without plumbing, gas, and electricity. This will be the ghetto. In October, the thirty thousand Jews of Riga who have survived the first onslaughts will be driven from their homes, empty-handed, to live in it. Hirschel, ironically, will finally be working again as a tailor, a slave laborer sewing Nazi uniforms. But the Nazis will decide that he is not among the most useful few thousand whose lives will be spared for now. And so on November 30, Hirschel, his sickly wife Dweira, Avrom, who is not yet three years old, and thousands of other Jews—old people, children, mothers with babies in their arms, cripples like Hirschel who limp, young men and women who are sound but show the exhaustion of famine and torture—all will be driven out of the ghetto by the German SS and the Latvian police who assist them. The Jews will be made to line up in one-thousand-person columns. Seven centimeters of snow will have fallen the night before, and the ground will be icy and slippery; but they will be forced to march toward the forest of Rumbuli, which is ten kilometers from the ghetto. There, pits will already have been prepared for them.

"Can't walk more, Mommy," Avrom will bleat as he scampers to keep up. He'll pull on his mother's dress and lift his little arms to her, but Dweira will be too weak and heartsick, dead already in her mind, to carry him.

"Shaa, Avromeleh, shaa," Hirschel will admonish softly, but he'll pick his son up quickly. He'll press him close to his heart, kiss his round little head, and then limp on, grasping the child very tightly to his chest and groin, as though he would reabsorb him into his flesh this minute, so that Avromeleh would not have to suffer his own death. The Latvian policemen will be shouting, "Faster! Faster!" and will lash their whips over the heads of the marchers. Those Jews who will be carrying packs on their backs, having thought perhaps they will merely be transferred to another ghetto and their few possessions might come in handy there, will abandon the packs on the side of the road so they can hurry along faster.

But none of the Jews will be marching fast enough to satisfy one of the German SS officers, who will fire directly into the crowd with an automatic machine-gun. He will mow down dozens of the exhausted marchers, who will fall in the path of the others. Those trying to push forward, away from the berserk SS man, will slip and slide in the blood of the fallen. In panic and confusion, they'll trample on the bodies of parents, children, siblings, aunts and uncles, lovers, friends, neighbors. This will be how my mother's beloved crippled brother and his wife and little son will die, two kilometers from the Rumbuli Forest.

Hitler never wrote condolence letters: *Dear Madam, I regret to inform you that we have massacred your family and their bodies are moldering in a Latvian ditch.* And I will not undertake to discover their fate until my mother has been dead for almost twenty years. Though she will never know for certain what happened to them, in her mind she will witness their murder almost every day of my childhood. "Zay hargenen Yidden!"—They're killing Jews—she will yell, seeing it right before her eyes, as if it is happening that instant, though the Jews will have long since been killed.

Because she will never know for certain, she will also believe that by some magical means, their fate might retroactively be in her hands. So if she does the right thing, it means they ran to safety; if she does the wrong thing, it means they're heaps of bones: If she takes her shop dress to work in a Macy's bag, as does Bertha, whose brother was killed by the Nazis in Vilna, it means her own brother Hirschel has been killed by the Nazis, too. If she avoids a Macy's bag, it means Hirschel is sitting in the sun in Argentina or Israel and does not write her only because he lost her address in the turmoil of escape. This is how she will pay for what she failed to do as a girl of seventeen.

July 1940. Mary is okay, because she has to be. About herself she doesn't care, but her baby will be here soon. Only let me be a good mother to my child, she intones to herself many times a day, as fervently as praying.

Ray sleeps in Mary's bed for a whole week, beginning July 10, because the Union Health Center doctor said that was when the baby might come. It's a week later, the morning of July 17, and butterfly wings start gently opening and closing in Mary's womb. She knows it's time.

"You don't have to come with me. I'm fine," she tells Ray.

"What do you think I slept here the whole week for?" Ray roars, and she runs to the corner to flag down a yellow cab. She rides back in it to the apartment house, where Mary is already waiting at the front door, her little cardboard valise in hand. Ray gets out while Mary, belly huge, gets in with difficulty. "Move over," Ray says, and slides back in.

Mary registers at the hospital as Mrs. Morris Federman. She stares down Ray's look of astonishment. Mary will not—not for the world—let her baby's birth certificate be stamped ILLEGITIMATE.

"And where is Mr. Federman?" the efficient nurse asks, but not unpleasantly.

"He had to work today," Mary says easily. Under the counter, she kicks Ray's foot, a warning to her to keep her mouth shut.

"Too bad," the nurse says, printing with block letters under "Father's Name," MORRIS FEDERMAN, just as Mary tells her.

"Yeah, his boss won't let him take the day off even when his wife is having a baby," my mother goes on, to make sure the nurse believes her. The opening and closing butterfly wings are transforming into a nipping dog, and she can't stifle a groan. By the time she's registered, she's feeling strong contractions every few minutes. Hold on, soon it will be over, she orders herself. She doesn't know for how much longer she can stand the pain.

In the labor room, a nurse examines her. A bespectacled, solemn-faced doctor comes in a while later and reads the nurse's chart. "Hmm, you haven't dilated much yet, Mrs. Federman," he says in a nasal voice. The two young interns who flank him hold clipboards and pens in their hands. They both examine the page on their clipboards, then scribble something on it intently, heads down, not looking at her.

Every few minutes she feels like her womb is being seared by a burst of flame. She bites hard on her lip, as though that pain can distract her from the worse one below. She feels a trickle down her chin, and with the back of her hand she wipes away blood.

They let Ray into the room to see her only once, because Ray takes one look at her sister's chalk-white color and screams, "Nurse, nurse, she's in danger! You gotta do something."

Mary is mortified. "Ray, shaa!" she hisses with energy she can't spare.

The no-nonsense-looking head nurse, who's examining the pulse of a patient that was just brought in, drops the girl's hand, marches over to Ray, and takes her by the elbow. "You're upsetting the patients, miss. You'll have to wait outside until we call you in again."

Ray lets the nurse lead her out, but she turns at the door to bellow, "I'll be right outside, Mary. Don't worry, you'll be okay. Call me when you want me."

Mary closes her eyes and nods because she's too weak to do anything else.

The others who are wheeled into the labor room throughout the day look like they're eighteen, nineteen years old, maybe early twenties at the most. She is old enough to be their mother, she thinks. "Been here long?" they say cheerily to Mary, who nods yes because she hurts too much to talk. Eventually, their young husbands come in to hold their hands. Before too many hours go by, each girl is wheeled out to the delivery room. Only Mary remains. She must push away fear that her womb cannot dilate enough to deliver her baby because she is almost forty-four years old. Through the little window, she can see the light leaving the sky and the stars coming in. Wolves are tearing her womb apart, but she won't let herself get scared. She doesn't want her baby to have a scared mother.

Every hour or so, one smiley young nurse comes in to check her dilation, and another one comes in to take her blood pressure and put a stethoscope to her stomach. About the time the stars are fading from the sky, the blood-pressure-and-stethoscope nurse stops smiling. "I'll call the doctor," she says to no one and hurries out.

I've struggled so hard to come into the world that I've wrapped the umbilical cord around my neck. I am slowly choking to death; I am choking my fetus-self back to the other world.

The old doctor has gone home and a new one hurries in, two new interns trailing him. Mary is too tired to follow what they're saying. "Break the amniotic sac now?" "Yes, then . . . and Scopolamine?" "No, first let's try . . . "

She feels herself being wheeled into the delivery room, but she keeps her eyes shut. She's too tired to open them. She could let herself drift away, out of pain, out of the world. *No.* Her baby. Hands pull her body one way and then another and then back. "Push! Push!" a voice that's far away says, but she has no more strength. She cannot push me out into air.

Let me come out, Mama, to where hands will help and I can breathe. Let me come out to be with you. Let me come out so I can remember them, Hirschel and Avrom and Hinda, all of them. Though I'll never see them, they won't be forgotten. Seventy years and more will go by, and still I won't forget, I swear it. That is not nothing, Mama. That is not total obliteration.

Slick as soap, I slide from her womb down to large waiting hands. "Oxygen!" a man's voice cries.

My wailing mouth, open wide like a baby bird's, is covered with something cold and I breathe.

Afterword

My mother's functional illiteracy in English probably accounts for the spelling of my last name as "Faderman," rather than "Federman": I imagine that in 1946, when she registered me for school at P.S. 62 in the Bronx, she told the registrar that my last name was Federman and was asked how to spell it. She must have said, "Like it sounds." My mother always pronounced the first *e* in Federman with a long *a* sound, as many Europeans do; and so the registrar spelled it "Faderman," and that is how my name appeared on my first-grade teacher's roster. It was she who taught me to spell my name, so I have been Faderman ever since.

In 1964, having just received my master's degree from UCLA and deciding to take myself to Europe for the summer, I applied for a passport. I was told I must show a birth certificate; but my mother had never gotten a copy of my birth certificate. I had to request one from the New York City authorities, who informed me that they had no records that showed a Lillian Faderman had been born—though based on my date of birth they were able to find a record for a "Female Federman," born to Mary Lifton and Morris Federman. No first name had been recorded. (I imagine my mother was so distracted by what was going on in Latvia in July 1940 that she could not think about obtaining a copy of the birth certificate, nor about having my first name put on it.) Looking at my birth certificate for the first time, at the age of twenty-four, I discovered that the name my mother meant me to have—a fairly common Jewish surname (as Faderman is not), and which the Bronx hospital receptionist knew how to spell—was Federman.

Throughout my childhood, I heard constantly about Morris Federman from my mother, who every once in a while went off in the evenings to see him—somewhere . . . I never knew where—until we left New York in 1948.

I saw Morris Federman only twice: once just before my mother and I were leaving New York to go live in Los Angeles; the second time in the summer of 1952, when my mother and I went back to New York. (Did she really still hope that Moishe might finally make an honest woman of her, if only he saw her again?) We went to the apartment where he'd lived with his parents, and there I briefly saw my paternal grandmother, a quite elderly woman who was clearly chagrined and would in no way acknowledge me; but, astonishingly, she did give my mother the address where her son could be found: it was a factory that made very upscale knitted sweaters and dresses. Morris Federman was the owner of the factory. Our meeting was short and very stormy, and my tearful mother and I took the train back to Los Angeles the next day.

Fifteen years later, the summer after my Ph.D. dissertation was approved and I became Dr. Faderman, I knew I had the emotional wherewithal to search for Morris Federman. I went back to New York but could find him nowhere; and soon, too caught up in my work as a professor and writer, I put the search aside. It wasn't until I retired from my career as a professor that I resumed it again. From the Ellis Island records of the steamship *Rijndam*'s "Manifest of Alien Passengers for the United States Immigration Officer at Port of Arrival," I was able to find exactly when he arrived in the United States. From the Social Security Death Records, I was able to find that he died in 1963, at the age of fifty-seven. I hired a New York private investigator, Denise Witzeman, who assisted me in uncovering more about this father I never knew. We discovered that he had married in 1950, and a daughter was born to him in 1951. (She was already eighteen months old that summer of 1952 when my mother wept and yelled at Morris in front of his elite knitting factory.) Denise then helped me find this daughter—Linda Federman Roosna—in Florida, and Linda is now my dear sister and friend. She's given me vivid details about our father's life, as well as pictures of him, remarkable in that I now have a clear physical image of this stranger in his prime, when he was the passion of my mother's life and helped make me.

Though my mother kept no emotional secrets from me, and I knew, because she told me, that she'd always lied to others about her age, she never did reveal, even to me, exactly how old she was. Going through her belongings after she died, I found that she'd actually taken a black ink pen to her citizenship certificate, obliterated her age, and put in a new number more to her liking, but I couldn't decipher what the original number had been. It wasn't until I sent for Moishe's Ellis Island documents that I thought also to send for hers: it was then that I found she was born in 1896 and had come to America in 1914. Not until that time did I know my mother had been almost forty-four years old when I was born.

What I have written in *My Mother's Wars* derives primarily from stories my mother or Aunt Ray told me or grumbled or grieved over aloud all during my childhood, though, as I suggest throughout this book, imagination has filled in precise details as well as various particulars: for example, because I do not know which non-union shop occasioned my mother's first strike experience, I invented "Alexander and Schwartz"—but the story of how the miserable working conditions she witnessed led to her marching on a picket line for the International Ladies Garment Workers Union is one she told me. Many of the historical details in this book have been provided by my extensive research about the period. It is the memories of my mother's and Aunt Ray's stories that have provided the emotional truth.

Resources

In addition to the newspaper and magazine articles and other documentary materials I relied on in constructing the *Time on the March* segments that begin each chapter (see below), I used the following sources in my research:

The Depression

Susan Currell. *The March of Spare Time: The Problem and Promise of Leisure in the Great Depression.* Philadelphia: University of Pennsylvania Press, 2005.

Laura Hapke. *Daughters of the Great Depression: Women, Work, and Fiction in the American 1930s.* Athens: University of Georgia Press, 1995.

Andria Taylor Hourwich and Gladys L. Palmer, eds. *I Am a Woman Worker: A Scrapbook of Autobiographies.* New York: Affiliated Schools for Workers, 1936.

Cathy Knepper, ed. *Dear Mrs. Roosevelt: Letters to Eleanor Roosevelt through Depression and War.* New York: Carroll and Graf, 2004.

David Kyvig. *Daily Life in the United States, 1920–1940: How Americans Lived through the "Roaring Twenties" and the Great Depression.* Chicago: Ivan R. Dee, 2004.

William Manchester. *The Glory and the Dream: A Narrative History of America, 1932–1972.* Boston: Little, Brown, 1974.

Eleanor Roosevelt. *My Days.* New York: Dodge, 1938.

Ann Schofield. *To Do and To Be: Portraits of Four Women Activists, 1893–1986.* Boston: Northeastern University Press, 1997.

Joel Seidman. *The Needle Trades.* New York: Farrar and Rinehart, 1942.

Studs Terkel. *Hard Times: An Oral History of the Great Depression.* New York: Pantheon, 1970.

Beth S. Wenger. *New York Jews and the Great Depression: Uncertain Promise.* New Haven, CT: Yale University Press, 1996.

Latvia during the Holocaust

In addition to the eyewitness testimonies taken in 1945, given to me by the mayor of Preili in 1996 and which I had translated from Russian, my scenes of the slaughter of Latvian Jews have been informed by the following accounts:

Andrew Ezergailis. *The Holocaust in Latvia, 1941–1944: The Missing Center.* Riga: Historical Institute of Latvia; Washington, DC: United States Holocaust Memorial Museum, 1996.

Max Michelson. *City of Life, City of Death: Memories of Riga.* Boulder: University Press of Colorado, 2001.

Frida Mikhelson. *I Survived Rumbuli.* New York: Holocaust Publications, 1979.

Bernhard Press. *The Murder of the Jews in Latvia, 1941–1945.* Evanston, IL: Northwestern University Press, 2000.

Gertrude Schneider, ed. *The Unfinished Road: Jewish Survivors of Latvia Look Back.* Westport, CT: Praeger, 1991.

Additional Latvian history

Mendel Bobe et al. *The Jews in Latvia.* Tel Aviv: Association of Latvian and Estonian Jews in Israel, 1971.

Josifs Steinmanis. *History of Latvian Jews.* Helena Belova, trans. New York: Columbia University Press, 2002.

Europe in the 1930s and what America knew

Yehuda Bauer. *American Jewry and the Holocaust: The American Joint Distribution Committee, 1939–1945.* Detroit: Wayne State University Press, 1981.

———. *Jews for Sale? Nazi-Jewish Negotiations, 1933–1945.* New Haven, CT: Yale University Press, 1994.

———. *My Brother's Keeper: A History of the American Jewish Joint Distribution Committee, 1929–1939.* Philadelphia: Jewish Publication Society of America, 1974.

Richard Breitman. *Official Secrets: What the Nazis Planned, What the British and Americans Knew.* New York: Hill and Wang, 1998.

Richard Breitman et al., eds. *Refugees and Rescue: The Diaries and Papers of James G. McDonald, 1935–1945.* Bloomington: Indiana University Press, 2009.

Richard Breitman and Alan M. Kraut. *American Refugee Policy and European Jewry, 1933–1945.* Bloomington: Indiana University Press, 1987.

Lucy S. Dawidowicz. *The War against the Jews, 1933–1945.* New York: Holt, Rinehart and Winston, 1975.

Leonard Dinnerstein. *Anti-Semitism in America.* New York: Oxford University Press, 1994.

Zvi Gitelman, ed. *Bitter Legacy: Confronting the Holocaust in the USSR.* Bloomington: Indiana University Press, 1997.

Raul Hilberg. *The Destruction of European Jews.* Chicago: Triangle Books, 1961.

Sidney Iwens. *How Dark the Heavens: 1400 Days in the Grip of Nazi Terror.* New York: Shengold, 1990.

Ronnie S. Landau. *The Nazi Holocaust: Its History and Meaning.* Chicago: Ivan R. Dee, 1994.

Laurel Leff. *Buried by the Times: The Holocaust and America's Most Important Newspaper.* New York: Cambridge University Press, 2005.

Deborah E. Lipstadt. *Beyond Belief: The American Press and the Coming of the Holocaust, 1933–1945.* New York: Free Press, 1986.

Haskel Lookstein. *Were We Our Brothers' Keepers? The Public Response of American Jews to the Holocaust, 1938–1944.* New York: Vintage Books, 1985.

Dalia Ofer. *Escaping the Holocaust: Illegal Immigration to the Land of Israel, 1939–1944.* New York: Oxford University Press, 1990.

A. J. Sherman. *Island Refuge: Britain and Refugees from the Third Reich, 1933–1939.* Berkeley: University of California Press, 1973.

Martin Small and Vic Shayne. *Remember Us: My Journey from the Shtetl through the Holocaust.* New York: Skyhorse, 2009.

American anti-Semitism in the 1930s

John Roy Carlson. *Under Cover: My Four Years in the Nazi Underworld of America.* New York: Dutton, 1943.

Charles E. Coughlin. *Am I an Anti-Semite?* Detroit: Condon Printing, 1939.

Lawrence Dennis. *The Coming American Fascism.* New York: Harper, 1936.

Glen Jeansonne. *Gerald L. K. Smith: Minister of Hate.* New Haven, CT: Yale University Press, 1988.

Sheldon Marcus. *Father Coughlin: The Tumultuous Life of the Priest of the Little Flower.* Boston: Little, Brown, 1974.

William Dudley Pelley. *No More Hunger: Presenting the Christian Commonwealth.* Asheville, NC: Pelley, 1939.

Michael Sayers and Albert E. Kahn. *Sabotage! The Secret War against America.* New York: Harper and Brothers, 1942.

Donald S. Strong. *Organized Anti-Semitism in America: The Rise of Group Prejudice during the Decade 1930–1940.* Washington, DC: American Council on Public Affairs, 1941.

Gerald B. Winrod. *The Hidden Hand: The Protocols and the Coming Superman.* Wichita, KS: Defender, 1933.

———. *Hitler in Prophecy.* Wichita, KS: Defender, 1933.

Rev. Frank Woodruff Johnson [Elizabeth Dilling]. *The Octopus.* Omaha, NE, 1940.

Immigrant life

Susan A. Glenn. *Daughters of the Shtetl: Life and Labor in the Immigrant Generation.* Ithaca, NY: Cornell University Press, 1990.

Andrew R. Heinze. *Adapting to Abundance: Jewish Immigrants, Mass Consumption, and the Search for American Identity.* New York: Columbia University Press, 1990.

Stefan Kanfer. *Stardust Lost: The Triumph, Tragedy, and Mishugas of the Yiddish Theater in America.* New York: Knopf, 2006.

Hannah Kliger. *Jewish Hometown Associations and Family Circles in New York: The WPA Yiddish Writers' Group Study.* Bloomington: Indiana University Press, 1992.

Lois Levine. *The Women's Garment Workers: A History of the International Ladies Garment Worker's Union.* New York: B. W. Huebsch, 1924.

Kathy Peiss. *Cheap Amusements: Working Women and Leisure in Turn-of-the-Century New York.* Philadelphia: Temple University Press, 1986.

Joseph Schechter. *Messiahs of 1933: How American Yiddish Theater Survived Adversity through Satire*. Philadelphia: Temple University Press, 2008.

Rose Schneiderman and Lucy Goldthwaite. *All for One*. New York: Paul S. Eriksson, 1967.

Abortion

Ellen Chesler. *Woman of Valor: Margaret Sanger and the Birth Control Movement*. New York: Simon and Schuster, 1992.

Angus McLaren. *Twentieth-Century Sexuality: A History*. Malden, MA: Blackwell, 1999.

Marvin N. Olasky. *The Press and Abortion, 1833–1988*. Hillsdale, NJ: Lawrence Erlbaum, 1988.

Leslie J. Reagan. *When Abortion Was a Crime: Women, Medicine, and Law in the United States, 1867–1973*. Berkeley: University of California Press, 1997.

Sources for Time on the March

New race in Reich: "New Race in Reich Starts with a Rush," *New York Times*, April 5, 1932.

New York governor Franklin Delano Roosevelt: Radio address, Albany, April 7, 1932.

Germany. Predictions are: Guido Enderis, "Expect Hindenburg to Win by 8,000,000 in Reich Vote Today," *New York Times*, April 10, 1932.

The United States. Between ten and twelve million: Norman Mattoon Thomas, "Third Parties: Repeal Unemployment!" *Time*, August 8, 1932.

This week, on every eminence: Frederick T. Birchall, "Victory for Hitler Is Expected Today," *New York Times*, March 5, 1933.

President Franklin Delano Roosevelt: Inaugural address, March 4, 1933.

All of Germany's Jews: H. R. Knickerbocker, *New York Evening Post*, April 15, 1933.

August Hoppe, Hitler Youth leader: "Germany: JaJaJaJaJaJaJaJaJa: Nein," *Time*, August 27, 1934.

Armories shelter thousands: *New York Times*, December 28, 1934.

Dr. John Becker: "Bail Denied to Doctor," *New York Times*, December 27, 1934.

Berlin. Organized gangs of youths: *Newsweek*, July 27, 1935.

Germany passes the Nuremberg Laws: *Newsweek*, September 21, 1935.

Congressman Fontaine Maury Maverick: American Neutrality Policy Hearings before the House Committee on Foreign Affairs, 74th Congress, 1st session, 1935.

New York. Three hundred thousand Americans: J. O. Reade, "Back to Panhandling," *New Republic*, October 9, 1935.

First Lady Eleanor Roosevelt: Excerpted from her nationally syndicated column "My Day," March 18, 1936.

Berlin is being beautified: Frederick T. Birchall, "Berlin Beautified for the Olympics," *New York Times*, July 13, 1936.

Rumania. Alexander Cuza: *New Republic*, December 30, 1936.

The curb on Jews is official: "Curb on Jews Held Official in Poland," *New York Times*, April 23, 1937.

Berlin. Third Reich schoolteacher: *A Picture Book for Great and Small,* quoted in Ralph Thurston, "Hitler Mobilizes 'Mother Goose,'" *Nation,* March 20, 1937.

Breadlines get longer: *New Republic,* April 21, 1937.

Budapest. Hitler's men: Henry C. Wolfe, "The Swastika in Hungary," *New Republic,* June 30, 1937.

Panic on Wall Street, again: "Stocks Drop to New 1937 Lows in Heavy Day," *New York Times,* September 25, 1937.

New York City. City employees: "WPA Groups Stage 3 Battles in Day," *New York Times,* July 2, 1937.

There are twenty-one: *Nation,* July 24, 1937.

Hitler enters his native Austria: "Hitler Comes Home," *Time,* March 21, 1938.

The Jewish quarter of Leopoldstadt: "Jews Humiliated by Vienna Crowds," *New York Times,* March 16, 1938.

The Gallup pollsters: March 1938 Gallup poll.

The picture is not bright: "Business: Depression Note," *Time,* May 2, 1938.

President Roosevelt convenes an international conference: Clarence K. Streit, "US Spurs Nations to Prompt Action at Refugee Parley," *New York Times,* July 7, 1938; *Proceedings of the Intergovernmental Committee on Political Refugees,* Evian, France, July 6–14, 1938 (London, July 1938).

Pleas by refugees: "German Refugees Fill Entry Quota," *New York Times,* September 13, 1938.

Pollsters: *Fortune* magazine poll, July 1938.

Berlin. Raiding Squads: "Berlin Raids Reply to Death of Envoy," *New York Times,* November 10, 1938.

Vienna. In the dingy streets: "All Vienna's Synagogues Attacked," *New York Times,* November 11, 1938.

U.S. senator Robert Rice Reynolds: 1938 speech to the U.S. Senate.

The latest Gallup poll: Gallup poll, January 1939.

The saddest ship afloat: "Refugee Ship," *New York Times,* June 8, 1939.

The Senate Committee on Immigration: "Congress Windup July 15 Predicted," *New York Times,* July 3, 1939.

Jerzy Potocki, Polish ambassador to the United States: "Poland Resolute, Envoy to New York Says," *New York Times,* September 2, 1939.

London. The British government has published: Raymond Daniell, "White Paper Says Practices Recall 'Darkest Ages,'" *New York Times,* October 31, 1939.

President Franklin Delano Roosevelt: Fireside Chat, September 3, 1939.

In New York City, every week: "Religion: No Picketing," *Time,* October 30, 1939.

News commentator Elmer Davis: CBS News broadcast, June 22, 1940, on the surrender of France to the Nazis.

Field Marshal Herring: *The Great Dictator,* directed by Charlie Chaplin, United Artists, 1940.